METHODS OF RESEARCH IN CRIMINOLOGY AND CRIMINAL JUSTICE

McGraw-Hill Series in Criminology and Criminal Justice

Binder and Geis: Methods of Research in Criminology and Criminal Justice
Callison: Introduction to Community-Based Corrections
De Forest, Gaensslen, and Lee: Forensic Science: An Introduction to Criminalistics
Klockars: Thinking about Police: Contemporary Readings
Walker: The Police in America: An Introduction

METHODS OF RESEARCH IN CRIMINOLOGY AND CRIMINAL JUSTICE

Arnold Binder
University of California, Irvine

Gilbert Geis
University of California, Irvine

McGraw-Hill, Inc.
New York St. Louis San Francisco Auckland Bogotá
Caracas Lisbon London Madrid Mexico City Milan
Montreal New Delhi San Juan Singapore
Sydney Tokyo Toronto

This book was set in Optima by Jay's Publishers Services, Inc.
The editors were Eric M. Munson and Susan Gamer;
the production supervisor was Rosann E. Raspini.
The drawings were done by Jay's Publishers Services, Inc.
The cover was designed by Mark Wieboldt.

**METHODS OF RESEARCH IN CRIMINOLOGY
AND CRIMINAL JUSTICE**

5 6 7 8 9 10 11 12 13 14 BKMBKM 9 9 8 7 6 5

ISBN 0-07-005286-7

Library of Congress Cataloging in Publication Data

Binder, Arnold.
    Methods of research in criminology and criminal
justice.

    (McGraw-Hill series in criminology and criminal
justice)
    Includes bibliographies and index.
    1. Crime and criminals—Research. 2. Criminal
justice, Administration of—Research. 3. Crime and
criminals—Research—Statistical methods.
4. Criminal justice, Administration of—Research—
Statistical methods. I. Geis, Gilbert. II. Title.
III. Series.
HV6024.5.B56 1983   364'.072   82-4670
ISBN-0-07-005286-7

CONTENTS

PREFACE   xi

1   RESEARCH METHODOLOGY AS A WAY TO MINIMIZE
HUMAN ERROR   1

Theory and Research   3
·Head, Body, and Crime: An Example of Long-Lasting
    Damage to Knowledge Resulting from Human Errors   9
Research Methodology as a Process   11
Essential Features of Research Methodology   13
    Comparison / Alternative Plausible Hypotheses
Basic and Applied Research   17
References   19

2   ETHICS IN CRIMINAL JUSTICE RESEARCH   21

Ethical Relativism   23
The Nuremberg Code   25
Anonymity and Deception   27
APA Standards   28
Research Posing Ethical Issues   31
    Behavior in a Simulated Prison / Tearoom Trade
References   35

3   RESEARCH IN CRIMINAL JUSTICE:
ISSUES AND PREPARATION   37

Research Issues   39
    "Bellow Like a Bull" / The Last Word / More Court
    Matters / Feedback from Probation Officers /
    Police and Weapons / Causes of Crime /
    Further Research Topics
Preparation for Research   51

Site Exploration and Related Details /
Review of the Literature
References   58

4   ON ALTERNATIVE PLAUSIBLE HYPOTHESES   60

Internal and External Validity   62
Subjects as Sources of Error   63
    "Center of Attention" Effects / Biological and
      Psychological Alterations / Selection
Pitfalls in Measurement Methods   76
    Reactivity / Pretesting Effect / Response Set /
      Changes in Measuring Instruments /
      Interviewer Effect
Situational Factors as Sources of Error   82
Experiments as Sources of Error   83
Problem in Crime Statistics   84
    Uniform Crime Reports / Unreported Crime—
      "The Dark Figure"
References   88

5   TECHNIQUES FOR AVOIDING ERRORS   90

Nonreactive Measures   91
    Erosion Measures / Accretion Measures / Physical
      Evidence / Archival Data / General Forms of
      Nonreactive Measure
Control Groups   102
    Ethical Considerations in Using Control Groups /
      Equating Treatment and Control Groups /
      Placebos as Controls
Dealing with Flaws in Crime Statistics   110
Victimization Surveys   111
    General Considerations / National Crime Survey (NCS)
References   116

6   STANDARD APPROACHES TO RESEARCH   118

Ways of Classifying Research   119
    Classification by Purpose / Statistical Classification /
      Temporal Classification / Classification by Control
      over Variables
Control and the Advancement of Knowledge   121
Systematic Observation   124
    Naturalistic Observation / Surveys: Questionnaires
      and Interviews / Physical Traces and Archival
      Records / Sociometry

Experimentation 140
The "True" Experiment / The Nonlaboratory
Experiment
References 148

7 PROGRAM EVALUATION 150

What Is Program Evaluation? 151
An Example: Evaluating "Scared Straight" 153
The Program / The Finckenauer Reports
Evaluator as Advocate 157
Issues of Generalizability 159
Assessing Process and Assessing Impact 160
Process Assessment / Impact Assessment
Issues of Economics 167
Conclusions 169
References 170

8 DESCRIPTIVE STATISTICS: CENTRAL TENDENCY
AND VARIABILITY 171

Measures of Central Tendency 173
Mean / Proportion / Median / Mode
Indicators of Variability 179
Variance / Standard Deviation / Mean Absolute
Deviation from the Median / Range
Standard Scores 183

9 DESCRIPTIVE STATISTICS: CORRELATION 188

The Product-Moment Correlation Coefficient 190
The Meaning of Correlation 196
Scatter Diagrams / Correlation in Everyday
Phenomena / Examples of Use of
Correlation Coefficients
Other Measures of Correlation 202
Curvilinear Relationships / Dichotomous Data /
Ranked Data
Correlation and Causation 214
References 215

10 PROBABILITY AND PROBABILITY DISTRIBUTIONS 216

Probability 216
Sample Space / Equal Likelihood / Mutually
Exclusive Events / Properties of Probability /
Probabilities in the General Case

Probability Distributions 227
Binomial Distribution / Normal Distribution

11 STATISTICAL INFERENCE 239

Sampling 239
*Simple Random Sampling / Stratified Sampling /
Cluster Sampling*
Statistical Inference 248
*The Logic of Statistical Inference / Estimation /
Testing Statistical Hypotheses*

INDEX 261

PREFACE

This book was first conceived when the faculty of the Program in Social Ecology at the University of California, Irvine, voted at an early stage in its development to initiate and require a course in research design (two members were in favor; one was opposed). Social Ecology is an interdisciplinary degree-granting unit that has, unashamedly, an applied orientation. At the present time, its 25-person faculty includes sociologists, who are primarily involved in urban sociology and criminology; psychologists, who work in community, environmental, and criminal subspecialties; lawyers; and planners. The faculty also has a few outliers, who focus on matters such as evaluation and water quality and make life more interesting for the rest of us.

The research design course, even in those early years, was expected to encompass both the basic principles of research methodology in the social sciences and the idiosyncracies of investigation in the various fields that ultimately were included in the curriculum of the program. The orientation was, of course, toward applied work rather than toward theory development.

One of the three members of the faculty at the time the research design course was established had considerable experience teaching statistics and experimental design, and so he became the reasonable person to inaugurate the course. Perhaps that explains why he cast the lone negative vote among the three.

No single book existed that seemed to satisfy the requirements of the course. At its first offering, therefore, several texts were included in the required list, with considerable reliance on that excellent book of examples of applied research work, *Statistics: A Guide to the Unknown*, edited by Tanur et al.

A natural next step was to plan to write that single, multidisciplinary applied book. The first stage consisted of recording and typing lecture notes during one of the quarters when the course was offered. Any instructor who conceives of himself or herself as coherent, profound, or both might try the exercise of recording a full quarter's or semester's lectures. It is a humbling experience. Most instructors will probably be forced to face the truth, as the instructor of that research methodology class was. It was, in short, a mess; and the result bred enhanced respect for the lot of students.

But rewriting, more rewriting, and still more rewriting occurred until the text could be handed out to students in mimeographed form: at first without cost; later, as budget cuts hit, at a nominal fee. This allowed the material to be sharpened and refashioned under actual classroom teaching conditions.

Later, at a luncheon discussion between the initiator of the course and a person he had worked with closely on other matters, the idea came up of a collaborative arrangement, focusing on criminal justice (our shared interest) and building on tested course materials. What you have before you is the product of that arrangement. It brought together two persons with different but overlapping talents. Both knew research methodology, but one of us had spent a large part of his professional career concentrating on mathematical aspects of social science research. Both knew and worked in the area of criminology and delinquency (indeed, we had collaborated on several projects), and one had specialized particularly in the broad area of criminal justice. One of us writes in a tight form; the other began adult life as a writer, until he fell from grace, and tends to embellish on matters a bit. It made for us a thoroughly pleasant collaborative arrangement, and we believe that it has resulted in the production of a sophisticated yet readable book on research methods in criminal justice.

As for the intent of the book, it is aimed primarily at the consumer rather than the designer of research. That is, it is intended for students who eventually will become directors of personnel departments, chiefs of police, developmental planners, managers of county agencies, prosecutors, defense attorneys, management-level police officers, management-level correctional officers, diversion counselors, and so forth. All such positions require a high degree of ability to make decisions—and the fodder for decision making is what this book is all about. In fact, the basic intent of this book is to provide the foundation for reaching decisions with a minimum of the typical human errors that can intrude on the process. This aim extends to evaluating results of other persons' work when such results affect policy.

The book will also be of value to those who will become research specialists by providing them with an introduction to, and an overview of, the methodological domain. We think that it offers a unique perspective on research methodology as systematic decision making and thereby provides a sound grounding for more specialized courses that might be taken subsequently.

In terms of coverage, we think that the full eleven chapters provide the right amount of material for a one-semester course. For a one-quarter course, it would seem most appropriate to drop the final two chapters (Chapters 10 and 11), which serve as an introduction to statistical inference. The essential features of research methodology in criminal justice—for the future consumer or the future practitioner needing an introductory overview—are covered in the first nine chapters.

We have tried to make the book readable and enjoyable, to overcome the reputation that a research course often carries among uninitiated students. There are, consequently, possibly more illustrations and anecdotes than some purists might prefer, but this is part of our deliberate attempt to make the introduction to the subject pleasant. We have throughout attempted to stress the pleasure that is involved in performing and understanding competent work that results in the acquisition of new knowledge, better information, understanding, and satisfactory policies, or the correction of fallacious, though commonsense, ideas that were founded on incorrect methods, misunderstandings, or misinterpretations.

Criminal justice research is an essential aspect of contemporary life. The phenomena of crime and delinquency are enormously complex, and their consequences are profound—both for the perpetrators and those close to them, and for the victims and those who share their suffering and deprivation. We believe that the best hope for alleviating the hurts and miseries commonly associated with criminal activity is skillful, scientifically sound scrutiny of all aspects of the behavior and those especial conditions associated with it. It is to this end that our book is dedicated.

A number of people were extremely helpful in the process of putting this book together. But the one person who stands out in importance as a coworker with the authors is Carol Wyatt. Her competence and wisdom were critical elements in the production of the final manuscript.

Arnold Binder
Gilbert Geis

METHODS OF RESEARCH IN CRIMINOLOGY AND CRIMINAL JUSTICE

CHAPTER 1

RESEARCH METHODOLOGY AS A WAY TO MINIMIZE HUMAN ERROR

CHAPTER OUTLINE

THEORY AND RESEARCH

HEAD, BODY, AND CRIME: AN EXAMPLE OF LONG-LASTING DAMAGE TO KNOWLEDGE RESULTING FROM HUMAN ERROR

RESEARCH METHODOLOGY AS A PROCESS

ESSENTIAL FEATURES OF RESEARCH METHODOLOGY
    Comparison
    Alternative Plausible Hypotheses

BASIC AND APPLIED RESEARCH

REFERENCES

Human beings, in order to remain alive, are constantly required to gather and sort facts, to form ideas and hunches, to reach conclusions, and to act in terms of their estimates of consequences. Some of the decisions that we make are routine, with few if any long-term consequences: Should I turn on the air conditioner or open the windows? Would it be wise to pack an umbrella in case it rains during the trip, given the look of the clouds forming to the east? Should I take this criminal justice course before another one, and in which instructor's section should I register? The person teaching the morning section is supposed to be more interesting and an easier grader; on the other hand, eight o'clock in the morning is quite early to get one's eyes open and mind going.

Other decisions may have critical consequences for ourselves and for others. Should I accept a job next week as a probation officer, or should I continue my graduate education? The tightening job market suggests that probation positions are going to be increasingly difficult to obtain. If I begin to work right now, in a few years I'll probably be earning a good deal more than I would get if I stayed in school and earned a master's degree. On the other hand, the higher degree could open up employment doors that would otherwise be forever closed to me. Similarly, as a medical patient, you may have to decide whether you will agree to double-by-pass surgery, with its risks, or choose to carry on as best you can under medication, with its risks. As the head of a police department, you may have to decide whether to use two-person patrol cars or restrict patrolling to one-person cars. And you undoubtedly will at some time have to decide whether Officer A or Officer B should be promoted to detective.

There is no clear distinction or dichotomy between very important and less-important kinds of decisions. There is a continuum, moving from the utterly trivial to the extremely critical decision. And, of course, our own position—who we are and where we stand—may determine how many persons are affected by our decisions and how deeply they are affected. Only certain individuals are able to decide whether to initiate prosecution against a major corporation for alleged fraudulent practices. On the other hand, in a democracy, where there is relatively free commerce in information, it is possible for anyone to attempt to influence decisions by marshaling persuasive evidence that what he or she is advocating makes much better sense than what those nominally making decisions are planning to do. If nothing else, most people can use the letters-to-the-editor columns of their local newspapers to try to persuade readers of their opinions, on the basis of their interpretations of available facts or their logic in connecting facts to conclusions.

Decisions and conclusions, no matter how trivial or profound, are based upon our understanding of the relevant state of the world and our expectations about their outcomes. We are constantly reorganizing our information set on the basis of new facts and insights, what someone tells us, what we read, what combination of stimuli intrudes into our lives. The process might well be equated to that by means of which a shrewd detective reanalyses clues in order to apprehend a suspect. In making decisions, therefore, it is desirable to have accurate and complete information, although decisions frequently must be made on the basis of insufficient understanding and limited relevant information. This is why persons sometimes make mistakes in judgment. Another reason, of course, is that they fail to interpret the available information adequately. A student need only consider his or her responses on a true-false test to appreciate how sufficient information can lead to success or how misinterpretation of known information or misreading of a question can lead to an unsatisfactory response.

The basic goal of this book is to provide a framework for increasing knowledge and understanding of criminal justice issues in a systematic manner that reduces the likelihood of errors. The material that we will present throughout this book will be directed toward providing an enhanced level of understanding and interpretation, so that more satisfactory and satisfying decision making will become possible. The framework that we will emphasize has its foundation in the social sciences, with their emphasis on theories of individual and group behavior.

THEORY AND RESEARCH

The purpose of a scientific theory is to summarize in a systematic and formal manner the available knowledge in a given realm of inquiry. A theory consists of a set of assumptions; concepts regarding events, situations, individuals, and groups; and propositions that describe the interrelationships among the various assumptions and concepts. A theory attains its status by drawing inferences from observations, deducing consequences from the inferences, testing these consequences (which are referred to as *hypotheses*), and then modifying the inferential structure (that is, the way we reach additional conclusions in accordance with the observed results of the tests).

To illustrate, Gross (1979:400–401) presents a theory of punishment which takes the following form:

> Punishment for violating the rules of conduct laid down by the law is necessary if the law is to remain a sufficiently strong influence to keep the community on the whole law-abiding and so to make possible a peaceable society. Without punishment for violating these rules the law becomes merely a guide and an exhortation to right conduct....The threats of the criminal law are necessary then, only as part of a system of liability ensuring that those who commit crimes do not get away with them. The threats are not laid down to deter those tempted to break the rules, but rather to maintain the rules as a set of standards that compel allegiance in spite of violations by those who commit crimes. In short, the rules of conduct laid down in the criminal law are a powerful social force upon which society is dependent for its very existence, and there is punishment for violation of these rules in order to prevent the dissipation of their power that would result if they were violated with impunity.

The theory states the seemingly paradoxical view that the purpose of punishment is to keep people who are currently law-abiding from committing crimes. It says that punishment does not deter established criminals who have no allegiance to prevailing social standards. Therefore, one conclusion that follows from this theory—assuming, of course, that the theory is correct, which it may or may not be—is that harsher and harsher punishment will reduce crime only when normally law-abiding people move into criminal activities. Accordingly, a legislator who relied on this theory would not introduce a bill calling for more restrictive forms of prison confinement on the basis that such a policy would serve to reduce the recidivism rate for established criminals.

Theories are sometimes capable of organizing facts that seem widely disparate into a position that explains all of them. For instance, a single theory—that of the operation of gravity—explains such diverse things as the movement of tides, the erect posture of trees, and the difficulty of writing on the ceiling with a ballpoint pen (Hirschi, 1973:168).

The purpose of theory is to summarize and organize knowledge. The purpose of research is to refine that knowledge. In criminal justice, we might want to know under what conditions the addition of new officers to police departments leads to decreases in crime, improvement in the morale of members of the department and, perhaps, more favorable attitudes among citizens about the adequacy of protection that they are being afforded. Perhaps all these ends will be achieved by increasing the number of sworn officers in departments. On the other hand, the crime rate may be reduced but morale may suffer because there now are too many newcomers in what earlier were smaller, more companionable groups of law enforcement officers. Moreover, it is likely that beefing up the personnel in a police department leads to other outcomes that were unanticipated in the initial planning of the research but, nevertheless, extremely important. For example, the heads of other units in city administration may complain about favoritism and create fusses that result in work slowdowns in, say, the fire department and the welfare office.

Because of the seemingly limitless possibilities for self-deception displayed by human beings, an elaborate set of procedures has evolved over the years to make the research endeavor as immune to human failings as possible. That set of procedures is widely referred to as *research methodology*. Some of the failings that research methodology seeks to guard against are the following.

1 *Errors of observation*. Humans not only fail to see important features in a given scene but often invent false observations. Attend any session of a court in your neighborhood and observe how inadequately witnesses remember the details of events and persons that they are attempting to describe. Experiments have been made which attempt to have people who report that there was an interval of two minutes between a first and second criminal episode close their eyes and not reopen them until they believe that two minutes have elapsed. Few can manage the assignment satisfactorily, though it should be noted that it is not altogether a fair trial, because the experiment introduces a kind of stress different from that which may have

been present during the initial observation. The importance of accurate observation has been graphically highlighted by Beveridge (1961:133):

> A Manchester physician, while teaching a ward class of students, took a sample of diabetic urine, and dipped a finger in to taste it. He then asked all the students to repeat his action. This they reluctantly did, making grimaces, but agreeing that it tasted sweet. "I did this," said the physician, "to teach you the importance of observing detail. If you had watched me carefully, you would have noticed that I put my first finger in the urine, but licked my second finger!"

2   *Selective observation.* It is notable that different people viewing the same event or phenomenon will notice different things, according to their interests and their biases. That is, we all tend at times to see those things that we want to see, rather than a true picture of what we are looking at. And we also select for observation matters that are of importance to us. A black observer of the behavior of the police, for example, may be especially alert to any sign of a racial slur or evidence of differential treatment based on race. And an ardent feminist is likely to be attuned to detecting signs that an individual being observed believes that differences between the sexes dictate policies of differential treatment. In this manner, all of us are particularly aware of things that have a special or important meaning for us.

3   *Errors of interpretation.* Our personal biases, our fears, and our inclinations determine not only what we observe but how we interpret what we have observed. Recently, a deaf-mute man was shot to death by a police officer when the man reached into a pocket and began to pull out an identity card. The officer said that he had interpreted the man's lack of responsiveness to his questions and directions as animosity. He said that he thought that the man's reaching into his pocket represented an attempt to draw a gun and open fire on him.

A further source of misinterpretation lies in failure to be aware of alternative explanations for the relationship between phenomena. For example, until the twentieth century, most medicines had no curative power whatsoever. Yet most people, including physicians, believed that the potions were effective. Indeed, changes often were observed in patients after they had taken the medicines. Such changes were, in fact, produced naturally (or perhaps psychologically) rather than by means of the biochemical actions of the medicine.

4   *Incorrect generalization.* This error results in large part from failure to attend scrupulously to the material which forms the basis of conclusions. It may involve an inadequate ability to think and reason logically, or it may involve a tendency to come to conclusions that are desired rather than those that are dictated by available information.

As an example, take the incorrect generalization that was derived from a report (*Project Identification,* 1976) of the Bureau of Alcohol, Tobacco and Firearms of the U.S. Treasury Department. On the basis of this report, it was widely believed that cheap guns—so-called Saturday night specials—were the weapons of choice among urban criminals. The report put the matter this way:

> Therefore, the only conclusion to be safely made from the...data is that a substantial majority of handguns used in street crimes is of low quality with a market value of less than $50. This conclusion is based on the fact that 5,336 (56 percent) of the handguns traced never exceeded $50 in value and of the remaining 4,176 at least some portion of this represents handguns, which although originally valued in excess of $50 had market values of less than $50 at the time of police acquisition (p. 9).

But a study by Wolfe (1977), covering essentially the same period, found that there was systematic exclusion of more expensive weapons in the survey of the Treasury Department bureau, leading to an overgeneralization regarding the role of cheap guns in street crime. Wolfe discovered, after a very careful survey in New York City, that 67.5 percent of the weapons confiscated after use in a crime were worth more than $60. The percentages of more expensive weapons (that is, those with values of more than $60) used in crimes were as follows: robbery—80.0 percent; assault—69.2 percent; burglary—100 percent; narcotics—33.3 percent; weapon possession—64.4 percent.

5 *Dependence on authority.* Many (if not most) of our beliefs are based on the statements of people we consider authorities. We may buy and horde gold because someone who has written a best-selling book says it is wise to do so, or we may go on a high-carbohydrate (or low-carbohydrate) diet because an "expert" with a goatee and an Austrian-sounding accent advises us that this is the surest way to shed 15 pounds painlessly. We look to authorities in religion and politics, in science and education. In some measure, this is because we assume that these persons have better information than we do, since they have presumably devoted their lives to its acquisition and are specialists in the field. Nonetheless, with their specialization often comes a vested interest in a particular point of view— their own—and a real or unwitting attempt to camouflage conclusions that might be contrary to the true ones. Sir Thomas Browne, a seventeenth-century writer, in his book *Vulgar Errors,* maintained that unthinking reliance on authority is the "mortallest enemy unto knowledge," since it involves a "resignation of our judgments" (Keynes, 1964:II, 275–276; II, 5–6).

In the instance of criminal activity, our decision making is frequently based on the positions of the chief of police or a prosecuting attorney rather than on careful analysis of events and relationships. In criminal trials, we tend to rely on what we read in the daily newspapers or see on the television newscasts. But note the observation of Felix Frankfurter, a former Supreme Court justice:

> It is my habit not to read accounts of trials as reported in the press unless the press purports to report the trial verbatim. My experience during those years

about trials in which I took part as I saw them reported even in the best papers was distortion, mutilation and at best an opaque account of what took place in the courtroom. If I was sufficiently interested in a trial, if I really wanted to know, I would try to get the stenographic minutes (Phillips, 1960:208).

6 *Inappropriate use of evidence.* Data may be based upon perfectly accurate observation and seem appropriate as evidence to support a certain decision, yet actually may misrepresent the phenomena of interest. To illustrate: if we are interested in measuring subsequent criminal behavior, we cannot rely with too much assurance on police statistical reports, because the police do not apprehend all offenders. And those persons that they do catch most certainly represent a particular kind of criminal or delinquent population. They are characterized, if by nothing else, by the fact that they were unskilled enough (or, in some instances, unlucky enough) to have been caught—or to have been suspected of a criminal offense.

If we resort to self-reports of criminal activity we are faced with a host of similar kinds of problems in obtaining accurate indications of criminal activity in order to conduct good research. For one obvious thing, some persons we talk to will lie to us, either out of uncertainty about what we intend to do with the information they are providing or, perhaps, because they want to exaggerate their "badness." For another thing, delinquency and criminality are basically legal categories, and the persons we are questioning might not be aware of or sensitive to the legal definition of behavior that they have engaged in. A middle-class boy might regard a street fight as "assault"; a working-class boy might define it as nothing more than a routine bit of horseplay.

Throughout this book we will specify these kinds of pitfalls for satisfactory decision making in the area of criminal justice and offer suggestions and advice on ways to overcome the problems they raise. It might be encouraging, in this regard, to appreciate that even in medical research, where vast amounts of money are committed to discovering cures for human disease and where the conditions for more controlled research are often superior to those in the area of criminal justice, imprecise and unsatisfactory conclusions are often reported. We can illustrate this matter by an example dealing with vitamin E.

The literature shows a number of claims by medical people that use of vitamin E helps to alleviate heart disease. Three Canadian physicians, for example, treated cardiac patients with large doses of vitamin E and reportedly noted startling improvements in their well-being. They reported that they were able to use a vitamin E regimen to move cardiac patients out of the hospital and into normal activities in a matter of a few days.

The results, however, were largely anecdotal, based upon observations of improvements in patients after administration of vitamin E, and not the product of systematic research procedures. There was no comparison over groups and no attempt to rule out other possible explanations. The startling improvements could have resulted from a placebo effect rather than from any pharmacological propensities of vitamin E. Indeed, the conclusions were repudiated when a careful study, under which a group of patients received the vitamin while a similar group did not, failed to find any difference between the two groups after two years.

Perhaps the ultimate tale of the true scientist, as opposed to a person relying carelessly on anecdotal evidence, is that of the two persons riding through the English countryside on a train during the spring season.

"How pretty," said one. "Look at all those sheep. They look naked. They must have just been sheared."

"Well," replied the other, always a most precise investigator, "at least we know that they've been sheared on one side."

This is the same kind of precision characteristic of the old Maine native, a man who had never gone farther than 10 miles from his home, who was asked if indeed he had spent his whole life in Maine. "Not yet," he replied.

To determine whether the sheep had truly been sheared on both sides, all you needed to do was to wait for one of them to turn around, unless you were the total skeptic who would insist that this proved only that this particular sheep had been totally sheared. At some point, most reasonable persons would be willing to grant that common sense ought to prevail, on the basis of knowledge of usual shearing practices and the visual evidence. But the story, combined with the example of vitamin E, illustrates the necessity for constant vigilance and scrupulousness in observing data and interpreting evidence. The systematic person will keep in mind the work of Blaise Pascal (1623–1662), who is credited with establishing the modern theory of probability. In 1648, when Pascal carried out an experiment for measuring the weight of air, he had a barometer carried some 3000 feet to the top of Puy-de-Dome, a mountain in central France, to demonstrate the loss of atmospheric pressure at the greater height. At the same time, he also provided for a second barometer to be kept at the foot of the mountain to make certain that it remained unchanged during the course of the experiment.

Sometimes investigators will undergo extraordinary personal sacrifice to uphold the integrity of their work. Phillip-Ignaz Semmelweis (1818–1865), a Hungarian physician, crusaded for the prevention of puerperal fever, a disease that affects women after childbirth when attendants fail to observe sterile obstetrical techniques. Semmelweis's colleagues refused to believe that it was their own hands that carried the fatal germ from patient to patient. To convince them, Semmelweis slashed his fingers and plunged them into the putrescent corpse of a fever victim. He proved his point by infecting himself and eventually died of the fever (Destouches,1937).

Research methodology did not arise one morning but evolved over hundreds of years as the sciences moved from primitive beliefs to theoretical systems that are repeatedly subjected to observational testing. Thus it is possible to have a belief system based upon authority and upon subjective observation, but it is not possible to maintain upon such foundations a scientific theory from which consequences will be deduced and tested. Conclusions that enter into the scientific structure must have been derived from procedures that minimized human errors. This is not to say that science is not at times mistaken; but when it is, it is almost always because it has failed to live up to its own best standards.

The aim of this book is to present certain basic principles of research methodology, with particular reference to criminology and criminal justice. These are principles that have been formulated over the centuries to minimize the kinds of human errors that we discussed in the earlier pages, errors which interfere with the accurate formulation of policy positions and effective decision making. The principles are derived from the methods of the sciences, but are useful in all aspects of decision making, from the laboratory to the street corner.

HEAD, BODY, AND CRIME: AN EXAMPLE OF LONG-LASTING DAMAGE TO KNOWLEDGE RESULTING FROM HUMAN ERRORS

The inventory of criminal justice research is filled with examples of inadequate investigation which, for a time, passes as satisfactory evidence. In the field of criminology, concerned with the causes of crime and the bases of criminal law, Cesare Lombroso, a physician and professor of forensic medicine at the University of Turin during a large part of his career, is generally regarded as one of the most renowned figures. But much of what he postulated, measured by modern research standards, borders on the nonsensical, largely because he ignored some basic dictates of sound method. It is worth noting that what Lombroso said seemed sensible in the light of information at that time, but it would not have gained credence had critics insisted upon decent standards of proof.

Lombroso thought that he was able to identify physical characteristics of offenders in the nature of facial, cephalic, and bodily anomalies. These anomalies—characteristics believed to be different from those of the "normal" or "average" person—were later to be referred to as Lombrosian "stigmata." They were, Lombroso suggested, indications that criminals were atavistic, that is, that they had not evolved as far as the rest of society from more primitive forms of hominids. Corresponding to these physical traits were retarded psychological characteristics, which he believed rendered such individuals incapable of adjusting to more highly advanced standards and were crucial in bringing about their criminal acts.

Lombroso and Ferrero (1895: 95,113–114) scorned armchair science and ventured forth with caliper and other measuring instruments to examine men and women in prisons. Lombroso produced volumes stuffed with descriptive cases. Of one female offender he noted: "a demi-type.... Her ears stand out, she has big jaw and cheek bones, and very black hair, besides other anomalies, such as gigantic canine teeth and dwarf incisors." He also engaged in rather tortured logic, such as his attempt to relate the fatness of prostitutes, which "strikes those who look at them en masse" to the obesity of Hottentots and then to relate both of these to a theory of atavism (inadequate progression along the evolutionary road).

The most trenchant criticism of Lombroso is that of a French anthropologist working at the same time, Paul Topinard (Tarde, 1912), who gave criminology its name. Topinard was shown a collection of Lombroso's pictures of supposedly strange-looking and odd criminals and then remarked wryly that the portraits looked no different from those of his own friends. It took many years, unfortunately, before the main body of criminal justice accepted the validity of this obvious criticism of Lombroso's work. Attention to the dictates of rigorous research methodology would have spared the field numerous fruitless attempts to expand and verify a fundamentally erroneous conjecture.

In this context, it is important to emphasize that research workers must not confuse highly sophisticated technical operations with useful scientific work. Appropriate quantitative skills, used intelligently, are frequently important for research in criminal justice. But the quantification of a concept in no way assures its scientific fruitfulness. Note, for instance, this example, provided by Edward Madden (1960:10):

> Consider the following concept: A "b" coefficient is the number of hairs on anybody's head divided by the number of years he has lived, raised to the fourth power. This concept is perfectly precise and quantitative but as far as I know, no one has claimed for it any scientific significance. It simply doesn't lend itself to any relation, functional or otherwise, with any other concept. It does not, in short, occur in any scientific law or hypothesis. The scientist needs mathematics, to be sure, but he needs, even more, a scientific genius for the formulation of useful hypotheses.

A good researcher must also appreciate that not all information, no matter how accurate and how scrupulously obtained, is worth the effort. Considerable intelligence must be brought to bear upon determining the likely value of research results before undertaking the expenditure of time, talent, and funds. Take, for instance, the episode of the man lost on a country road who approached a farmer in his quest for orienting information. "Where am I?" inquired the motorist. "You're in your car," the farmer answered. The farmer's answer is accurate, and it has been derived by means of the use of all the necessary canons of scientific reasoning, but it sheds absolutely no light on a fundamental issue of importance. Too much scientific work is much like the farmer's response in terms of its utility for the criminal justice system.

RESEARCH METHODOLOGY AS A PROCESS

Research methodology is not simple. It requires skill and sophistication merely to determine the kinds of results that you want to examine and what to make of them. Take the subject of heroin addiction. Suppose the state or a private agency has begun a program designed to secure jobs upon their release from prison for persons with a history of narcotics addiction. You are asked to determine if the program is "successful" by the methods of evaluation research. You decide that you will concentrate on the number of persons who are not using drugs after two years in the program. At that time you find 70 percent of the clients have relapsed and are using heroin again. Is this to be regarded as satisfactory or unsatisfactory? Is the employment program a success or a failure? It might be regarded as a dismal failure if a different type of intervention—say one that used intensive counseling as its major treatment—produced a drug-free clientele of 50 percent after two years of work with clients much the same as yours in age, general background, and previous history of crime or use of drugs. But suppose that your program had cost only half as much money as the counseling program; and suppose that the average earnings of persons in your program were four or five times larger than those of clients in the counseling program. How are these considerations to be balanced in order to reach a final judgment? And, particularly important, what other matters must you gather information about in order to have a useful summary portrait of the work of the treatment regimens for the former heroin addicts?

You might, for instance, have decided that a better measure of success of the program to secure employment would be the number of months that your clients remain drug-abstinent compared with their previous records. You may discover that, despite the 70 percent "failure rate," your clients, on the average, were drug-free 18 of the 24 months following their involvement in your program, 6 months longer than they had gone earlier. In this evaluation approach, you regard heroin addiction as a "chronic" condition, with the goal not necessarily total "cure" but rather a gradual lengthening of the periods of drug-free existence.

It can be seen that research methodology requires experience and information about the topic being examined. You must know as much as possible about the ins and outs of agency operations and the structure of a particular agency in order to conduct research on program innovations or to measure the impact and importance of existing operations. Unless you, or others with whom you can consult freely, are thoroughly acquainted with the organization, you may overlook some very important results of the work or of the change that you are interested in examining. Research work requires not only the technical skills that this book presents but also persistence, judgment, substantive information about the subject, and a great deal of doggedness and curiosity. We will try, as we go along, to provide illustrations of tactics that should prove valuable for making the most effective use of the technical information we present.

This book will not provide you with many of the mathematical skills necessary to conduct sophisticated research. Primarily, it will stress the logic of research methodology, the kind of thinking that is required so that you do not stumble into pitfalls that trap the unwary. Poor research is particularly treacherous because it parades under the trappings of science, tending to mislead laypeople and, when challenged, to bring research itself into disrepute. Besides, inadequate research is not as easily disputable as ideas that are clearly labeled as someone's opinion or personal preference.

If, for instance, someone favors a program of intensive probation for lawbreakers in which probation officers see their clients in person at least once every day, you might believe that such an approach will do little to reduce crime. You may think that such a program will make probationers angry because they feel that they are not trusted, and that this anger will produce short tempers and a larger number of crimes of personal violence. Good research can resolve the difference between the viewpoints by supplying reliable information on the attitudes and the offenses of the persons who are involved in the program. But it would be highly misleading research if it failed to make absolutely certain (and this has happened) that the probation officers actually saw their clients each day and did not simply talk to them on the telephone or skip seeing them for weeks at a time.

Research methodology may be considered a set of procedures designed to achieve clear thinking. It is common practice in books setting out research methods to indicate a series of steps that the "ideal" research program ought to take, from the formulation of a hypothesis to the interpretation of conclusions. This represents a shorthand and simplified attempt to reduce to formula what we regard as a much richer kind of intellectual experience. There are indeed standard and accepted procedures by which research moves, but their most fundamental attribute cannot be captured in any formula, because the essence of research is that the worker attacks the problem confronting him or her with intellectual integrity and ingenuity. We will, of course, set forth the common means by which research is done, because it is important that the student understand and rely upon these when necessary. But we want to avoid conveying any impression that research is a matter that can be carried out by rote, once the proper procedure is understood. The nature of research methodology is that it involves the search for truth and understanding, and these priceless results can be achieved by a vast variety of approaches that cannot be expressed as a preordained, simple formula.

Research must avoid the types of human failings discussed earlier in this chapter. Research is essentially a process of systematic decision making, whether the decision is concerned with choosing a theoretical formulation or with the relative merits of different kinds of programs for heroin addicts. To achieve the goals of clear thinking and systematic decision making, procedures to be employed always use observable data collected in a manner that others can duplicate.

Research methodology contrasts with approaches that involve such things as folk tales and anecdotes, in which persons tell stories about particular episodes and derive conclusions from the material. The conclusions may or may not be accurate, but the support upon which they rest does not constitute satisfactory systematic groundwork. Hunches or intuition may turn out to be correct predictors of later events, but they cannot be confirmed by others.

Sometimes, we ought to warn you, a pretense of logical reasoning can be employed to undermine rather than to advance the cause of a systematic approach. In the field of criminal justice, an apt illustration is provided by the seventeenth-century witch trials in England. Village pests, generally old crones on the dole, were sometimes accused of witchcraft by their neighbors, particularly when children died (as they so often did in this period of high infant mortality) after contact with the alleged witches. In one such case, one of the country's most famous judges charged the jury in the following terms:

> That there were such creatures as witches he made no doubt at all, for first, the scriptures had affirmed so much. Secondly, the wisdom of all nations had provided laws against such persons, which is an argument of their confidence of such a crime. And such hath been the judgment of this kingdom, as appears by that Act of Parliament which hath provided punishment proportionable to the quality of the offense (Hale, 1682:55–56).

At first glance, the judge's statement seems to have certain validity. He is inferring from observable data; that is, the biblical injunction that "Thou shalt not suffer a witch to live" and the enactment of statutes in England and other countries against the practice of witchcraft. Others can, if they desire, check the accuracy of his observations. The problem, of course, is that the material he uses is not responsive to the real question that is being asked: "What proof is there that there really are people who engage in the practice of witchcraft?" The scriptural references and the statutes only reinforced the prejudice of the judge himself, since they were based on no better evidence than that available to him; they neither prove nor disprove the basic question by systematic procedures. The terrible significance of erroneous logic and poor research can be attested to by the deaths of thousands of persons accused of witchcraft and burned or hanged after members of the Inquisition (on the European continent) or jurors (in England) declared them guilty as charged.

ESSENTIAL FEATURES OF RESEARCH METHODOLOGY

There are two characteristics of the process of research methodology that need to be stressed: comparison and alternative hypotheses.

Comparison

First, research methodology always involves comparisons between sets of observations, such as comparing test scores of adjudicated delinquents or adult felons before and after they are exposed to a certain treatment, say a program of group counseling run by persons of the opposite sex. Without a base or control comparison, a given set of observations simply cannot be used to reach any defensible conclusion. Comparison is implicit in any judgment that we make. Note the observations of a scientist who met a colleague on the elevator and was asked how his wife was feeling that day. The answer emphasizes the point we are making: "Compared with what?" the scientist wanted to know.

We can readily determine whether shoplifters, for instance, score high or low on a psychological or sociological test, but the information is worth little unless we know how others do on the same test, particularly other persons who share characteristics with the shoplifters we are examining (characteristics that might bear upon the test results, such as age, sex, and religious background). Indeed, comparison is the essence of human existence, and some philosophers suggest that all of us would suffer mercilessly if we did not have varying standards against which to measure change—that is, if everything were constant. Good health, it is maintained, becomes much more precious because it can be compared with memories of periods of illness or depression.

Comparison can be of endless variety. We can compare any two persons or groups of persons with each other. We might find that arsonists, for example, tend as a group to produce more responses on a Rorschach test that signify "fire" or "red" symbolism. More often than other persons, they see in the Rorschach cards figures with lipstick, devils, or ashes. We also can match our sample with standardized scores. We know that an average intelligence quotient (IQ) is defined as 100. Anything below or above that point is readily interpretable; it provides a comparison score. If a sample of arsonists score 112 on an IQ test, we can assume that as a group they are somewhat more intelligent than the average person.

It is necessary when making comparisons to be extremely careful that distinctions between the things being examined are not a function of something other than what you want to know about (an error of interpretation). Note, for instance, a well-known study of the differences between black armed robbers and other blacks convicted of different kinds of property offenses (Roebuck and Cadwallader, 1961). The researchers observed that the armed robbers used weapons in their juvenile offenses more often than the property offenders did and that they had an early pattern of stealing from their parents, at school, and on the streets. By comparison with property offenders, they also had a history of greater numbers of muggings and purse snatchings. As far as it goes, the study provides some interesting information about the incarcerated armed robbers from whom the information was derived. It remains possible, however, that the imprisoned armed robbers were the more impulsive types who therefore were more frequently caught by the police. Nor do we have sufficient information to determine whether the armed robbers differed from the rest of the black population in addition to their distinction from other black property offenders. Depending upon the use to which the research information will be put, such kinds of data may be essential.

Alternative Plausible Hypotheses

A second basic characteristic of the process of research methodology is that it involves selection among two or more alternative plausible hypotheses. The data must be collected in such a way that all hypotheses but one are ruled out or controlled satisfactorily. By satisfactory control, we mean that the experiment or investigation is so designed that the conclusion can permit but one plausible interpretation.

Consider the following example. You are told that the police are biased against blacks and hispanics because they shoot them at a proportionately higher rate than they shoot whites. It is pointed out that Jenkins and Faison (1971) found in their study of 248 fatal police shootings in New York City that young blacks and hispanics were killed far out of proportion to their numbers in the general population of that city. On the basis of these findings, one observer (as reported in Fyfe, 1978:41–42) argued:

> This preliminary report demonstrate[s] without question that the problem of police killing in general and the specific problem of disproportionate killings of minorities cannot be explained in terms of chance or reasonable extenuating circumstances. There is a permeating racial and ethnic discriminatory pattern in these police killings. Something must be done to reverse this outrage.... The New York City police must be taught to pay them the respect as human beings which whites ordinarily receive.

Similarly, Milton et al. (1977), in a study that covered seven police departments, found that 79 percent of the victims of police shootings were black, while only 39 percent of the population over the seven cities was black. Harding and Fahey (1973) discovered that 75 percent of the people fatally shot by the police in Chicago were black, at a time when that city was only 33 percent black.

But the issue before us is the question whether the method of data collection and comparison allows an alternative plausible hypothesis for these findings.

Consider for a moment that police officers do not ordinarily shoot professional baseball players, very young children, ministers, dentists, or shoppers in department stores. Rather, they tend to shoot people who have committed crimes or who are prepared to commit crimes and who seem to be threats to the officers or to other people. The point is that proportionate representation in a general population may not be a valid basis for comparison; proportionate representation in the pool of potential opponents of the police would seem more appropriate.

An alternative plausible hypothesis, then, to the conjecture that police shoot more minority group members (especially blacks) than whites because of a "racial and ethnic discriminatory pattern" is that the differential rates of shooting may result from differential rates of exposure and threat. And, indeed, Fyfe (1978) found, for New York City, that about half the minority opponents in police shootings were armed with handguns, while under a third of the white opponents were so armed. He found, furthermore, that of all incidents where the police used deadly force, almost half involved blacks and hispanics armed with handguns, rifles, machine guns, or shotguns; under seven percent of the incidents involved whites with one or more of these four types of weapons. The minority group members, therefore, clearly represent a disproportionately high threat to the police.

A similar pattern emerges when the shooting data of Milton et al. (1977) are compared with those of Harding and Fahey (1973), using disproportionate involvement in serious crime rather than the proportion of the persons in the population. Over the seven cities examined by Milton et al. (1977), 73 percent of the individuals arrested for serious crime were black (not far from the rate for shootings of blacks, which was 79 percent). For Chicago during the period of Harding and Fahey's study (1973), 73 percent of those arrested for violent crimes were black (their victimization rate in police shootings was 75 percent). On the face of it, then, the police shootings appear to be responsive to confrontations with street crime. It may be argued, of course, that the arrest rates themselves are a function of discriminatory patterns. That may be true in terms of differential rates of arrest for white-collar crimes (committed largely by whites, who hold positions of power), but not likely for offenses such as robbery, in which the police tend to be color-blind.

In addition to demonstrating the importance of controlling for alternative plausible hypotheses in research methodology, the preceding examples show the importance of archival sources (the use of public records) in criminal justice research. Too frequently, experimentation is regarded as the prime method of research, but the experiment is only one of the available approaches to knowledge and understanding. There is, for example, no reasonable way that a research worker can adequately examine use of deadly force by the police solely by experimentation.

Setting up a study or an experiment or an investigation in a manner that allows for the ruling out of alternative plausible hypotheses is referred to as *design*. It is extremely important that a researcher employ all his or her imaginative and analytical skills to make as certain as possible that only one explanation is possible for the results achieved. Otherwise, a great amount of investigative effort can go to waste, though sometimes alternative explanations suggest further designs which permit more discriminating conclusions. A not inconsiderable amount of criminal justice research is flawed because interpretations which appear to be "commonsense" explanations turn out under later research to be spurious, as, perhaps, in the interpretation of discrimination in shootings by the police, and explainable by some of the more subtle ideas that did not occur to the original research worker.

A particularly revealing story of the pitfalls of failure to consider alternative explanations carefully is that of the professor who places a frog on the laboratory table in front of the class. "Jump" he yells at the frog. It does. He then cuts the legs off the frog. Again, he yells at it to jump. This time there is no movement from the animal. The professor then conveys to the class the results of his scientific inquiry: "You see, this illustrates that when you sever the legs of a frog, it grows quite deaf" (Rubin, 1958:230).

In considering alternative hypotheses, criminal justice researchers should understand that whatever is done is likely either to favor or to be opposed to a particular position. There is rarely such a thing as "neutral" research, though, as we have indicated, there sometimes is trivial research. Charles Darwin, the founder of the theory of evolution, makes the point well in a letter to a friend in which he observes: "How odd it is that anyone should not see that all observation must be for or against some view if it is to be of any service" (Darwin, 1887; I,395). Lawrence Durrell (1961: 77) reduced the idea of "total objectivity" and "uninvolvement" to the kind of caricature that it often represents. Durrell observed that the British Foreign Office insisted on objective reports from its field representatives, leading to dispatches from remote stations such as the following: "While it is true that the inhabitants eat each other, nevertheless, the food consumption per head is remarkably high."

For Darwin, scientific endeavor of the highest quality was an obsession. As William Irvine (1955: 74) remarks, Darwin became "attached to the problem rather than to the solution of the problem and could therefore live with the facts until they *had* to yield up their meaning." Darwin provides another hint to criminal justice researchers when he observes in an autobiographical note that he had to record very carefully those findings that did not agree with his ideas, though he always remembered clearly those that confirmed them (Guttmacher and Weihofen, 1952: 371).

BASIC AND APPLIED RESEARCH

The archival studies on use of deadly force by the police dealt with the very "here and now" issue of the use of firearms by officers. Yet, embedded in the research were elements that carried implications for higher levels of abstraction—such as the relationship between personal discriminatory attitudes and day-to-day behavior. Higher-level abstractions are the building blocks of theories. In this book, though at times we will attend to both higher- and lower-level abstraction, much of our attention will be directed to the latter kind, and particularly to "here and now" questions. This type of research is frequently called *applied research*. Applied research requires careful blueprinting so that specific important research questions are asked and inquiries are directed at providing answers which can be implemented.

One type of applied research that has become particularly important in recent years is called evaluation research. As the name implies, evaluation research is aimed at assessing the effectiveness of a social program—the degree to which the program fulfills its goals and the manner in which it does so or fails to do so. Several of the examples in earlier parts of this chapter fall in the category of evaluation research, for instance, the example in which the effectiveness of a job program for narcotics addicts released from prison.

Much criminal justice research to date, especially in criminology, which aims to seek the cause of crime in general or of particular crimes, has lacked direct practical application. Consider, for example, the outpouring of work in the past 30 years on gang behavior among juvenile delinquents. Work on juvenile gangs has been carried out in Boston (Cohen, 1955; Miller, 1958), New York (Cloward and Ohlin, 1960; Spergel, 1964; Yablonsky, 1962), and Los Angeles (Klein,1971). The most readily identifiable effort in this genre to evolve practical ideas for public policy efforts was that by Cloward and Ohlin. They focused on a "total community approach," regarding delinquency as the consequence of a sense of frustration arising among youths because of structural conditions within the community, such as poor schools and the difficulties of securing jobs. Gang members were said to be unable to compete successfully in the society's legitimate "opportunity structure." Moreover, some could not even gain access to the world of illegitimate enterprise. The authors pointed out that it is just as difficult, if not more so, to become entrenched in an organized crime syndicate as it is to become entrenched in the higher ranks of major corporations such as General Motors or General Electric. Violent behavior, which is an important component of the Cloward and Ohlin schema, is traced to membership in a "conflict" subculture, one marked by the absence of both legitimate and illegitimate opportunities. The call is for elimination of these conditions. This is both a monumental task and a very vague one. It illustrates what we do *not* have in mind in regard to applied research, where the aim is to specify with some precision the nature of the problem and the character of the solution.

The difficulty of drawing practical conclusions from research that is primarily theoretically oriented can be illustrated further by examining the picture of murder and assaultive crimes painted by Wolfgang and Ferracuti (1967) in their description of a "subculture of violence." These writers find violence to be the product of values in a society which favors its use under a variety of circumstances, such as when you or a member of your family presumably has been insulted or when you are challenged in any way. To reduce violence, Wolfgang and Ferracuti believe efforts need to be undertaken to disrupt, disperse, or disorganize the subculture where such values prevail.

What is a policymaker to do with such diverse reports? The two descriptions—one by Cloward and Ohlin and the second by Wolfgang and Ferracuti—reach widely different conclusions with respect to the phenomenon of violence and offer different suggestions for policy: the first, to provide more legitimate opportunities for persons prone to violence; the second, to disorganize the groups to which such persons belong. Neither approach provides more than a mere glimmer of an outline for an action program—and no clue as to what might happen beyond the immediate consequences of any attempt to change things.

Though applied research has specific, manageable goals, it needs emphasizing that there often can be considerable overlap between it and research directed toward advancing scientific theories. A research project may contain both scientific and applied implications. For example, an investigator might be primarily interested in the effects of a program of regular urinalysis on the relapse rate of drug addicts but could state the results of a particular experiment in conceptual terms with implications for a general theory of social control.

REFERENCES

Beveridge, H. I. B. 1961. *The Art of Scientific Investigation*. New York: Vintage Books.

Cloward, R. A., and Ohlin, L. E. 1960. *Delinquency and Opportunity: A Theory of Delinquent Gangs*. New York: Free Press.

Cohen, A. K. 1955. *Delinquent Boys: The Culture of the Gang*. New York: Free Press.

Darwin, C. R. 1887. *The Life and Letters of Charles Darwin*, F. Darwin (ed.). London: Macmillan.

Destouches, L. F. 1937. *Mea Culpa: The Life and Work of Semmelweis* (R. Allerton, trans.). Boston: Little Brown.

Durrell, L. 1961. *Mountolive*. New York: Dutton.

Fyfe, James J. 1978. *Shots Fired: An Examination of New York City Police Firearms Discharges*. Ph.D. Dissertation, State University of New York at Albany.

Gross, H. 1979. *A Theory of Criminal Justice*. New York: Oxford University Press.

Guttmacher, M. S., and Weihofen, H. 1952. *Psychiatry and the Law*. New York: Norton.

Hale, M. 1682. *A Tryal of Witches at the Assizes Held at Bury St. Edmonds*. London: William Shrewsbery.

Harding, R. W., and Fahey, R. P. 1973. "Killings by Chicago Police, 1979–70: An Empirical Study." *Southern California Law Review*, **46**: 284–315.

Hirschi, T. 1973. "Procedural Rules and the Study of Deviant Behavior." *Social Problems*, **21**:164–173.

Irvine, W. 1955. *Apes, Angels, and Victorians*. New York: McGraw-Hill.

Jenkins, B., and Faison, A. 1974. *An Analysis of 248 Persons Killed by New York City Policemen*. New York: Metropolitan Applied Research Center.

Keynes, G. (ed.) 1964. *The Works of Sir Thomas Browne*. London: Faber and Faber.

Klein, M. W. 1971. *Street Gangs and Street Workers*. Englewood Cliffs, N.J.: Prentice-Hall.

Lombroso, C., and Ferrero, W. 1895. *The Female Offender*. New York: Appleton.

Madden, E. 1960. *The Structure of Scientific Thought*. Boston: Houghton Mifflin.

Miller, W. B. 1958. "Lower Class Culture as a Generating Milieu of Gang Delinquency." *Journal of Social Issues,* **14**:5–19.

Milton, C. H., Halleck, J. W., Lardner, J., and Allbrecht, G. L. 1977. *Police Use of Deadly Force*. Washington, D.C.: Police Foundation.

Phillip, H. B. (ed.) 1960. *Felix Frankfurter Reminisces*. New York: Reynal.

Project Identification: A Study of Handguns Used in Crime. 1976. Washington, D.C.: Bureau of Alcohol, Tobacco and Firearms, U.S. Department of the Treasury.

Roebuck, J. B., and Cadwallader, M. L. 1961. "The Negro Armed Robber as a Criminal Type: The Construction and Application of a Typology." *Pacific Sociological Review*, 4:21–26.

Rubin, S. 1958. *Crime and Juvenile Delinquency: A Rational Approach to Penal Problems*. New York: Oceana.

Spergel, I. 1964. *Racketville, Slumtown, Haulburg: An Exploratory Study of Delinquent Subcultures*. Chicago: University of Chicago Press.

Tarde, G. 1912. *Penal Philosophy* (R. Howell, trans.). Boston: Little, Brown.

Wolfe, J. L. 1977. *Firearm Abuse: A Research and Policy Report*. Washington, D.C.: Police Foundation.

Wolfgang, M. E. and Ferracuti, F. 1967. *The Subculture of Violence*. London: Tavistock.

Yablonsky, L. 1962. *The Violent Gang*. New York: Macmillan.

CHAPTER 2

ETHICS IN CRIMINAL JUSTICE RESEARCH

CHAPTER OUTLINE

ETHICAL RELATIVISM

THE NUREMBURG CODE

ANONYMITY AND DECEPTION

APA STANDARDS

RESEARCH POSING ETHICAL ISSUES
    Behavior in a Simulated Prison
    Tearoom Trade

REFERENCES

Ethical principles refer to matters of "right" and "wrong." Sometimes the principles are supported by laws and regulations which prohibit various kinds of behavior; at other times they are part of less formal understandings about how things ought to be done.

In criminal justice research, for example, government regulations do not allow the use of federal prisoners for experiments by either social or natural scientists. The reasoning behind this stipulation is that prisoners are not able to give their free consent to involvement in research. Such consent is said to be too readily dictated by hope of an early parole or perhaps by fear of the authorities. Therefore, it is argued by those who favored the regulations, prisoners will often agree to participate in research that is dangerous or which they would not have become involved with had they not been incarcerated.

Many prisoners oppose the regulations which debar them from acting as research subjects. They maintain that projects such as those mounted by pharmaceutical companies to test new drugs or by criminal justice experimenters to obtain information about sociometric patterns (that is, which persons associate with which others) break some of the terrible monotony of prison life; provide at times some learning that they would otherwise not obtain; and, on occasion, allow them to earn a little money. The possibility of impressing a parole board also seems to some inmates a reasonable basis for agreeing to engage in experiments. Nathan Leopold, who was involved in 1924 in perhaps the most sensational murder ever committed, the coldblooded slaying of a 12-year-old casually picked up on the Chicago streets, ultimately gained his freedom from the Illinois State Penitentiary in part because of his participation in an experiment testing antimalarial drugs, drugs which proved to be of particular value for American troops engaged in combat in the Pacific area during the Second World War.

Ethical issues, then, may be debatable, in particular in terms of the value of the research in relation to the risk to which the subject is exposed. There also is the matter of consent on the part of the subject—whether this consent is freely and voluntarily given under conditions in which the subject has adequate information regarding all relevant details of what the experiment will involve. In some instances, there have been clashes between the research community and persons charged with seeing that certain ethical standards are maintained. Take, for example, an experiment attempting to determine if the use of marijuana will prove helpful in alleviating the awful pain that accompanies terminal cancer. The experiment would best be conducted by giving some patients marijuana under "blind" conditions— that is, under conditions in which they are not aware that they are receiving the drug. But is it ethical to administer a drug to a person who is dying and who might have moral or other objections to the drug? However, if the person is told, then the experiment falls short of scientific standards, because it may be the knowledge of the drug rather than the drug itself that brings about the response.

In one instance, a researcher agreed that it would not be acceptable to administer marijuana to unknowing cancer patients but asked that he be allowed to have them sign a consent form stipulating that they were to be given a dosage of "THC," the abbreviation for tetrahydrocannabinol, the constituent ingredient of marijuana. He argued that this in fact was what was being done and that if the patients had any reservations, they were free to ask about THC; otherwise, the research process could go on unabated. He also maintained that the likely results, if it were found that the drug was effective as an anodyne (a painkiller), were so significant for persons in agony with cancer pains that any ethical reservations should give way in the face of the possible extraordinary value of the results. How would you decide this ethical research issue?

ETHICAL RELATIVISM

Ethics, then, are at times controversial. They also involve matters that can vary from place to place and over time. De Mause (1974) reports that infanticide—the deliberate killing of newborn children—was commonly practiced throughout the Middle Ages in western culture even with legitimate children, and into the nineteenth century with illegitimate children. Today the deliberate killing of an infant is regarded as a heinous offense, though the assumption also prevails that for a mother to kill her infant indicates very serious stress that should be taken into account when judging the way the case should be handled by the authorities. Child murder is no longer common and no longer regarded as acceptable ethical or legal behavior. Today, of course, intense debate centers on the matter of abortion, with different groups in American society trying to pin legal and ethical definitions on the behavior in accordance with their views about the time when life begins, the rights of women, medical decisions, and a wide array of other considerations. Ethics obviously can be a hotly disputed matter.

The past 20 years have witnessed dramatic changes in our social attitudes toward individual and human rights. In the realm of criminal justice, these changes have been manifest in such phenomena as the virtual abandonment of capital punishment (though it remains permissible in many states of the United States); the use of the exclusionary rule at federal and state levels, under which evidence obtained by searches and seizures in violation of the federal Constitution becomes inadmissible in court; the requirement that the police warn an arrested individual of his or her rights, including the right to the assistance of an attorney (the *Miranda* warning); and the imposition of almost full "due process" rights in the juvenile court, even though these rights had been considered contrary to the philosophy and spirit of the juvenile court in the almost seven decades of its existence (it began about the turn of the century).

These changes may not be as dramatic as the change in attitudes toward infanticide and toward executing persons because they hold dissident political opinions. But the climate of concern for human welfare that is evident in society today has come about during a relatively short period and is extremely pervasive in its reach. The bases for the general concern are too complex for discussion here, but it seems clear that a major source of concern about research with human subjects can be traced to the moral outrage that came in the wake of the Second World War and the revelations that unfolded during the Nuremberg trials about Nazi atrocities in the concentration camps. In particular, the use of camp prisoners—Jews, gypsies, communists, common criminals—for barbaric medical experiments by licensed German physicians turned the stomachs of all decent persons who came to know of it, and provided a basis for actions designed to make researchers more sensitive to the permissible limits of such work.

Experiments that were hardly questioned when they were carried out years ago are scorned in the current era of concern for human rights, or, as the matter is rather more indelicately put, human subjects. An example is the so-called Tuskegee study, begun in the 1930s. Some 400 poor black men diagnosed as having syphilis were examined for about 30 years by officials of the U.S. Public Health Service. The subjects were studied periodically to determine the nature and course of their disease; but they were not treated, even after 1945, when penicillin had become available as a safe and recognized cure for syphilis. An estimated 107 subjects died from the effects of the disease (Jones, 1981). The indifference to humane considerations in the pursuit of knowledge in the Tuskogee study is totally unacceptable today, and indeed public discussion of it leads to expressions of public indignation.

Another example of changing standards is found in the work of Hartshorne and May during the 1920s. Hartshorne and May (1928–1930) gave children opportunities to lie, to cheat, and to steal in many different types of settings, under instructions by the experimenters that often were blatantly dishonest and deceptive. While Hartshorne and May raised questions about the moral conduct of the children they were using as experimental subjects, modern standards lead to questions about the moral conduct of the investigators. But it must be appreciated that concerns about the propriety of lying to subjects and deceiving them in other ways were not brought up during the era of the Hartshorne and May studies or for a substantial period thereafter. In those days the status of researchers tended to insulate them from such criticism; today it may be that more education and the proliferation of rights movements, starting with the civil rights campaign, may have made people more aware and more sensitive about such matters. Many researchers feel that the ethical movement in regard to research has gone too far, that essential work is handicapped unnecessarily by ethical restraints; other persons disagree and insist that strict ethical requirements are more important than scientific inquiry. The most common position probably is that there are conflicting values in society and that, depending on the case at hand, they have to be balanced in a sensible and responsible manner.

Another example of an experimental condition that would no longer be acceptable—at least not without considerable disputation—involves the work of Watson and Rayner (1920). They created a conditioned fear in Albert, a 9-month-old child, frightening him by making a loud noise (striking a hammer against a steel bar) whenever he played with a white rat that he had been given. The child naturally was afraid of the loud noise; the repeated pairings of noise and the presence of the rat led to his associating his fear with the rat. Moreover, owing to generalization effects, that fear also became associated with animals and objects similar to the white rat, such as rabbits. The child thus became fearful of things which had previously been pleasant or neutral. The effects of the experiment were never extinguished by the persons who carried it out; that is, they did not reverse the learning experience that they had induced in Albert. No attention was paid at the time to the ethical aspects of the experiment: the matter had no obvious priority in the concerns of experimenters or those who attended to their work and how it was carried on.

THE NUREMBERG CODE

While the concerns about the welfare of little Albert and the children in Hartshorne and May's experiments are important, there have been vastly more blatant abuses of humans in the name of research. We will present further examples of some of the most questionable of these instances shortly.

Questionable research practices, together with the general spirit of concern for individual and human rights in the present era, have led government agencies and professional societies to consider systematically the responsibilities of researchers working with human subjects and to promulgate guidelines for the conduct of such work. The grandparent of this approach is the Nuremberg Code of 1946. That code came in response to knowledge of atrocities by Nazi researchers in concentration camps, acts of almost inconceivable brutality.

Some points of the Nuremberg Code are the following (see Reynolds, 1979, appendix 2, for a more complete listing):

- Voluntary consent is critical to involvement in an experimental program.
- The research must have a clear social value not obtainable by an alternative, more benign method.
- The procedure should avoid all unnecessary physical and mental anguish.
- The degree of risk must be less than the humanitarian gain from the experiment.
- The utmost care and skill are necessary throughout any research procedure.
- The human subject must be free to terminate the research at any time.
- The human subject must be protected against even a remote possibility of injury or disability.

Rules, of course, are neither self-fulfilling nor self-interpreting, and a careful reading of the foregoing guidelines will indicate a number of points about which reasonable persons can disagree, even though they are dealing with the same set of facts. How voluntary is voluntary? We have noted that there is now some belief that under no conditions can prisoners voluntarily consent to participate in an experiment. Can a person under the age of 18 voluntarily offer consent? Is mental retardation a barrier to informed consent? Is true consent given if the person is in dire need of money and knows that there will be a fee attached to participation in the experiment? Is true consent given if participation gains the approval of the experimenter and failure to participate annoys or even outrages the experimenter?

One of the elements of many students' experience is the common requirement that if they are enrolled in introductory classes or in research courses they have to participate in experiments, which usually are carried out by graduate students completing theses or dissertations or by faculty members. The rationale for such participation is that being a subject in an experiment is part of a learning experience, that the student comes to see how research is conducted and comes to get a fine feeling of being part of something beyond the classroom. Others maintain that the activities are no more than exploitation of students in order to serve the ends of the graduate students and the faculty. In some college and university departments, failure to participate in such outside work carries with it a grade penalty; in others, the student is given an extra assignment, such as watching a movie or writing a paper, that is supposed to be as time-consuming as the experiment. There are those who maintain that for the participation of the student to be truly voluntary there must be no reward, such as a grade, and no penalty, such as an additional assignment. But under such conditions, probably comparatively few students would choose to participate in such research work, and the goal of obtaining a true sample of the class would be undermined.

Similar kinds of considerations prevail for each of the other provisions of the Nuremberg Code. It is easy enough to know when an experiment is blatantly unethical or when it clearly is within the bounds of any reasonable ethical system. The marginal instances are the ones that cause the most trouble, when phrases such as "unnecessary physical and mental anguish" and "degree of risk" and "remote possibility" have to be interpreted in terms of a particular research investigation.

Take, as a further illustration, the ethical standard that the participant must be "free" to terminate the research "at any time." How can this condition be satisfied adequately? In most experiments, the research worker merely tells the subject that this condition is to prevail, usually in words such as: "If you want to stop at any time, please let me know and we will be pleased to release you from the experiment." But there are all sorts of subtle and direct pressures on a person to continue as part of a project once the involvement has been initiated. Should the person be reminded a certain number of times of the freedom to leave? And, of course, virtually any researcher will, even in the face of his or her best conscious intentions, try to structure a situation so that the subject continues with the experiment; otherwise, the time taken up to that point is lost and the sample is distorted by a withdrawal. Obviously, ethical codes are not self-operating; they require a good deal of attention and clarification.

ANONYMITY AND DECEPTION

More recent statements of concern for human subjects and guidelines for appropriate research procedures have encompassed issues such as the right to anonymity and confidentiality and the right to be as free as possible from deception.

In criminal justice research in particular the question of anonymity can be of preeminent importance. A person may reveal to a research worker information about his or her involvement in a criminal offense and be in considerable jeopardy if such information comes to the attention of the police. The research worker is put in a delicate position, trying to keep channels of communication open so that accurate and complete information will be forthcoming while at the same time knowing that the information secured can be subpoenaed by law enforcement agencies by means of court processes. In general, the best procedure appears to be to inform a subject directly of the risks—they tend to be minimal, but they can be extremely harmful—that are involved in conveying damaging information. In some cases when criminal justice researchers have reported on corruption in police departments, district attorneys have attempted to gain possession of their field notes, in which the actual names of persons camouflaged in the later reports would be found. It should be emphasized that researchers do not enjoy the privilege of confidentiality that is accorded lawyers, physicians, and religious conselors, though there are some persons who favor such protection (for an opposing view, see Sagarin and Moneymaker, 1979).

One of the methods that has recently been used by criminal justice researchers to guarantee anonymity to subjects is to code their materials to cover actual names and identities and then to send the original data with the actual names out of the country (to a colleague in Canada, say), thereby protecting the information against court processes in the United States. It is often necessary to have some place where the true names are retained so that follow-up studies can be done or some matching can be made between two sets of information.

The right to be free from deception lies at the heart of many ethical dilemmas in research. In criminal justice work with a psychological bent, there often is the need, as seen by the experimenter, to deceive the subject; otherwise, the subject would react in a manner contaminated by knowledge of what was being done. There is no way out of this bind, except to plead that the results of the experiment are of more significance than any possible harm that might result from a mild deception. Researchers now routinely "debrief" their subjects after an experiment; that is, they tell them what was truly done and why it was done, and respond to any inquiries about the process.

In field work, issues of deception can be more pronounced. Is it ethical to participate as a researcher in gang activities which violate the law, listening and recording the comments of the gang members unbeknownst to them? Or should the gang members be told the true role of the person in their midst? How far should a researcher go in collaborating in illegal plans or activities in order to obtain information? Should persons who are objects of research share in the income—say, royalties for a book—from that research, and if they do not, are they being used as objects, without gain to themselves? Minority group members have increasingly come to demand that they come to share in some of the wherewithal that surrounds research, such as the salaries of the workers and the glory of the subsequent publication and career advancement. They may demand research jobs, recognition, and similar boons as a prerequisite to their cooperation.

APA STANDARDS

A representative set of ethical principles for research with human subjects is that published by the American Psychological Association (APA) in 1973. These principles were developed over several years by a committee that consulted widely and repeatedly with members of the APA. Similar statements have not yet been promulgated by the criminal justice community, though a great deal of formal and informal consideration of the matters has been manifest at meetings of organizations such as the American Society of Criminology and the Academy of Criminal Justice Sciences. The full set of APA principles reads as follows (Ad Hoc Committee, 1973):

1 In planning a study the investigator has the personal responsibility to make a careful evaluation of its ethical acceptability, taking into account these Principles for research with human beings. To the extent that this appraisal, weighing scientific and humane values, suggests a deviation from any Principle, the investigator incurs an increasingly serious obligation to seek ethical advice and to observe more stringent safeguards to protect the rights of the human research participant.

2 Responsibility for the establishment and maintenance of acceptable ethical practice in research always remains with the individual investigator. The investigator is also responsible for the ethical treatment of research participants by collaborators, assistants, students, and employees, all of whom, however, incur parallel obligations.

3 Ethical practice requires the investigator to inform the participant of all features of the research that reasonably might be expected to influence willingness to participate and to explain all other aspects of the research about which the participant inquires. Failure to make full disclosure gives added emphasis to the investigator's responsibility to protect the welfare and dignity of the research participant.

4 Openness and honesty are essential characteristics of the relationship between investigator and research participant. When the methodological requirements of a study necessitate concealment or deception, the investigator is required to ensure the participant's understanding of the reasons for this action and to restore the quality of the relationship with the investigator.

5 Ethical research practice requires the investigator to respect the individual's freedom to decline to participate in research or to discontinue participation at any time. The obligation to protect this freedom requires special vigilance when the investigator is in a position of power over the participant. The decision to limit this freedom increases the investigator's responsibility to protect the participant's dignity and welfare.

6 Ethically acceptable research begins with the establishment of a clear and fair agreement between the investigator and the research participant that clarifies the responsibilities of each. The investigator has the obligation to honor all promises and commitments included in that agreement.

7 The ethical investigator protects participants from physical and mental discomfort, harm, and danger. If the risk of such consequences exists, the investigator is required to inform the participant of that fact, secure consent before proceeding, and take all possible measures to minimize distress. A research procedure may not be used if it is likely to cause serious and lasting harm to participants.

8 After the data are collected, ethical practice requires the investigator to provide the participant with a full clarification of the nature of the study and to remove any misconceptions that may have arisen. Where scientific or humane values justify delaying or withholding information, the investigator acquires a special responsibility to assure that there are no damaging consequences for the participant.

9 Where research procedures may result in undesirable consequences for the participant, the investigator has the responsibility to detect and remove or correct these consequences, including, where relevant, long-term after-effects.

10 Information obtained about the research participants during the course of an investigation is confidential. When the possibility exists that others may obtain access to such information, ethical research practice requires that this possibility, together with the plans for protecting confidentiality, be explained to the participants as a part of the procedure for obtaining informed consent.

These principles are quite detailed, but the same problems exist that we noted earlier in regard to interpretation. Even with the clearest and most comprehensive guidelines, reaching clear-cut decisions about what is proper and what is unacceptable will prove difficult. In its broadest terms, the ethical problem involves balancing the possible value of a given research project to all humankind against the cost or possible cost to individual subjects. Often, though, there is little indication of what the research will produce—indeed if we knew, we might not be as interested in undertaking it.

To illustrate the difficulty of resolving ethical issues, we present opposite perspectives on two issues. In one case, Warwick (1981) argues in the following vein:

> In order to facilitate the collection of data, or to advance man's knowledge, or to help the oppressed, researchers condone deception in the laboratory, on the streets, and in our social institutions. They deliberately misrepresent the extent of their experiments, assume false appearances, and use other subterfuges as dubious means to questionable ends. *These tactics are unethical and unjustified.* They are also dangerous, because they may spread to other segments of society (italics added).

On the other hand, Rubin (1981:41) presents the following argument after considering essentially the same research as that which prompted the previous writer's remarks:

> To eliminate all deceptive experiments would be a mistake. I am convinced that many are of potentially great scientific and social importance.

Similarly, Galliher (1973:98) has taken the position that confidential information from a research subject may be disclosed if "it is evident that the gain by society and/or science is such that it offsets the probable magnitude of the individual discomfort." Warwick (1981:367) is scathing in his repudiation of that position. He notes in his rebuttal to Galliher:

> At present we too often dispose of ethical questions quickly so that we can get on with the real business of theory and research. The time has come to examine not only the techniques, but the moral implications of social research....Social scientists who do not hesitate to point an accusing finger at [political examples of immorality] are too quick to shrug off their own complicity in moral decay.

Obviously, feelings run strong on these issues, and adjudication can be extremely complicated. We still do not truly have any clear definition of what Rubin calls "potentially great scientific and social importance" or any sense of how many experiments would have to be of such a calibre in order to justify "deceptive experiments." Indeed, exactly what level of deception needs to be reached in order to have the experiment defined as "deceptive" is not obvious either. All of us deceive others—not to mention ourselves—in order to achieve certain ends. We make excuses, invent explanations, and generally tend to put the best light on things, even though we might actually know or suspect otherwise.

Reynolds (1979) has devoted an entire book to providing an inventory of modes of analysis and strategies for resolving ethical problems in social research of the kinds that will occupy persons working in the field of criminal justice. Where deception appears to be absolutely necessary for the conduct of a study, Reynolds advocates getting "surrogate informed consent," that is, consent from people who are thoroughly knowledgeable about all aspects of the research. He also favors providing a comprehensive debriefing of all subjects following participation in the research. The surrogate would have to be a person with a dispassionate relationship to the work: researchers, it seems evident, tend to be biased in favor of an experimenter and do not always consider the best interests of the subject. Lawyers may make fine surrogates, in the sense that they are professionally sensitive to the possibility of harm and the consequent liability that the imposition of such harm may involve.

Debriefing is a kind of "dehoaxing," in the sense that the participants in the research are told all details of the deceptive practices. Even here we may find ourselves confronted with an ethical issue. The debriefing may indeed point out to the person in the experiment that he or she was rather simple-minded in not being able to comprehend that duplicity had been involved. Is it ethically acceptable to ruin a person's self-image as a shrewd and aware person? Or the debriefing may destroy a person's trust and confidence in the professional who carried out the research. Distrust of authority probably is a healthy attitude, but the experimental subject did not volunteer for the research knowing that this would be the outcome.

RESEARCH POSING ETHICAL ISSUES

Let us now turn to examples of research that have led to vigorous criticism on ethical grounds. Later in this book, we will also attend to ethical issues when they are relevant to the particular forms of research being discussed.

Behavior in a Simulated Prison

Haney, Banks, and Zimbardo (1973) undertook a study of the behavior of "prisoners" and "guards" as a function of the roles defined for persons occupying such positions. The investigators selected 24 male subjects from a pool of 75 who responded to a newspaper advertisement asking for volunteers to participate in an inquiry about life in prison. Selection was based upon answers to questionnaire items covering family characteristics, previous experiences, and health history and upon personal interviews. The subjects who were selected were presumed to be the fittest and best adjusted members of the total pool. Twelve were assigned the role of guard and 12 the role of prisoner.

The subjects had been told that they could be assigned either role, and they agreed to participate for up to two weeks for pay of $15 a day. They were assured that they would receive adequate physical care, but they were also warned that the prisoner role would entail loss of privacy and some curtailment of basic civil rights.

The subjects designated as guards were given instructions on appropriate behavior for guards, and they practiced routine tasks associated with that role in the simulated prison complex on the day before the introduction of the prisoners into the setting.

The guards were deceived by statements that the investigators were primarily interested in studying prisoners' behavior. Actually, they were equally interested in learning what they could about the effects of the environment upon the guards.

The guards worked on 8-hour shifts, three men at a time, and remained in the prison environment only during work assignments. On the other hand, the prisoners remained in the simulated prison 24 hours a day throughout the study. Each cell was 6 x 9 feet and contained only a cot. A nearby unlit closet, 2 by 2 by 7 feet, served as a room for solitary confinement.

The procedures involving the prisoners started quite realistically. A real police officer "arrested" the subjects at their residences on charges of suspicion of burglary or armed robbery. They were given *Miranda* warnings, those rules we noted earlier as resulting from the growing concern for civil rights. Then they were handcuffed, searched (often with the neighbors looking on curiously or suspiciously), and transported in the rear of the police car to the police station. At the station, they were fingerprinted and placed in a detention cell, where they were stripped, sprayed with a "delousing" substance (actually, a deodorant), and then required to stand alone and naked in the prison yard for a period of time.

Prisoners were made to memorize the rules of the prison and were told that they must follow these rules. They were referred to only by the numbers marked on their uniforms. These uniforms were loose-fitting smocks; the prisoners were not given underclothing. Each day, the prisoners were served three bland meals, allowed three supervised visits to the toilet, and given two free hours for reading and letter writing. They were allowed two visiting periods each week and certain rights to attend movies and participate in exercise periods. They were lined up for a count once during each guard shift, and at the beginning they were tested on their knowledge of the rules during this lineup.

Concealed video equipment recorded the counts, meals, visits by friends and relatives, a "prisoner rebellion" and other occurrences for about 12 hours each day. Concealed microphones recorded interactions between guards and prisoners for a total of 30 hours. The guards recorded their observations following each shift, and the experimenters who were running this program maintained diaries of their own.

That the mock prison experience had a marked impact on participants is evident from the fact that it was necessary to release five prisoners from the study because of such acute reactions as crying, depression, anxiety, rage, and psychosomatic symptoms.

The major result was that the respective roles imposed upon guards and prisoners led to behavioral differences by the end of the study that exceeded even the most radical expectations. The persons recruited as guards became arbitrary, abusive, and aggressive, while the prisoners became subservient, passive and disorganized. It must be remembered that the subjects were assigned to the roles randomly, which makes it reasonable to conclude that these apparent personality and behavioral differences were environmentally determined. The behaviors resulted primarily from shared stereotypes regarding prisons, prisoners, and guards and the power and the absence of autonomy associated with the respective roles in the institutional setting.

The transformation of the persons involved in the research took place very rapidly. Indeed, because of the intensity of emotional reactions in the study, it was terminated at the conclusion of six days, despite the initial intention to continue into a second week. Even in the brief period of time that the experiment had lasted, harassment by the guards had escalated to the point of being unbearable to many prisoners.

Encounter sessions aimed at debriefing were held for the guards and prisoners separately. Haney, Banks, and Zimbardo (1973:88) state:

> Subjects and staff openly discussed their reactions, and strong feelings were expressed and shared. We analyzed the moral conflicts posed by this experience and used the debriefing sessions to make explicit alternative causes of action that would lead to more moral behavior in future comparable situations. Follow-ups on each subject over the year following termination of the study revealed that the negative effects of participation had been temporary, while the personal gains to the subjects endure.

Despite the disclaimer in the final sentence, a reader can hardly help wondering about the long-term effects of the experiences upon the participants. The humiliations and the indignities suffered by the prisoners were powerful, as was shown by statements after the study as well as by the necessity for terminating the experiment early (and releasing five of the prisoners even earlier). Beyond that, it appears possible that even the guards felt some long-range stress based on guilt stemming from reflecting on the types of individuals they were capable of becoming. It was just this kind of self-revelation that had led to strong objections to earlier work by Milgram (1974) in which he found that subjects would be willing to inflict pain on innocent people if they were ordered to do so by someone who appeared in the role of an authority. There may be a bit of the fascist in all or most of us, the critics of the experiment said, but persons volunteering for an experiment said to be measuring something else had not agreed to find this out about themselves.

Whatever the longer-range effects in the research of Haney et al., participants unquestionably reacted to the immediate environment in an intense manner. It seems clear that the ethical justification for subjecting humans to even short-term psychological suffering of the type involved in the prison study requires, at least, unequivocal presentation of overriding gains to be won on the basis of the work.

For the experimenters, the overriding gains, as they saw the matter, lay in the direction of ultimate connection between what they referred to as the deplorable and dehumanizing conditions in our penal system and how such conditions influence the persons exposed to the system, either as keepers or as captives. In a subsequent report, Haney (1976:188) posed the ethical issue in the following form:

> It seems disturbing and perverse that we might refrain from engaging in the kind of research which is needed to effectively demonstrate the dehumanizing effects of certain social environments and rebut the localization of pathology within individuals, because the necessary research is too dehumanizing. It seems equally ironic that persons moved by a deep concern over the effects of dehumanizing environments on people would engage in research which is similarly harmful in kind if not in degree. For me personally there is a paradox in the recognition that now my own sensitivity to these issues might well preclude performing the research which produced it.

Indeed, Haney argues, the importance of the outcome of the prison study depended on "the *extent* that the effects on subjects were painful." If the effects had been slight or nonexistent, the lesson about the impact of institutional conditions would have been different.

There was a large degree of deception in the prison study. But most persons commenting on the ethical aspects of research grant that a certain amount of deception may be tolerable (see, for instance, principle 4 in the APA statement). They insist, though, that the deception is not to be too gross and that there be a poststudy effort to explain the reasons for it to all subjects. The prison study might well have been within ethical boundaries on this dimension, though Warwick (1981) clearly would not agree with such a judgment.

The participants undoubtedly were volunteers, respondents to a newspaper advertisement, and they freely signed a consent form when they were selected. But it is less sure that the information given to them in regard to the mock prison and the possibility of their assignment to the role of guard or prisoner gave them an adequate feel for what participation truly meant.

Tearoom Trade

We can conclude the chapter by noting an additional study that created a furor of response based upon ethical considerations. Later in the volume we will tell more about the details of the investigation, published as *Tearoom Trade* and written by Laud Humphreys (1970), who carried out the fieldwork while a doctoral student at Washington University in St. Louis. It involved observing homosexual episodes in restrooms in public parks. Humphreys would station himself as a lookout while the activity occurred and would record details of what went on. Later, Humphreys, who had taken down the license numbers of the cars of the participants, disguised himself and visited the men's homes, saying that he was conducting a door-to-door survey. Humphreys said that he did everything possible to make sure that the names of the men whose secrets he knew would never get out. He writes (1975:179):

> I kept only one copy of the master list of names and that was in a safe deposit box. I did all of the transcribing of taped interviews myself and changed all identifying marks and signs. In one instance, I allowed myself to be arrested rather than let the police know what I was doing and the kind of information I had.

The work drew a stinging rebuke from Nicholas van Hoffman, a columnist for the Washington Post, who noted that "we're so preoccupied with defending our privacy against insurance investigators, dope sleuths, counterespionage men, divorce detectives and credit checks, that we overlook the social scientists behind the hunting blinds who're also peeping into what we thought were our most private and secret lives." Hoffman particularly discounted Humphreys' claims that his work was well-intentioned, noting that "everybody who goes around snooping on people can be said to have good motives." In the same vein, Warwick (1973) weighed the pros and cons of Humphreys' work and concluded that the potential harm to other persons was in no way worth whatever contribution, if any, the study had made to science.

This brief overview of the ethical issues in criminal justice research indicates that there are broad boundaries and very complex questions involved. The aim of a good and decent criminal justice researcher is to be aware of the ethical considerations in the work that is undertaken and to be as certain as possible that the research falls within acceptable limits in regard to any possible harm to human subjects.

REFERENCES

Ad Hoc Committee on Ethical Standards in Psychological Research 1973. *Ethical Principles in the Conduct of Research with Human Participants.* Washington, D.C.: American Psychological Association.

Galliher, J. F. 1973. "The Protection of Human Subjects: A Reexamination of the Professional Code of Ethics." *American Sociologist,* **8**:93–100.

Haney, C. 1976. "The Play's the Thing: Methodological Notes on Social Simulations." In P. Golden (ed.), *The Research Experience.* Itasca, Ill.: F. E. Peacock.

Haney, C., Banks, W. C., and Zimbardo, P. G. 1973. "Interpersonal Dynamics in a Simulated Prison." *International Journal of Criminology and Penology.* **1**:69–77.

Hartshorne, H., and May, M. A. 1928–30. *Studies in the Nature of Character:* vol. I, *Studies in Deceit;* vol. II, *Studies in Self-Control;* vol. III, *Studies in the Organization of Character.* New York: Macmillan.

Humphreys, L. 1970. *Tearoom Trade: Impersonal Sex in Public Places,* enlarged ed. Chicago: Aldine.

Jones, J. H. 1981. *The Tuskogee Syphilis Experiment.* New York: Free Press.

de Mause, L. 1974. *The History of Childhood.* New York: Psychological Press.

Milgram, S. 1974. *Obedience to Authority: An Experimental View.* New York: Harper & Row.

Reynolds, P. D. 1979. *Ethical Dilemmas and Social Science Research*. San Francisco: Jossey-Bass.

Rubin Z. 1981. "Jokers Wild in the Lab." In T. C. Wagenaar (ed.), *Readings for Social Research*. Belmont, Calif.: Wadsworth.

Sagarin, E., and Moneymaker, J. 1979. "The Dilemma of Researcher Immunity." In C. B. Klokkars and F. W. O'Connor (eds.), (pp. 75–193). *Deviance and Decency*. Beverly Hills, Calif.: Sage.

Von Hoffman, N. 1970. "Sociological Snoopers and Journalistic Moralizers." In L. Humphreys, *Tearoom Trade*. (pp. 177–181). Chicago: Aldine.

Warwick, D. P. 1981. "Social Scientists Ought to Stop Lying." In T. C. Wagenaar (ed.), *Readings for Social Research*. Belmont, Calif.: Wadsworth.

Warwick, D. P. 1973. "Tearoom Trade: Means and Ends in Social Research" *Hastings Center Studies* 1:27–38.

Watson, J. B., and Rayner, R. 1920. "Conditional Emotional Reactions." *Journal of Experimental Psychology*, 3:1–14.

CHAPTER 3

RESEARCH IN CRIMINAL JUSTICE: ISSUES AND PREPARATION

CHAPTER OUTLINE

RESEARCH ISSUES
   "Bellow Like a Bull"
   The Last Word
   More Court Matters
   Feedback From Probation Officers
   Police and Weapons
   Causes of Crime
      Schools of thought on causation
      An example: Arson as a research issue
   Further Research Topics
PREPARATION FOR RESEARCH
Site Exploration and Related Details
Review of the Literature
REFERENCES

A fundamental impetus for research is curiosity. Someone wants to know something, to learn something. The resulting information may be used by the person discovering it or by others for good or evil or for indifferent purposes. Scientific democracy is committed to the view that individuals and the social system itself both are likely to be better off if they have accurate information on which to base policy and personal action. People ought to know the truth about the crime rates in different parts of their home city, the utility of capital punishment, the relationship between expenditures for law enforcement and their personal safety. With such information, they (and we) believe, they will be able to make more decent kinds of decisions.

Some research is undertaken because an agency wants an answer to nagging questions before it proceeds with policy or expenditures of funds. Perhaps members of a legislative oversight committee want to learn whether victims of crime are making better adjustments to their deprivation under a compensation program than they had previously. Or perhaps the head of a department of corrections wants to find out whether a new effort in programmed learning in a youth corrections facility is producing the kinds of benefits that reasonably seem to justify the cost of personnel and equipment. In such cases, the thrust of the research inquiry will be dictated by the policy requirements of the progenitor of the work. But astute research workers will always keep an open mind when they do such work. Other things that nobody had anticipated might happen when a new program is operating, and unless the researcher is on the lookout for so-called serendipitous effects, some major considerations will not find their way into the research report.

There are other forms of research and evaluation that are prompted by the worker's personal or professional interest in discovering an answer to a question. The stereotype is that of the scientist who awakes suddenly in the middle of the night, struck by the force of an idea. The next morning the researcher rushes to the laboratory or into a field setting to attempt to verify or reject the inspiration by empirical methods, that is, by a sophisticated research inquiry.

Where do such ideas come from? Some, of course, are flashes of insight, perhaps based on a long history of consideration of matters that concern the researcher. For instance, the worker may have been pondering more effective methods to reduce the rate of burglary and got the idea that an intensive campaign which requires people to write down the serial numbers of all their possessions—such as typewriters and stereos—will inhibit burglary because it will make "fencing" the property (that is, selling it to an intermediary) more hazardous. The next step is to establish a satisfactory method of testing this assumption.

The possibilities for constructive and useful research in criminal justice are almost limitless, once the student acquires the skills to do a competent job. Acquiring an answer to a problem that no one has yet solved can prove enormously satisfying.

Reading is one sure method for gaining ideas about researchable matters. Many writers make statements that a good researcher will ponder in a questioning manner, asking: Is this really true? And, if so, under what conditions and with what reservations is it an accurate statement? How could I demonstrate the point—or refute it? Is it an important enough issue to occupy my time? And how might I tie it to larger questions of general theoretical concern, questions that can be illuminated by a small-scale experimental effort?

Let's look at some possibilities gleaned from writings in the field of criminal justice. We will not go into detail about the requirements for research on each of the topics, since that will be covered later. Besides, the pride and pleasure of constructing your own research designs and inquiries is one of the particular appeals of independent research. You might try to imagine for some of the topics below how you would investigate questions that are directly or indirectly posed. After you've gone further in this book and through a research methods course, you could perhaps apply some of the new ideas you've learned to these and similar issues.

RESEARCH ISSUES

"Bellow Like a Bull"

Courtrooms offer especially attractive research sites. The drama of court proceedings, often with high stakes, involves fundamental principles of our society. The distinction between the principles and actual practice can sometimes create disillusionment. In other respects, when the task is to structure better and more effective ways of judging guilt and innocence, some of the strengths of the adversary system of American justice begin to stand out.

The fact that trials, with rare exceptions, must be public is a great benefit to a research worker. He or she can sit unobtrusively in a courtroom and count and observe those things of investigative interest. The dynamics of courtroom performance has been relatively unexplored. There is a great deal of work on juries, but most of it involves simulations, often using college students. Such laboratory work has the advantage of being conducted under tightly controlled experimental conditions, but it lacks verisimilitude; that is, the atmosphere is far different from that of an actual courtroom scene, and the results may not be generalizable from experiment to reality. The English have attempted to overcome this particular problem by recruiting members of what they call a "shadow jury," persons who have been empaneled for jury duty but are not serving in a particular case (McCabe and Purves, 1974). These persons observe and listen to the same trial that the regular jury is adjudicating. Later, researchers monitor closely the deliberation of the shadow jury members and attempt to establish rules by which such groups reach their decisions. This work builds upon some classic earlier American inquiries which employed mock juries for cases that had been artificially constructed or tape-recorded (Kalven and Zeisel, 1966).

There are almost limitless questions about the operation of courts and their personnel that could occupy the talents of a good researcher. Take, for a simple illustration, the observation of a veteran trial lawyer, advising a newcomer to the business:

> "If you have a strong case in law—talk to the judge. If you have a strong case in fact, talk to the jury. If you have no case in law or in fact, talk to the wild elements and bellow like a bull" (Botein, 1952:112).

In its essentials, the folklore advice suggests that the courtroom styles of lawyers should vary with the type of case. Certainly, we can suspect that the nature of a case, the kind of charge, the qualities of the judge, the mix of jury members, the tactics of the opposing attorneys, and the social climate in the community at the moment (including such things as the crime rate, the stance of the mass media, unemployment, welfare costs, and even the weather) will all blend to determine the outcome of a criminal trial. All or any one of these matters can form the basis of important research work.

The Last Word

Take another courtroom issue, the question of who gets the last chance to address the jury in a criminal trial. A famous English barrister suggests that the right to talk to the jury last in a criminal trial represents a particular advantage to the lawyer who has it. His biographer notes:

> Mr. Birkett always liked the last word to the jury.... He once said: "You may think that one of the reforms one day will be that counsel for the defense shall always speak last, so that he can reply to everything that is said" (Bowker, 1949:237).

In all European countries except England, the defense addresses the jury last. In America and England, the reverse is true for criminal trials: the prosecutor speaks last. The only exception is the state of Minnesota, which by statute adheres to the continental model. The French believe that Americans "have no conception of fair play to the accused," but instead possess "the souls and minds of hangmen," because we do not have a rule such as *l'inculpé a le dernier la parole* ("the accused is entitled to the last word").

Commonsense would indicate that the French view of things is probably correct. Most of us would probably guess that jury members will retire to their deliberations with the comments of the person they heard last more prominent on their minds. Also, the final speaker has an opportunity to counter arguments made by the other attorney, but what he or she says remains unchallenged. This is particularly true in the United States, where judges cannot comment on the trial as freely as their English counterparts do.

Competent research that bears on this question challenges common-sense views, however. Experimental work indicates that jurors might well adhere to an "ideal of consistency", that is, they may make up their minds about the guilt or innocence of the accused immediately after they have heard the first lawyer make the final presentation. Thereafter, they are reluctant to change their minds, no matter what else is said to them. To alter their opinion makes them feel inconsistent, wishy-washy, and indecisive. So it may be that what lawyers typically regard as a decided advantage is a very considerable disadvantage.

But the matter is far from adequately settled. The gap between experimental research conducted under tightly controlled conditions and actual trials in courtrooms is considerable. And a generalization may be true for things such as formal debates but inaccurate for the more complicated business of a criminal trial. Besides, numerous other considerations, including those we mentioned earlier (such as the respective talents of the attorneys and the nature of the charge), can have different effects on the importance of the order of presentation of final arguments. Research probes that could give acceptable answers to this particular question would provide interaction between a general scientific issue and a particular aspect of criminal court proceedings. It also would allow better determination of the question whether, at least in regard to who speaks last, Anglo-Saxon or continental trials are "fairer."

The distinctive procedures used on the European continent and in Anglo-Saxon countries for the order in which attorneys address juries in criminal trials also appear in a number of other approaches to matters of law and justice. In France, it is considered unacceptably cruel to let a condemned person know the date of the execution; not until the morning when the governor of the prison comes into the cell does the prisoner know that he or she will die that day (Bedford, 1961:297). On the contrary, in the United States, though we aim at making the death penalty as humane as possible, we usually allow the condemned person to know far in advance when the execution is to be. Which method produces the desired consequences? Or is there a procedure better than either?

Similarly, in Italian criminal trials, if two witnesses offer contradictory testimony, they may be forced to confront each other in an open courtroom. Quite often the result is a violent emotional outburst that elicits the actual truth of the matter (Young, 1958:214). Is this process tailored exclusively for the presumed national character of Italians, or is it an admirable, useful way to achieve the truth in a courtroom trial that most basically is very similar to an athletic contest? Good research could go a long way toward providing an answer.

More Court Matters

The intricacies of courtroom maneuvers offer a further variety of puzzling research issues. Take, for example, the ageold Anglo-Saxon doctrine that hearsay evidence is not admissible in a criminal trial and that evidence will not be used if the defense cannot cross-examine the person offering the testimony. But the law also states that "a dying declaration...is a statement of material facts concerning the cause and circumstances of a homicide, made by the *victim* when dying and under the belief of impending death."

Such a statement is admissible in court on the assumption that a person facing death will not dare to tell other than the truth. The principle arose in a social system which was deeply religious, with citizens mortally afraid of eternal punishment and perdition were they to die as unredeemed sinners. But does the underlying theme hold true today? It does not take much imagination to picture a leading figure in organized crime, fatally wounded, malevolently accusing another enemy rather than the true perpetrator, in order to obtain last-minute vengeance. Or someone, even while dying, might try to protect a close friend or relative from a homicide indictment by naming someone else as the killer.

How might a curious researcher, seeking to make suggestions either for keeping the ancient doctrine regarding dying declarations or for abandoning it, go about investigating its current legitimacy? Certainly, a first step would be to determine how often the practice occurs in contemporary jurisprudence. Then an effort might be made to investigate its consequences. Various kinds of experimental inquiries could be mounted, though this, obviously, is one of those situations where duplication of the circumstances lies beyond the abilities of any possible research simulation.

Similar kinds of uncertainty surround another, more common courtroom vignette. Rules of proper procedure insist that when something is said during a trial that should not have been uttered, the judge must interrupt the flow of evidence to issue a solemn warning to the jury that its members ought not to pay any attention to the material that should not have been placed before them. But it has been suggested that such an approach is worse than nothing:

> Most lawyers and judges think that the accused will be better off if the judge does not give the jury such a warning. For that sort of warning tends to rub in the very fact the jury is cautioned to disregard; it asks the jury, said a great judge, to engage "in a mental gymnastic which is beyond not only their powers, but anyone else's." It recalls the classic story of the young boy told to stand in the corner and "not to think of a white elephant" (Frank and Frank, 1957:113).

The discrepancy between common understanding and empirical evidence in regard to the last word to the jury, which we discussed earlier, indicates that we ought to be wary about taking at face value the impressionistic views of lawyers and judges about the actual effect of any courtroom procedure. The commonsense view appears to have much to be said in its favor. But is it really accurate? It probably is under certain conditions, and probably is not under others. It is likely, for instance, that a stern warning by an impressive judge under particular kinds of conditions would be notably effective in leading jurors not only to try to ignore the stated point but to lean over backwards to make certain that they have not been biased by it. Under other conditions, the analogy with the boy and the white elephant probably prevails. A good researcher would probe all these contingencies plus those which involve the particular rule and the entire courtroom process. Both scientific theory and the administration of criminal justice would be better off for the results of such an inquiry.

Feedback from Probation Officers

Let's move to another realm of the criminal justice system for additional illustrations. Probation involves attempts by city, county, or state employees to supervise persons who have been convicted of criminal offenses or have been adjudicated in juvenile court. Its aim is to keep the offenders from further violations by watching over them and also by offering them various kinds of assistance. Such assistance can include counseling, job placement, budget management, and a host of other matters. The skill of the probation officer in doing those things that will assist his or her charge becomes the measure of the value of the service. But probation officers rarely learn how successful or unsuccessful they have been. As one of them notes:

> I cannot think who is so handicapped as is the probation officer by having no opportunity to study the effects of his labors. To evaluate his work on the day the case is closed is not enough, no matter how brightly successful it seems to be. The real test is in the long pull after that, for the treatment given the probationer does not fulfill our farthest hope unless it is of permanent effect. Yet we have usually no way of knowing what is now happening in the lives we touched ten, twenty, or more years ago. They may have done well after a slow start, and somewhere now are successful beyond any hope we had for them when last seen. Just as possible—the man who showed the most promising success while on probation may since have proved unable to hold the gains and, unknown to us, have later failed more miserably than before (Keve, 1954:257).

The foregoing statement implicitly assumes that better information on the long-term effects of their work will make for better probation officer efforts. This itself is a researchable issue: the information that they would get might prove so discouraging that many officers would abandon strenuous efforts, knowing too well that they will not have much impact. On the other hand, of course, reliable data could produce much finer tuning in what the officers emphasize. The obstacles to satisfactory adjudication of the numerous issues in this field are formidable. Can you say, for instance, that what an officer did 10 years ago, even if it seemed to have been marvelously valuable, will now be of similar utility? The officer has changed, the probationer is a very different person, and society has undergone considerable alteration. The whole chemistry of the interaction of probation may be altogether altered.

How would you attack the kind of problem that the probation officer raises? We have offered some hints earlier in this chapter: it is our aim in this book to provide the means of thought and analysis and the tools by which questions such as these can be handled skillfully.

Police and Weapons

Police work offers the criminal justice research worker an extraordinary range of opportunities for both applied research (particularly evaluation research) and original experimental efforts tied to more general scientific hypotheses. How, for example, is human behavior in general affected by the interaction between persons in authority and the general population? Geoffrey Gorer (1955), a British social anthropologist, insists that one of the reasons why the British people are so agreeable in their public behavior (why, for instance, they so commendably get onto the ends of lines rather than attempting to crash into the front) is that the police, at least in earlier times, have provided constant examples of cooperative social behavior. Do human beings respond in such a manner to models that are set before them? If so, do the pornography and violence in our mass media trigger imitation of the portrayed activities? Or do the representations allow easier sublimation of aggressive kinds of impulses?

Another British writer finds similar benefits from the fact that British police go about without weapons, except for particularly dangerous kinds of assignments. Martienssen (1951:3) writes:

> Partly because of their civilian status and partly as a safeguard against the possible abuse of power, the police are unarmed. It is almost impossible to exaggerate the good which Britain has gained from insistence on this principle. The fact that the policeman is discouraged from using force means that he must do his work by tact and persuasion. Blustering or shouting only makes a British crowd laugh or jeer, and the policeman learns that good humor and pleasant courtesy are essential if he is to do his work well. British crowds were not always as good-humored and tolerant as they are today, and it is not going too far to say that the improvement owes much to the police, whose non-violent methods of controlling a crowd have slowly taught the British that public behavior which is justly admired by foreign visitors. The amiability of a British crowd...springs from an awareness of what is reasonable behavior on public occasions, and this is chiefly due to the use by the police of persuasion rather than force.

The glowing portrayal by Martienssen may be a bit overdone. It is not unlikely that the behavior of British crowds and the fact that the police are able to go about unarmed are both a consequence of precedent factors. Among such factors might be the smallness of the nation, its ethnic homogeneity, its rather rigid class distinctions, and its low crime rate—the last item perhaps also a consequence of other considerations.

Few American authorities would advocate unarmed police, largely because of their belief that to take weapons away from law enforcement officers would unreasonably expose them to lethal consequences produced by criminal offenders. Perhaps few British would advocate unarmed police for America if they were aware of conditions here. But the issue poses intriguing research possibilities, because so much might be at stake. Do criminal offenders tend to kill and injure American law enforcement officers because they know that the officers are armed and a serious threat to their own well-being? Might they rather run than stay and shoot if the police went unarmed? And, if this were to prove to be true, what would the price be in a possibly lower number of apprehended criminals? Above all, for our purposes, how might answers to questions such as these and related issues be obtained? Where, for instance, might we find police officers under today's conditions who would be willing to carry out their assignments without weapons? And, even if we could obtain such volunteers, would these exceptional experimental circumstances be satisfactory for answering our questions? Perhaps we would, at first, require only some slight indications of possible outcomes before we would feel comfortable trying to mount a more elaborate investigation. Or perhaps today public policy dictates that this is not a matter for which systematic inquiry is appropriate.

Police work itself is based upon a good deal of scientific insight. The resolution of complicated cases may depend on scrupulous laboratory work with fibers or footprints or similar detritus of the criminal scene. The spate of murders of black children in Atlanta in 1980 and 1981 produced an arrest based upon microscopic comparisons of fibers from some victims' clothes with similar fibers allegedly located in the automobile and apartment of the apprehended suspect. Or a solution might be reached by means of careful inferential logic on the part of investigating detectives. Jonathan Rubinstein, in an observational study of police work, provides a number of stories about the manner in which certain clues are employed by the officers. He notes, for instance, that ex-convicts and other persons who have been confined in institutions often learn to walk with their toes curled while they are incarcerated, because they are denied the use of shoelaces. The laces are taken away from them because of a fear of suicide or even because it is believed that they might be used as a weapon in a strangling. Not unusually, a released inmate will continue to forgo laces. When police officers see people without shoelaces on the street, the officers are likely to assume these are people whose past histories make them worthy of further scrunity (Rubinstein, 1973:248).

The interplay of scientific logic on the police beat is further illustrated by the practice in some cities, where it is very cold in the winter, for officers on a beat to "hide out" in a neighborhood store. They set up a system whereby they are warned from headquarters when their supervisor is about to come into their territory. But the supervisor may put an arm about an officer's shoulder in a seemingly friendly gesture and "accidentally" touch the badge, whose temperature will reveal at once whether the officer has been walking a beat or keeping warm indoors. The officers themselves are not without counterstrategies. Some men carry two badges, leaving one outside when they go inside (Rubinstein, 1973:19).

Such slight vignettes of police experience, to have real meaning, would have to be tied to more significant research questions. It might be worthwhile to learn more accurately, for instance, the relationship between performance of officers and trust on the part of supervisors, as contrasted with constant surveillance of and suspicion about officers' activities. Trust may breed superior performance, or it might encourage the subordinate to take advantage of the opportunity to perform less well. We might thereafter want to tie the conclusions we reach to broader research questions that bear upon performance in other bureaucracies, such as business and educational institutions. The results could also be related to the ways in which children are raised in terms of disciplinary patterns.

Another example from the realm of law enforcement shows how carefully a research worker must monitor all relevant considerations when examining an intervention program. The police introduced a more effective burglar alarm system in a particular city. Because of the high level of false alarms, they previously had rarely responded to alarms that were registered or reported to them. Under the new system, however, burglars soon began to break into a store, trip the alarm, and then congregate nearby to see whether the police would respond. When they did show up, an alternative target would be chosen. One set of figures showed that the new alarm system was singularly effective in reducing the number of burglaries in those places which had the system. But what did not appear in the preliminary reports was information that places in neighboring jurisdictions and those without the alarm, had suffered a very considerable increase in the rate of burglaries during the same period (Maltz, 1972:22).

Causes of Crime

Schools of Thought on Causation Explanations of criminal behavior have been something of an elusive holy grail sought by criminal justice workers. There are a number of schools of thought about the best way for criminal justice research to deal with the issue of causation—or *etiology*, as it is more formally known. One proposes that criminal behavior is the product of the same kind of processes that produce noncriminal behavior and that adequate explanations of crime must await breakthroughs in all the behavioral sciences concerning what makes people behave as they do. It is noted, for instance, that since we really do not understand why some persons do *not* steal, kill, rape, and rob—even if sometimes they might be able to do so without penal consequences—we are not likely to learn why other persons do engage in such acts. At the same time, though, it is possible, and may be worthwhile to learn what differentiates individuals who commit crimes from those who do not. If we find that an overwhelmingly large number of homicides are committed by very young persons (say, ages 15 to 24), we can begin to scrutinize correlates of this age span for more precise causative factors.

Some writers believe that causation is the essence of criminal justice investigation. Edwin H. Sutherland, in his pioneering textbook examination of the field of criminology, indicated, for instance, that "the most important thing to know about crime is the mechanisms by which it is produced" (Sutherland, 1924:86). He thought that such understanding could best be obtained by the use of case studies, a method widely employed in earlier days but rather out of fashion today, though it has much to recommend it as a means of comprehending the details and nuances of criminal biography. Sutherland believed that a single explanation should be sought for all crime. Robert Rice (1956), among many others, believes, however, that the terms *crime* and *criminal* are too general and vague to allow for worthwhile research into any single causative factor. Rice observes that the dictionary defines a *criminal* as "one who has been found guilty of a crime," and he maintains that the following portrays the shortcomings of such a definition:

> Any definition that in nine words, eight of them monosyllables, is able to effectively blanket such assorted personalities as John Dillinger, Harry K. Thaw, Loeb and Leopold, Waxey Gordon, Robert Whitney, Lizzie Borden, and Robin Hood is pretty primitive, and is no more enlightening than the observation that whales, giraffes, two-toed sloths, and disc jockeys are all mammals, or that quail, deliquescence, pique, and cumquat are all common nouns containing the letter "q" (p. xiii).

Robert K. Merton, one of the luminaries of social science theory, has gone further and pointed out that grouping a wide constellation of acts— such as those behaviors defined as *crime*—into a single category has the consequence of directing the nature of the research that will be conducted. Merton (1957:27) observes that it "naturally leads us to assume that it is what these behaviors have in common that is more relevant, and this assumption leads us to look for an all-encompassing set of propositions which will account for the entire range of behavior." He believes that such an endeavor is like trying to find a single theory of disease, rather than distinct theories, to explain tuberculosis and arthritis and typhoid and syphilis.

The idea of seeking particular constellations of explanations for particular kinds of crime seems to make a good deal of sense. Within general categories of crime, such as homicide, there is a vast array of different forms of action: infanticide, the killing of parents, the murder of a spouse for insurance, and killing during a robbery. To try to find a common ingredient which would help to explain so varied a range of killings may be unfruitful.

It should be appreciated, too, that causal research is by no means "better" or necessarily more useful than more pragmatic work. Karl Popper (1966:291) sarcastically noted if we focus all our attention on trying to find precise causes of crime rather than simultaneously enacting and effectively enforcing laws, it would be much like only studying the causes of cold weather in order to remove them, rather than wearing heavy clothing at the same time.

An Example: Arson as a Research Issue We turn to the offense of arson to illustrate etiological research associated with one general category of crime.

Pyromania, or pathological fire setting, is said to be a mental condition marked by an irresistible impulse to set fires. Nolan D. C. Lewis (1951), a psychiatrist, who has examined persons caught committing acts of arson, says that his work leads him to believe that most are of low intelligence and are physical cowards. He points out that arson is an excellent means of destruction, with a spectacular effect being produced merely by the use of a match. Most conspicuously, it is a crime committed by adolescents and young adults, with the most common age of offenders being 17 years. The arsonists Lewis studied described their feelings before they set fires as mounting tension, restlessness, an urge for motion, and what psychiatrists call conversion symptoms—such as headache, ringing in the ears, heart palpitations, and a general sense of unreality. Lewis observes that targets for arson among his study group included baby carriages. From a psychiatric perspective, he interprets this as the product of aggressive and hostile feelings of arsonists toward their siblings. Finally, he put forward the following idea as an integral explanation of what he believes to be the condition of pyromania:

> A desire for exhibitionism is the factor most common to each of the men described, as though they began life with an exaggerated wish to become leading participants in the contemporary drama, and then, when it was realized fate had relegated them to insignificant roles, they secretly staged a drama of their own, in which they were author, stage director, and the leading actors (Lewis, 1951:117).

Are there propositions in Lewis's postulation that are testable by research methods? Against whom are the captured arsonists being compared? All of us generally find at one time or another that we are not getting quite the attention that we are certain we deserve, but only very, very few of us set fires. What might be special about the select group of arsonists? Certainly, we can tabulate the targets of fire setting and determine whether such objects as baby carriages occur more often than we might expect by pure chance. It is important to note that various conjectures offered by psychiatrists, particularly those with psychoanalytic leanings, sometimes are unverifiable by research methods.

Research workers looking intently at the crime of arson will come across a rather puzzling reported relationship betwen epilepsy and fire setting. The relationship was summed up by a New York fire marshall who said: "Epilepsy is found in an important number of persons found to be pyromaniacs. I am sorry to have to bring this point up, and as far as I have been able to determine, there is no medical opinion on the reasons for the tendency of epileptic pyromaniacs" (*New York Times,* April 4, 1953). The reluctance to speak of the possible relationship between epilepsy and arson very likely reflected in part a reaction against a long and unfounded tradition in criminology, begun by Cesare Lombroso, which insisted that epilepsy and crime inevitably went hand in hand. It was not until C. L. Anderson (1936), conducting an obvious kind of research probe, found that there was no significant difference between the extent of epilepsy among prison inmates (250 out of 100,000) and the general population (210 out of 100,000) that the hoary hypothesis was called into doubt.

The failure to establish a direct tie between epilepsy and crime is not surprising when we delve further into the dynamics of the situation. There are between 500,000 and 1,500,000 epileptics in the United States—the range of variation is partly due to uncertainty about proper definition—and about 80 percent are able to control their seizures through the use of medication. Lombroso's concentration on epilepsy as a "degenerative" disease reflects little more than a traditional attitude toward a badly misunderstood condition. The Bible related epileptic seizures to visitations by the Devil (Luke 9:37–43), and the early Greeks labeled it as the "sacred disease." Such outstanding persons as Buddha, Socrates, Alexander the Great, Julius Caesar, Mohammed, Peter the Great, Feodor Dostoyevski, and Napoleon are all reported to have been epileptics. Epilepsy today is regarded not as a disease but as a symptom of various kinds of disorders.

These facts do not explain very satisfactorily, however, the relationship, if any exists, between epilepsy and arson. Gustav Aschaffenburg (1913) simply observed that "epilepsy, arson, mysticism, cruelty, and sexual excitement are all interrelated," taking in rather haphazardly a very large piece of behavioral territory. Lewis (1951:386) has doubted that epilepsy and arson are very much, if at all, interrelated, concluding that "the type of firesetting seems to depend entirely on the basic personality trends...and there is no special pattern for the epileptic as such."

The material above illustrates, for the criminal justice student seeking meaningful kinds of research tasks, just one of the numerous areas where important controversy still prevails. Despite the enormous growth in the past two decades of the number of persons performing research in criminology and criminal justice, there remain a vast number of unaddressed problems. Some day, some investigator may provide us with an acceptable, scientifically impregnable explanation of pyromania (assuming that such a condition even exists) and of the relationships, if any, between personal or biological conditions and crime, particularly the crime of arson. That the answers are not yet in place indicates not so much a lack of interest or curiosity about the issues as the absence of trained criminal justice workers intent upon finding correct answers to these and other important questions.

Further Research Topics

A few more illustrations of research issues in crime causation might be noted before we conclude this section. Observe, for instance, the classical explanation by Lindesmith (1952:8) of the essential element in the use of opiates that transforms the casual user into an addict. Lindesmith notes that "the critical experience in the fixation process is not the positive euphoria produced by the drug but rather the relief of the pain that invariably appears when a physically dependent person stops using the drug." Other research- ers insist, to the contrary, that addiction is reinforced by the continuing euphoria, the good feelings, that drugs such as heroin induce in the user. Obviously, here is a fine opportunity for work to determine what effects are produced and what significance such effects appear to have on the continuing career of the user.

Note, finally, two hypotheses in the realm of criminalized sexual activity. Kate Millett (1971:94) offers the following possible explanation of the motive of customers of prostitutes:

> It is not sex the prostitute is really made to sell; it is degradation. And the buyer, the john, is not buying sexuality, but power, power over another human being, the dizzy ambition of being lord of another's will for a stated period of time—the euphoric ability to direct and command an activity presumably least subject to coercion, and unquestionably most subject to shame and taboo. That's a very considerable impression of power to purchase for ten or fifteen dollars.

Is Millett accurate in her ideas regarding the motivation of men who patronize prostitutes? If so, does the idea hold true for all patrons or only some proportion of them? Or has Millett intruded her own theories of male- female relationships into the subject without any supporting data to buttress her conclusion? What alternative explanation might illuminate the role of prostitution in our society and the motivations of participants in the behavior? And how can a researcher investigate questions such as these?

We might observe in this connection the interesting hypothesis offered by a pair of married graduate students at the University of California, Berkeley, who participated in the North Beach culture of San Francisco as part of the research for the wife's dissertation. They indicated that in recruiting members of a "stable" of women, pimps in the area use psychological principles that seem almost to have come out of a textbook on the practice of brainwashing:

> When you turn a chick out, you take away every set of values and morality she had previously and create a different environment. You give her different friends. You give her instead of squares of bookkeepers or secretaries, clerks, and so forth for friends, professional hos [whores] (Milner and Milner, 1972:95).

Here again we find the germs of research propositions. And note the possible interrelationship between the Milners' material and Millett's ideas. Do prostitutes who work for pimps do what they do because of the introjection of a different set of values, values which allow them to play in a yielding manner the slave role that Millett insists is a prime characteristic of their work?

Let us close this segment of the chapter with two quotations providing succinct insight into the research task. The first is Pierce's definition of truth: "the opinion which is fated to be ultimately agreed to by all who investigate" (Hartshone and Weiss, 1934:V, 408). The second stands as a warning against being trapped into error by our own preconceptions or biases. We should not, Oliver Wendell Holmes warned, "be proper geese led by our propaganda."

PREPARATION FOR RESEARCH

We have noted earlier that a primary task of criminal justice research workers is to gain thorough understanding of the subjects that concern them. Such understanding involved things such as perusal of whatever has been written by others regarding the matter and immersion in the research setting. In this section, we will provide some specific information regarding how such tasks might be accomplished.

Site Exploration and Related Details

There is no substitute for personal familiarity with the research site and the persons who are involved in what is being examined. If the job is to evaluate how a halfway house for paroled narcotics addicts operates, then as much time as possible must be spent probing into all aspects of that particular facility. The research worker should visit it at all hours of day and night. He or she should talk as much and as often as possible with all personnel associated with the effort. Questions should be both standardized (that is, the same question should be addressed to all individuals in order to compare and cumulate answers) and open-ended (that is, general kinds of inquiries). The research worker must learn how to be a good listener. Too often young researchers feel compelled to keep the conversation moving, and they interrupt too readily or ask the next question too quickly. An uncomfortable silence can sometimes produce, from the person being interviewed, information that otherwise would not be forthcoming.

It is difficult to appear sympathetic to all parties involved in a research effort. The narcotics addicts living in the halfway house may put forward a litany of complaints about the treatment that they are receiving. Staff members for their part may have a roster of criticisms of the residents. And members of both groups may seek sympathy from the research worker, particularly if they appreciate that the final report may reflect (or omit) their viewpoints and may hurt their advancement or their positions. A research worker of intelligence and understanding inevitably will form judgments about who is "right" and who "wrong" in any such dispute, but it probably is the best strategy to keep such feelings to oneself. Otherwise, one or another group will soon identify the worker as an antagonist and will withhold or distort pertinent kinds of information. It is possible, of course, to discard any attempt at neutrality and to portray a program from the viewpoint of one or another of the groups or persons involved. But such a posture tends to result in the kind of effort caricatured by the fable of the blind men and the elephant—each of the blind men had a distorted picture of the elephant; one, grasping only the trunk, thought that an elephant was much the same as a snake, and so on.

Two points need to be made about the accumulation of data acquired through site exploration, before the more formal research probe. First, it is essential that all notes be written down as soon as possible after a discussion. Otherwise, despite the best of memories and the noblest of intentions, much of the flavor and much of the content of what was learned will surely be forgotten. Sometimes it is possible to record things during a conversation or while an event is occurring, but such scribbling is likely to inhibit the participants or make them self-conscious. Sometimes it will be possible to tape-record discussions, so that the precise flavor of what was said is preserved for later examination. But it is tedious to transcribe tape recordings, and researchers are likely to become too rushed in their work to take the time and effort to do this or to have it done. But our main point must be stated with emphasis: Write down anything and everything that seems likely to be pertinent to the formulation of the research inquiry and the discussion of its results. And keep up to date on such recording. Organize it systematically, in a manner that will allow it to be used when it is required.

A research worker in criminal justice should appreciate that much pertinent information can be acquired by assiduous attention to what persons acquainted with the subject say. Sometimes the key points will be located not in their precise words but in the nuances of their speech, in the things they emphasize, and perhaps in what they do not say.

One more point should be made about the preparation for a research task. It will often prove enormously helpful if all possible details of the research endeavor are set down very specifically before work gets underway. Many stories of research investigations are filled with episodes of misunderstandings among collaborators, arguments between sponsors and workers, and similar unfortunate experiences. Friendships among research workers have ended sorrowfully because one or the other person thought that his or her name ought to appear first on any published reports. Anger has erupted when a research worker finished a task and found that the sponsoring agency believed that it had the right to censor the material, that is, to keep it as a confidential internal document rather than to publish it more widely, or even to omit or alter parts of the report. Considerations such as these ought to be spelled out in very precise detail. At the outset of research, all parties tend to believe in the goodwill of all concerned and in the ability of decent human beings to resolve amicably all possible conflicts. This is particularly true if the research has been funded and everybody is suffused with the glow of success and well-being. This honeymoon period probably is the best time to pound out the precise details of everybody's rights and duties in regard to the research task.

Review of the Literature

There is a vast amount of material written about most issues in criminal justice. Much of it is readily recoverable by the research worker who needs a thorough understanding of the relevant things that have been written about the subject of concern. But there also is considerable amount of ephemeral material—reports, pamphlets, and similar items—which is not so easy to obtain. We will offer a few suggestions here about how the criminal justice researcher might best obtain the materials on his or her subject.

By far the simplest way, though in many regards the least satisfactory, is to inaugurate a computer search focused on a particular topic. A good library generally has the resources to provide assistance in mining the computer sources that will print out the material you seek. If, for instance, you are concerned with the subject of "police training," a computer search is apt to yield a very large pile of printouts which list books and articles on this subject. There is also likely to be a summary of the contents of the material, attempting to highlight major findings and conclusions.

On a nationwide basis, the National Criminal Justice Reference Service (NCJRS) will provide the researcher with document citations and abstracts from its computer file. In addition, NCJRS supplies reports, monographs and similar documents from its extensive file.

Such materials can offer a starting point, but our experience to date is that the coverage from computer searches is erratic and incomplete. Important material on "police training," for instance, might be missing because it was classified under another heading, such as "police organization."

There are, however, a number of index services available in the field of criminal justice that are invaluable. Perhaps the handiest is the *Social Science Citation Index*(SSCI). The SSCI is a relatively new research tool, which has not yet been employed to the extent that it would warrant. There are a variety of volumes in the SSCI, but we have found that the most useful is the author index. This segment lists, for any published author in the field of social science, every time a particular piece that he or she wrote has been cited in another journal. The SSCI now goes back to 1966, and there are five-year cumulative volumes for the periods 1966 to 1970 and 1971 to 1975.

Suppose that you are interested in work on homicide. You identify as a key contribution on the subject Marvin E. Wolfgang's *Patterns in Criminal Homicide*, a now-classic study that was published in 1958. Wolfgang analyzed the epidemiology (that is, the distribution and characteristics) of the homicides that had taken place in the city of Philadelphia between the years 1949 and 1952. Among other things, the study originated the concept of "victim precipitation," the idea that in some crimes the victims appear almost similar to the offenders in background characteristics and that who kills whom seems almost a matter of chance.

Now suppose that you are interested, as a criminal justice research worker, in determining for a different site and more than 20 years later the extent of "victim precipitation" in homicides. You could begin to gain control of other research on the topic by consulting the SSCI under "Wolfgang," since you can reasonably assume that anybody else writing on this topic would have made note of Wolfgang's findings and compared their own with his. For the purpose of illustration we will look at the SSCI for 1970. Under "Wolfgang," we find the entries shown in Figure 1.

The shorthand of these references is easily interpreted, though it would not be amiss to take along a good magnifying glass when trying to cope with the SSCI.

The first point that can be observed regarding Figure 1 is that entries for the author in whom we are interested occur in three different places—first for WOLFGANG, later for WOLFGANG M, and finally for WOLFGANG ME. The book *Patterns in Criminal Homicide* is the first entry under the author's name. The 58 to the left stands for 1958, which is the year of publication. Let us select the second entry for further scrutiny. It reads WALDO GP, the name and initials of the article's author. Then J CRIM LAW and finally, to the right, three numbers: 61 60 70. These all add up to a reference to Gordon P. Waldo's article "The 'Criminality Level' of Incarcerated Murderers and Non-Murderers," appearing in the *Journal of Criminal Law, Criminology, and Police Science*, volume 61, beginning at page 60, and published in 1970. Waldo's study examines differences between murderers and other offenders in a prison setting along a number of dimensions; it does not deal with the concept of "victim precipitation."

A later entry—the fourth under WOLFGANG ME—is "Patterns of Criminal Homicide: A Comparison of Chicago and Philadelphia," by John Hepburn and Harwin L. Voss in *Criminology*, volume 8, at page 21, the May 1970 number. It contains (on pages 35 to 37) a thorough discussion of "victim precipitation." Among other conclusions, it is noted that the number of victim-precipitated criminal homicides which occurred when intoxicants were present or in which the victim was killed by a friend or member of the family do not differ notably in the two cities. Overall, though, Chicago shows more such slayings than Philadelphia. The Hepburn and Voss article also provides us with additional references which perhaps can be fruitfully

```
WOLFGANG........................................
  58 PATTERNS CRIMINAL HO
    ENGLISH P      CRIM LAW R      1970    249 70
  58 PATTERNS CRIMINAL HO         168
    WALDO GP       J CRIM LAW       61     60 70
  62 J CRIM LC PS    53   301
    GOLDBERG AJ    HARV LAW RE      83   1773 70
  64 MEASUREMENT DELINQUE
    BROWN BS       J CRIM LAW       61     71 70
  65 MINN L REV    50   223
    JACOB BR       J CRIM LAW       61    152 70
  67 SUBCULTURE VIOLENCE
    BAKER BC       CRIMINOLOGY       7      2 70
    SHASKOLS.L     FED PROBAT       34     44 70
    ZELLICK G      CRIM LAW R     1970    188 70
  67 STUDIES HOMICIDE          279
    BROWN BS       J CRIM LAW       61     71 70
  69 ANNALS   381   119
    GOLDFARB RL    GEORGE WASH      39    175 70
  69 VIOLENCE STREETS
    ZELLICK G      CRIM LAW R     1970    188 70
WOLFGANG A......................................
  68 J ABNORM PSYCHOL    73   336
    ZIMET CN       ANN R PSYCH  R   21    113 70
  69 PSYCHON SCI    14   175
    WRIGHT JMV     SC J PSYCHO  R   11     21 70
WOLFGANG M......................................
  ** EXTENT CHARACTER DEL
    MONAHAN TP     PHYLON           31    129 70
  58 PATTERNS CRIMINAL HO
    BEDAU HA       J CRIM LAW       61    539 70
  62 SOCIOLOGY CRIME DELI
    LEONARD WN     LAW SOC REV       4    407 70
  67 STUDIES HOMICIDE     271
    BLAKE JA       SOCIOL Q         11    331 70
  67 SUBCULTURE VIOLENCE        CH 5
    NEWMAN G       BR J CRIMIN      10     64 70
  70 CRIME RACE CONCEPTIO     100
    MILLER AS      LAW CONT PR      35     69 70
WOLFGANG MA....................................
  62 SOCIOLOGY CRIME DELI
    SOLOMON PH     J CRIM LAW   R   61    393 70
WOLFGANG ME...................................
  ** CITED INDIRECTLY
    FERRACUT.F     B PSIC APPL    1970     33 70
  57 J CRIM LAW CRIMINOL    48    1
    FISHER G       BR J SOCIAL       9     54 70
  58 PATTERNS CRIMINAL HO
    DYNES RR       ISSUES CRIM       5    181 70
    FATTAH EA      CAN J CRIM       12     97 70
    FERRACUT.F     B PSIC APPL    1970     33 70
    HEPBURN J      CRIMINOLOGY       8     21 70
    KENDELL RE     ARCH G PSYC      22    308 70
  59 J CLINICAL EXPERIMEN   20   335
    SEIDEN RH      PSYCHOL TOD       4     24 70
  63 U PENNSYLVANIA LAW R    3   708
    WARD P         J RES CRIME       7    207 70
  64 CRIME RACE CONCEPTIO
    GREEN E        AM SOCIOL R      35    476 70
  64 MEASUREMENT DELINQUE
  66 RISS   18   219
    PICCA G        REV FR SOC       11    390 70
  66 SOTSIOLOGIIA PRESTUP
    SOLOMON PH     J CRIM LAW   R   61    393 70
  67 STUDIES HOMICIDE
    FATTAH EA      CAN J CRIM       12     97 70
  67 SUBCULTURE VIOLENCE
    FERRACUT.F     B PSIC APPL    1970     33 70
    IGLITZIN LB    J SOC ISSUE      26    165 70
    KRAUSS S       BR J SOC PS       4    106 70
    MAURA JR       GOVT OPPOS        5    456 70
  68 CRIME CULTURE ESSAYS
    GROSSMAN JB    LAW SOC REV  R    4    613 70
    OSBORNE HW     AM SOCIOL R  B   35    154 70
  68 ETABLISSEMENT INDICE
    PICCA G        REV FR SOC       11    390 70
  69 PSYCHOLOGY TODAY    3    54
  69 PSYCHOLOGY TODAY    3    72
    SEIDEN RH      PSYCHOL TOD       4     24 70
  69 VIOLENT BEHAVIOUR
    COHEN S        SOCIOLOGY    B    4    284 70
  70 SOCIOLOGY CRIME DELI
    BILES D        AUST NZ J C  B    3    188 70
WOLFGANG R.....................................
  68 KULTURELLE RELATIVIS
    WEIDKUHN P     ANTHROPOS    B   65    290 70
```

FIGURE 1

Entries under Wolfgang in the *Social Science Citation Index. (SSCI, 1970.)*

explored. Fairly soon, we ought to have located most, if not all, of the relevant written materials on the subject of interest to us. Experienced researchers often comment on the moment when everything that other writers are referring to represents something that they themselves have read. It is most certainly the moment when they feel quite prepared to venture forth on their own research explorations.

There also exists a *Science Citation Index,* which provides similar kinds of reference material for the natural sciences. It is generally a good idea to trace your authors through these volumes as well—a matter that can be accomplished with very little expenditure of time and effort—in the event that studies bearing on the subject have been published in journals in fields other than social science.

There is no equivalent method for expeditiously locating books that bear on your topic, though the subject index of the Library of Congress catalog, which is also likely to be held by most good libraries, will probably satisfy your requirements.

Beyond this, there are a host of excellent reference works which allow you to gain control of material that has appeared which deals with the subject of your concern. The most current and comprehensive bibliography in the field today is *Criminology and the Administration of Criminal Justice: A Bibliography*, edited by Leon Radzinowicz and Roger Hood and published in 1976 in London by Mansell. Earlier bibliographies are: (1) *Criminology—A Bibliography: Research and Theory in the United States, 1945–1972.* Philadelphia: Center for Studies in Criminology and Criminal Law, University of Pennsylvania, 1974. (2) Dorothy Campbell Tompkins, *The Offender: A Bibliography*. Berkeley: Institute of Governmental Studies, University of California, 1963. (3) Dorothy Campbell Tompkins, *Administration of Criminal Justice, 1949–1956.* Sacramento: California Board of Corrections, 1956. (4) Dorothy Campbell Tompkins, *Sources for the Study of the Administration of Criminal Justice.* Sacramento: California Board of Corrections, 1949. (5) Dorothy Campbell Culver, *Bibliography of Crime and Criminal Justice, 1932–37.* New York: H. W. Wilson, 1939. (6) Augustus Frederick Kuhlman, *A Guide to Material on Crime and Criminals.* New York: H. W. Wilson, 1929.

The publication *Current Contents,* which is issued every week, can be of considerable value to a researcher who wants to keep abreast of work being published in the field of criminal justice. The social and behavioral sciences edition of *Current Contents* reproduces the table of contents of each of the major criminal justice and legal journals (among many other periodicals) at almost the same time that they are issued. *Current Contents* also includes a topic index, as well as a list of addresses of the authors listed in each edition. Researchers can send a postcard to the author of any article that they want to have, requesting a reprint, and most scholars will be more than pleased to send it. Sometimes, they will also include other material that they have published on the same topic. *Current Contents* also publishes editions relating to (1) life sciences, (2) clinical practice, (3) physical, chemical, and earth sciences, (4) engineering, technology, & applied sciences, (5) arts and humanities, and (6) agriculture, biology, & environmental sciences. Some of these may include material of interest to a criminal justice researcher with a specialized subject interest. The volumes are published by the Institute for Scientific Information (ISI), 325 Chestnut Street, Philadelphia, Pennsylvania 19106.

Additional bibliographic sources include *Index Medicus,* which provides information about research of interest to physicians. It contains a good deal of material on topics such as criminal insanity, the treatment of sex offenders, and narcotics, among other matters that could concern a criminal justice worker. The *Index to Legal Periodicals* lists articles published in almost 200 law journals. These writings are likely to be useful to a person who wants to get a very comprehensive analysis of a criminal justice subject from a legal perspective. They are usually meticulously researched and very extensively footnoted, though somewhat weak on behavioral science insight. Law journals are usually edited by third-year law students, and the quality of the best is extremely high indeed.

An excellent source, in particular because it is strong on foreign materials and also because it provides an abstract of the contents of each article listed, is *Abstracts on Criminology and Penology,* published by the Criminological Foundation in the Netherlands. Volumes 1 through 8 (1961–1968) of the *Abstracts* bear the title *Excerpta Criminologica,* with the current title beginning on March 1969. The *Abstracts* are issued bimonthly, in January, March, May, July, September, and November. A companion volume, *Abstracts on Police Science,* began publication in 1973.

Abstracts of articles may also be found in *Criminal Justice Abstracts* (called *Crime and Delinquency Abstracts* before 1976), published by the National Council on Crime and Delinquency. The abstracts are organized by topics such as "law and the courts" and "correction." In addition, there is a subject index in the back of each issue. For example, a recent issue of the *Criminal Justice Abstracts* contained the following items under "juvenile offenders," with appropriate page references: commitment to delinquency; correction; effect of detention; female; female, self-mutilation; hard-core, definition; inmates, U.S.; intelligence and theft; interrogation by police; Massachusetts, recidivism; thought content; violent (see "violent offenders"). In addition to the abstracts, each issue of the journal contains a review of a timely topic in criminal justice. Various newsletters are published that provide overviews of current developments in criminal justice. They emphasize newsworthy items for practitioners—for example, congressional budgetary hearings for the funding of criminal justice agencies and projects—and these matters are frequently of potential importance for the researcher. The newsletters include summaries of statutory and case law bearing on criminal categories, reviews of recent books or major articles, and evaluative reports on projects in crime and delinquency. The *Criminal Justice Newsletter,* published by the National Council on Crime and Delinquency, is an example of a newsletter with general coverage; the *Juvenile Justice Digest,* published by Washington Crime News Services, is an example of a newsletter with more restricted coverage.

Other sources of information on criminal justice issues include *Psychological Abstracts, Public Affairs Information Service*(PAIS), *Reader's Guide to Periodical Literature, Social Science and Humanities Index* (before 1965 titled *International Index*), and *Sociological Abstracts.* Finally, there are several sources of information about federal government publications. Among these are *Index to U.S. Government Periodicals, Guide to U.S. Government Publications,* and *Monthly Catalog of United States Government Publications.*

Researchers and criminal justice students might also find helpful Martin Wright (ed.), *Uses of Criminological Literature* (London: Butterworths, 1974), which includes bibliographical review chapters on a number of basic criminal justice topics, such as alcoholism and crime. Nicolette Parisi's *Sources of National Criminal Justice Statistics: An Annotated Bibliography,* issued by the U.S. Department of Justice in 1977, is another valuable source book. Worldwide listings of journals in the field can be found in Charles P. McDowell, Gerald L. Russell, and Theodore C. Hines, *International Guide to Periodicals in Criminal Justice* (Greensboro, N.C.: North Carolina Justice Institute, 1979) and in Roy M. Mersky, Robert C. Berring, and James K. McCue, *Author's Guide to Journals in Law, Criminal Justice, and Criminology* (New York: Haworth Press, 1979). Finally, an invaluable compendium of a wide variety of statistical information appears in *Sourcebook in Criminal Justice Statistics,* published annually by the U.S. Department of Justice.

REFERENCES

Anderson, C. L. 1936. "Epilepsy in the State of Michigan." *Mental Hygiene,* **30**:441–462.

Aschaffenburg, G. 1913. *Crime and Its Repression,* A. Albrecht (trans.). Boston: Little, Brown.

Bedford, S. 1961. *The Faces of Justice: A Traveller's Report.* New York: Simon and Schuster.

Botein, B. 1952. *Trial Judge.* New York: Simon and Schuster.

Bowker, A. E. 1949. *Behind the Bar.* London: Staples Press.

Frank, J., and Frank, B. 1957. *Not Guilty.* New York: Doubleday.

Gorer, G. 1955. "Modification of National Character: The Role of the Police in England." *Journal of Social Issues,* **11**:24–32.

Hartshone, C., and Weiss, P. (eds.), 1934. *The Collected Papers of Charles Pierce.* Cambridge, Mass.: Harvard University Press.

Hirschi, T. 1973. "Procedural Rules and the Study of Deviant Behavior." *Social Problems,* **21**:164–175.

Kalven, H., Jr. and Zeisel, H. 1966. *The American Jury.* Boston: Little, Brown.

Keve, P. W. 1954. *Prison, Probation, or Parole?* Minneapolis: University of Minnesota Press.

Lewis, N.D.C. 1951. *Pathological Firesetting (Pyromania).* New York: Nervous and Mental Diseases Monographs.

Lindesmith, A. R. 1952. *Opiate Addiction.* Bloomington, Ind.: Principia Press.

McCabe, S., and Purves, R. 1972. *The Shadow Jury at Work.* Oxford: Blackwell.

Maltz, M. D. 1972. *Evaluation of Crime Control Programs.* Washington, D.C.: National Institute of Law Enforcement and Criminal Justice, Law Enforcement Assistance Administration, U.S. Department of Justice.

Martienssen, A. 1958. *Crime and the Police.* London: Secker & Warburg.

Merton, R. K. 1957. *Social Theory and Social Structure.* rev. ed., New York: Free Press.

Millett, K. 1971. *The Prostitution Papers.* New York: Basic Books.

Milner, C., and Milner, R. 1972. *Black Players.* Boston: Little, Brown.

Popper, K. 1966. *The Open Society and Its Enemies*. Chapel Hill: University of North Carolina Press.

Rice, R. 1956. *The Business of Crime*. New York: Farrar, Straus, and Cudahy.

Rubinstein, J. 1973. *City Police*. New York: Farrar, Straus, and Giroux.

Sutherland, E. H. 1924. *Criminology*. Philadelphia: Lippincott.

Young, W. 1958. *The Montesi Scandal*. New York: Doubleday.

CHAPTER 4

ON ALTERNATIVE PLAUSIBLE HYPOTHESES

CHAPTER OUTLINE

INTERNAL AND EXTERNAL VALIDITY

SUBJECTS AS SOURCES OF ERROR
   "Center of Attention" Effects
   Biological and Psychological Alterations
   Selection

PITFALLS IN MEASUREMENT METHODS
   Reactivity
   Pretesting Effect
   Response Set
   Changes in Measuring Instruments
   Interviewer Effect

SITUATIONAL FACTORS AS SOURCES OF ERROR

PROBLEMS IN CRIME STATISTICS
   Uniform Crime Reports
   Unreported Crime—"The Dark Figure"

REFERENCES

This chapter considers factors that generate alternative plausible hypotheses in criminal justice research. It was noted earlier that conclusions reached when there are alternative explanations call into question the value of the research endeavor and may even prove highly counterproductive. We may, for instance, report that a certain intervention program has reduced the amount of crime in the area where we carried out our experiment. But it is possible that because of the intervention project, criminal activity merely moved elsewhere or perhaps persons reported crime less often, though just as much of the same behavior had taken place. We must be both knowledgeable and sensitive in ferreting out reasonable alternative explanations if our work is to have merit and integrity.

The factors that undermine reliable conclusions operate in such a way that continuous alertness is required to keep them from mocking the decision-making process. Procedures to control or neutralize possible sources of error must be adopted if we expect to have an unambiguous basis for decision making. There are some standard pitfalls that previous experiences (and research disasters) have warned us about. In criminal justice research, these may involve adaptive strategies used by offenders and intricacies in the statistical information that we often must rely upon. After all, we will never know the *actual* number of crimes that are committed, only those which by one means or another come to our attention. Therefore we must be continuously alert to make certain that when we are concerned with crime rates our results are not merely reflecting reporting variations.

Take, for example, a commonsense experiment which attempts to evaluate the effectiveness of extra police officers who walk the beat in a ghetto area largely populated by older persons. After six months, contrary to expectations, there is a very much higher rate of crime recorded in police headquarters for the area. This is particularly startling because no change of any significance has occurred in adjacent neighborhoods (where no extra law enforcement personnel were added), and no change was introduced in patroling patterns. Are we to conclude that the addition of beat officers encouraged crime? That hardly makes sense. It is only when we come to understand that the introduction of beat patrols provided an opportunity for the neighborhood residents to approach the officers personally and tell them about depredators (things about which they had not wanted to inform the more distant, bureaucratic-seeming headquarters in the past) that we can understand the paradoxical outcome of the experiment. Crime may indeed have gone down, perhaps dramatically, but the manner in which we are measuring it was notably insensitive to the work we were doing.

Our discussion here of research problems is only a start in the direction of clear thinking about designing experiments and other kinds of approaches to derive data for decision making. Knowledge of the possible sources of error will protect us from some pitfalls; and a standard working rule, as we have noted, is that deep immersion in the research subject and the research area should help greatly in sensitizing the researcher to many other hazards.

INTERNAL AND EXTERNAL VALIDITY

When all hypotheses except the one of central concern have been ruled out, an investigation is said to be "internally valid," (see in particular Webb et al., 1981; Campbell and Stanley, 1966). Let us see how an internally valid study is mounted.

Suppose we are interested in discovering how well two different methods of dealing with juvenile delinquents succeed in producing a variety of outcomes which have been stipulated. These outcomes might include the effect of the programs upon the participants' school grades, the number of school days during which they are absent, reports by their parents on their behavior at home, and their subsequent delinquent activities (self-reported and reported by the police).

We can designate the first treatment regimen as *method F*. Each member of the group subjected to method F must report daily for two hours after school for intensive counseling. The second treatment approach we call *method R*. Under its terms, all members of the group involved are to spend five hours one day a week and all day Saturday or Sunday engaged in community service projects, such as park and highway cleanup, shopping for elderly or immobilized residents, and similar activities.

If the participants in the study are selected with scientific care and if the details of the investigation are otherwise well-designed and well-executed, then differences found in the outcome measures between persons in groups F and R can be said to be the result of the methods of handling the groups. The investigation is said to be internally valid because differences in the obtained outcomes can be attributed to the variable manipulated, that is, to the treatment method.

Alternative hypotheses, such as the idea that the persons in group F are smarter than those in group R, could not have produced the difference, because our method of selection of the participants had ruled out that possibility in the first place.

The expression *internal validity* is almost always used in conjunction with the term *external validity*. The latter refers to the generalizability of the results. In the foregoing example, external validity has reference to the issue of whether the confirmed effect of the two kinds of treatment for the delinquents will hold true for other groups of juvenile offenders, perhaps in another county or throughout the state or nation. Difficulties concerning external validity in criminal justice are manifold. Take our example, for instance. It may be true that the counseling sessions showed better results than the community service approach for the youngsters with whom we had worked. But it is believed among workers in the criminal justice area (though definite research support is lacking) that some members of ethnic groups strongly resist counseling and that the results for them are likely to be counterproductive with regard to the aims of treatment. Mexican-Americans, for example, sometimes find it undignified to talk about their personal and their family problems and will balk mightily at being pressed to do so. Therefore, if we were to take our results and try to use the same approach in a neighborhood with a large chicano population, we might well discover the limits to generalizability.

Similar kinds of difficulties might bear upon the issue of external validity in regard to the setting of the study. Suppose, for instance, that the place in which it was conducted was marked by very high unemployment rates and that it was virtually impossible for juveniles to get part-time work. In that event, the enforced period of community service would hardly interfere with any kind of wage earning that the youngsters might be involved in. But if the study were transplanted to another setting, where youths were generally holding jobs, the participants might define the community service as a very real deprivation, since it was costing them income. In this second locale, their attitudes might be reflected in considerably poorer results for members of this treatment group. Generalizability is again clearly affected.

The hypotheses that are being tested may refer to a large group (or *population,* as it would be called) from which a sample has been taken for the purposes of the research. Or we may be interested in the results only as they bear on the small group, or sample, itself. Plausible hypotheses, or explanations, that are alternative to the hypotheses about the population of inferential concern are said to interfere with external validity—or, to put it another way, they produce external invalidity. Thus, in our example, the employment rate might interfere with the generalizability of results of counseling and community service. Plausible—that is, reasonable—hypotheses or explanations that are alternative to the one being investigated and refer only to the particular sample are said to produce internal invalidity.

SUBJECTS AS SOURCES OF ERROR

Human behavior is obviously a complex function of many interacting events and processes. Our inability to foresee how our friends are going to behave at all times and in particular situations tells us clearly how difficult a science of human behavior becomes. There are persons who we are certain will end up on death row; but somehow they turn out to be the wardens of the prisons in which youngsters we thought were destined for better things come to be imprisoned. Can you tell for certain, given all the information that you know about yourself, whom you are going to marry or, if you are married, whether that marriage will last until death do you part—or even a date a good deal earlier than that?

The following factors figure importantly in how human beings will behave.

1 *The individual's life history, both long-range and short range.* One of the most interesting areas of research investigation concerns the relationship between the background of a person and the way he or she responds to legal postulates. It is notable that women, for instance, very rarely commit what might be called impersonal crimes of violence, crimes such as mugging and armed robbery. Successful armed robbery takes a good deal of nerve, or recklessness, but not much strength. In theory, women would be just as likely as men to be successful armed robbers, since they can readily intimidate their victims with handguns. But they do not do so.

The *Uniform Crime Reports* (UCR), which is published annually, contains a summary of a wide range of information about criminal activity in the United States. A recent report shows that there were 122,514 arrests for robbery in the United States. Of these, 113,309 were of men and only 9,115 of women. The percentages by sex are: men, 92.6 percent; women, 7.4 percent. Women are even less equally represented in arrests for burglary, with a total of only 6.0 percent of the arrests. Obviously, there is something in the way that women are raised, something in their general training (and perhaps in their biological makeup as well—a matter we will consider in a moment) that inhibits their engagement in the crime of robbery.

Some of these factors may be long-range phenomena, such as the relatively nonaggressive manner in which female children are brought up in the United States. They traditionally have been taught to use tactics other than direct confrontation in order to achieve those things they desire. They have been trained in general to be careful rather than carefree. Some people may believe that such training has kept women from effective participation in many desirable aspects of adult life, but seemingly it has also kept them out of the ranks of robbers. Whether new styles of raising girls and socializing women will alter the distribution by sex for robbery is an intriguing issue that only time will resolve.

2 *The individual's biological equipment.* It often goes unobserved, but there are certain physical prerequisites for committing certain kinds of crime. Agility is required, for instance, to scale fire escapes in urban apartment houses in order to break and enter for criminal purposes.

Undoubtedly, the most obvious of the criminal categories in which biological equipment is almost a sine qua non is rape. In 1980, there were 29,431 arrests for rape, with 29,161 (99.1 percent) being of men. The 270 females arrested for the offense were almost all accessories to the act. In many states, the criminal statutes do not provide for an act of a female raping a male, but all jurisdictions proscribe acts in which women are accomplices of men in rape, such as when they hold a gun on another female while the man engages in the forced sexual intercourse.

3 *The individual's methods of forming constructs and the biases that intrude into such constructs.* There are striking variations in how each of us perceives what we believe to be "reality." The manner in which we do so is probably a function of an uncertain mix of our heredity and environment. It is often astonishing how different persons view the same event. A standard strategy used to train criminal lawyers is to stage in law school classrooms episodes that unfold rapidly. In one such vignette, for instance, a person may run into the classroom in the middle of the professor's lecture, wave his or her arms in the air, shout something, and then speed out through another door. Thereafter, each student is asked to write down what seemed to have happened.

The discrepancies between the reports usually are eye-opening. Persons will misidentify the intruder in regard to all physical characteristics—height, weight, hair color, and even sex. There are likely to be even stranger variations in the reports of what went on. Some persons will insist that they clearly heard every word that was said, but they will differ greatly in what they report hearing. Others will maintain stoutly that nothing at all was said.

The assumption behind such strikingly different perceptions of a "real" event is that because of either physical inadequacies (poor hearing, poor eyesight, poor memory) or personal ideas (that is, people very often see not what happens but what they would like to believe has happened), individuals distort situations.

A particularly fine example of such distortion in the area of criminal activity is found in the study done by Charles Winick (1961) among students in one of his classes. At the time, New York City was plagued by a person who had come to be labeled in the media as the "mad bomber." This person was holding the city in terror by leaving explosives at various places throughout the area. Winick asked members of his class to guess what the bomber would prove to be like when (and if) captured. Their characterizations of the presumed culprit covered an enormous range but were particularly marked by their great divergence from the truth, when it finally unfolded. Students were likely to see the "mad bomber" as an angry young man, motivated by political forces, and diabolical in his cleverness in outwitting the law enforcement agencies. Instead, the bomber proved to be a quiet old man with a grudge against the electric company for some wrong he believed it had done him. The students in the class, like all of us, had pictured the situation as they thought that it ought to be.

4 *The array of events and conditions immediately preceding a given set of behaviors.* One of the most difficult problems for social scientists, including criminal justice research workers, is to grasp and take into account the idea of a continuum of causality for human behavior. Perhaps it is the lingering influence of the Freudians, who are likely to insist that very early experiences are sufficient to explain and to predict later behavior, that leads to contemporary misunderstanding of this phenomenon.

The easiest illustration that we can think of to demonstrate the compelling significance of immediate events in the determination of human behavior concerns the legal doctrine of "irresistible impulse." The doctrine maintains that a person is not to be regarded as criminally responsible for what is done under the pressure of an impulse which is defined as "irresistible." Such an impulse corresponds in certain jurisdictions to other defenses such as insanity, mental retardation, or nonage (being under the stipulated legal age of responsibility for a criminal act). But virtually no one would be likely to commit a crime if several law enforcement officers were standing there watching, no matter how irresistible the presumed impulse, until a more propitious moment presented itself. It is not, in this circumstance, anything that happened in infancy or anything that happened even yesterday, but the circumstances of the very moment that are especially influential in determining the course of the person's conduct.

In summary, then, human behavior results from a complex interaction among the following factors: life history, biological composition, personal biases and modes of forming constructs, and the environmental context. We turn now to consideration of how these factors can be sources of alternative plausible hypotheses in research investigations.

In experiments or investigations where people are the objects of interest, we typically observe behavior or performance in conjunction with a change in the internal or external environment. A possible sequence is: observe behavior, introduce experimental event, observe behavior. A specific case of the sequence might be: test subjects' driving ability, give subjects a specific dosage of marijuana under carefully controlled circumstances (time of day, number of persons about, smoking instructions, and so forth), and then test driving ability again. In this example, interest lies in the effects of the experimental event—the ingestion of marijuana—on the subsequent driving behavior.

But differences in driving behavior between the two testings could have resulted from events, factors, or conditions other than the experimental event of direct research interest, that is, the specific dosage of marijuana.

Certain nuisance events (nuisances in the sense that they generate alternative plausible hypotheses) are created by the measurement process that is inherent in the investigation or by the change in the overall context necessitated by the investigatory process. Other nuisance events can be entirely incidental to the investigation and might have occurred even if the experimental study had not been carried out.

In our example of marijuana and driving behavior, a nuisance event would be created if several of our subjects individually decided to attempt to compensate for any effects of the drug by making an unusually strong effort and paying particularly close attention. Unfortunately for the experimenter, it is not possible to fool a person who has smoked marijuana before into believing that a substitute is the drug. The persons in the experiment, then, might well be able to figure out what the research worker is trying to determine. Perhaps they want the results to show that marijuana is not dangerous in regard to highway safety, and so they devote unusual attention to being particularly careful.

Another confounding nuisance event would be created if several subjects had a few bottles of beer before the investigation. Or perhaps they might have taken amphetamines in order to prepare themselves (they believe) for what could be a difficult test. If this is the case, the experimenter is not truly conducting a test of the consequences of using marijuana but rather (and perhaps unknowingly) is securing results which measure the impact of a combination of marijuana and another drug on driving ability.

We shall employ a three-part classification of the factors which may intrude into the purity of criminal justice research. The three categories are: (1) "center of attention" effects, (2) biological and psychological changes, and (3) selection.

"Center of Attention" Effects

This is a broad category that encompasses all changes in the people under investigation that result from the contextual aspects of the study. Changes produced by the experimental event of direct interest, such as the administration of marijuana in the foregoing illustration, do not of course constitute untoward effects but rather are part of the experimental design itself. "Center of attention" effects include all changes in a subject that result from the subject's being aware that he or she is being systematically observed. Subjects may try to make a good impression—for example, prison inmates involved in an experiment may hope that their particularly cooperative attitude will later be worth points with the parole board. Some subjects may even respond in ways that are deliberately unpredictable. This is obvious in many laboratory experiments with college students, in which the subjects, out of pique or friskiness, respond in an erratic fashion in order to "screw up" the experiment. Persons involved in experiments in which their liberty might be in danger, such as criminals and delinquents, sometimes are motivated to try as hard as they can to obscure the very things that the experimenter is seeking to discover. If, for example, offenders believe that they are likely to get a better break in court by appearing somewhat unintelligent, they may act quite strangely when participating in an experimental program that is being carried out in the jail where they are held.

The best-known example falling into this category is the well-established Hawthorne effect: the name comes from the location in which it was first systematically observed about 50 years ago—the Hawthorne plant of the Western Electric Company in Chicago. In the overall research, the investigators tried to determine the effects of variations in work conditions (such as differing lengths of rest periods, various kinds of lighting, hours of work, and methods of pay) on productivity. One experiment was aimed at determining the best level of illumination for groups of workers. Strange results were observed. For example, significantly increased production was found when the illumination was increased from 24 footcandles to 72 footcandles for one group of workers, but production also increased for another group whose members were treated similarly except that the illumination was actually maintained at 24 footcandles.

In a key concluding experiment, workers were asked to comment on the effects of different intensities of illumination. When an electrician came in on a daily basis to change bulbs and increase the level of illumination, the workers commented favorably on the changes. The electrician was then told to act *as if* he were changing the bulbs, but actually to put the same bulbs back. The workers commented as favorably as when the illumination did increase. It was clear that the workers were reacting strongly and positively to the attention they were getting as part of the experiment. Whatever positive effects, if any, produced by the actual changes in illumination were being overwhelmed by the effects of being the center of attention.

Similar results were observed throughout the experimentation. Productivity increased whether rest periods were fewer or more frequent, whether work hours were lengthened or shortened, and so on. The workers clearly were responding positively to being a special group. The effects of the experimental variables of central interest to the experimenters, such as the work hours and rest periods, were being masked by the phenomonen subsequently called the *Hawthorne effect* (Roethlisberger and Dickson, 1939).

Similar kinds of effects have cropped up in a number of studies of criminal justice processes. In one city, there was a flow of complaints about the ineffectiveness of the burglary squad in solving crimes against property. Citizens said that the department was poorly led and that its tactics in tracing goods and maintaining surveillance over pawnshops and other possible sources of fenced goods were not satisfactory. The department instituted a program of training for the officers in public relations, informing them how to deal in a more cordial and sympathetic manner with persons whose houses they entered. It was pointed out to the officers that the victim is undergoing an unusual and sometimes quite frightening experience and may feel that he or she has literally been invaded by the offender. For the officer, it is just another routine burglary in a long series of rather unexciting events, where the likelihood of solving the case is quite low.

The public relations training proved somewhat effective, though an unsatisfactory level of dissatisfaction remained among victims. Then officers were instructed to take a bit of extra time trying to locate fingerprints, even if such an effort seemed absolutely hopeless. Thereafter, victims' discontent dropped significantly. It was believed that the person who suffers a burglary wants at least to have something to talk about to his friends and neighbors; that is about all the pleasure that a victim will be likely to get out of the event (unless, and alas, he or she is one of the many burglary victims who exaggerate losses to the insurance company). The drama of the search for fingerprints, even though it left many smudges about the house that had to be cleaned, added something extra to the victim's story and provided a bit of vicarious involvement in an exciting event. It is likely that the same results would have been produced had the officers used not fingerprint powder but mere talcum.

Another important "center of attention" effect has to do with the set of cues provided by the experimenter and the experimental context that define the behavior expected of the subject. Orne and his colleagues (Orne, 1962; Orne and Scheib, 1964; Orne and Evans, 1965) have studied the phenomenon extensively, calling the cues defining expected roles "demand characteristics of the experimental situation."

The phrase *demand characteristics* refers to the role called for by the experimental context. The very reason for the experiment is to create certain conditions of control that do not exist in the natural state. The measured dosage of marijuana; the laboratorylike setting in which the marijuana is to be smoked; the precise instructions in regard to how much of the cigarette should be used; and, of course, the artificial manner in which the driving test is administered (since the subject cannot, without putting the experimenter in considerable peril of liability, be allowed to drive on the city streets)—all these create demands, in the sense that they convey to subjects a sense of something special and an insistence that they behave in unusual ways. The factors of the experiment are being carefully controlled in order to rule out sources of alternative plausible hypotheses. But this very control introduces the artificial context that must be interpreted and responded to by the subject.

To the extent that the role played in the experimental context differs from the real-life behavior to which we would like to generalize our research conclusions, the usefulness of the experiment is diminished.

It is essential that investigators remain fully alert to the differences between responses to questions in a laboratory or other "unreal" context and the actual behavior that will take place under less constrained conditions. Take the following example, for instance. There is a test that has been developed which is used to evaluate police discretion, that is, the way law enforcement officers make decisions about how they will handle any given case with which they are confronted. The test makes use of cards which have written on them descriptions of criminal incidents and a portrayal of the characteristics of the offender. The police officer being tested is handed a card, asked to digest the information on it, and then asked to tell the person administering the test what would be done with the offender in this particular instance. Will an arrest be made or will the offender merely be warned?

The person administering the cards then tabulates responses and suggests that the results provide an accurate inventory of how law enforcement officers will behave in a variety of situations with a variety of different offenders. To us, this generalization seems a bit far-fetched. Investigators who assume that the responses to the cards under the artificial conditions are interchangeable with behavior on the streets are fooling themselves, those who read their results, or both. In the research setting, using the cards, the officers' behavior is strongly influenced by the demand characteristics of that setting. In short, they tell the experimenter what they believe the experimenter would prefer to hear. Law enforcement officers most certainly know, for instance, that graduate students or professors are likely to feel strongly on matters of racial prejudice. An officer who is biased against blacks, or whites, or women, or men knows that it is sensible to keep such ideas concealed. And all of the subjects can readily figure out what the "proper" response is to each of the cards. On the street, matters may be quite different—in fact, none of the items on the card may be of particular strength in influencing the officer's decision on what procedure to follow.

Furthermore, the cards construct a situation in which the risks are likely to be very different from those facing officers in their day-to-day assignments. In the test situation, status and self-image are at risk, and these must be protected by "proper" responses. In the street, it may be life that is in danger, and the niceties of experimental protocols will probably be handled in a very different manner.

Biological and Psychological Alterations

Another difficulty in research has to do with time elapsed. It is evident that no two moments in time are exactly alike: even as you have read this sentence, or a fragment of it, you have aged and perhaps you have changed in some very slight way. If the time gap is elongated, the change is likely to be more significant and it must be taken into account in research work in the field of criminal justice.

In an experimental situation, we may want to intrude some intervention and then determine whether the person being tested has changed in any manner during the time interval between our first examination and our later examination. But if the initial point, point A, and the subsequent point, point B, are far apart in time, factors such as maturation and aging may be more responsible than anything else for the variations that we are likely to document. In infants, maturational changes appear over very brief time spans. If points A and B are relatively closer together for older subjects, factors such as maturation and aging may be of much less consequence. But short-term effects such as boredom, fatigue, and hunger can be very much in evidence. And these factors rather than the factor that interests the researcher can be highly influential on dictating the results of the inquiry.

If, then, an investigator evaluates the subject at time A, introduces an experimental treatment between times A and B, and reevaluates the subject at time B, the result can be confounded by the lapse of time.

Consider the following absurd example, which illustrates the operation of these biological and psychological conditions frustrating the unwary investigator. Suppose it has been claimed by a research team that they have developed an instrument which will teach babies to talk. To prove their point, they enroll 100 subjects, all of whom are 1 year old. A recording is played each night from the time the infants are placed in their cribs until the moment that they fall asleep. The infants' speaking ability is tested at 1 year of age, time A, and then again at 3 years, time B. The babies are found to be talking quite well at time B, and the researchers announce that they have "scientific" support for their original claim.

Few people in our culture, of course, would find the contention of these researchers plausible, despite the seeming "proof." Everyone knows that a young child typically develops language skills between 1 and 3 years of age; this is a maturational and learning process. It goes on whether recordings are played, trumpets are blared, or the researchers stand on their hands for two hours each day or wag their fingers in front of the infant's nose. If researchers were interested in a serious test of the value of their training instrument, they would have to set up a much more sophisticated experiment in order to rule out the alternative hypothesis of maturational learning.

The foregoing example is admittedly absurd, because the alternative hypothesis is so widely and clearly recognized. But some events are much less obvious. Let us consider an example in which the operation of the equivalent of biological and psychological change is not so evident.

Suppose, for example, we are interested in determining the accuracy of a group of law enforcement officers on the pistol range after members of the group have been given special instructions on how to hold and aim the gun and how to compensate for factors such as recoil. The members of the group are tested at time A. There are five persons in the sample, all young men. They are given instructions and then retested a few hours later. The suprising results are shown in Table 1, which indicates a deterioration between the first and second test.

What could have gone wrong? It is perfectly possible, of course, that the instructions were so confusing (or just plain wrong) that they served to reduce the accuracy of the men on the target range.

In this case, however, further investigation leads to the discovery of an artifact at work. It is common among young males in our culture to drink rather large quantities of beer at times. The police officers had done just that during the interval between their first round of practice and the time that they had been brought together for firing instructions. The biological effects on a 150-pound male of drinking four or so bottles of beer are not insignificant. Blood alcohol concentration can reach 0.10 percent, with the

TABLE 1
TARGET-SHOOTING ACCURACY OF FIVE POLICE
OFFICERS (100 Is a Perfect Score)

Officer	Time A	Time B
A	73	61
B	81	42
C	65	68
D	71	58
E	76	72
Total	366	301
Mean	73.2	60.2

precise percentage depending most particularly on the rapidity with which the beer is consumed. For the average person oxidation will decrease the blood alcohol concentration by approximately 0.015 percent an hour. Therefore, after three hours of no drinking whatsoever, the blood alcohol concentration of a 150-pound beer drinker could still be as high as 0.055 percent. It takes about seven hours for oxidation to totally eliminate the alcohol from the system. At the same time, we know that a blood alcohol concentration of as low as 0.04 percent can affect human performance in such areas as perceptual discrimination, speed of reaction, automobile driving ability, attention span—and firing performance on a rifle range.

It seems apparent that the results achieved in the target-shooting experiment tell us virtually nothing about the issue that we wanted to examine—the effect of training on performance. An uncontrolled factor had intruded into our experiment and has undermined—indeed, seriously distorted——the value of what we had hoped to find out.

It is worth noting that not all the scores registered by the officers declined. Officer C, we can observe from the table, did better on the second trial than he had done on the first. Here we have another illustration of how human subjects can compensate for experimental conditions. This officer was probably relatively unmotivated at test time A, and his score of 65 turned out to be the worst in the pack. The low score also offered him rather more room for improvement than was available to his colleagues. It may also be true that this officer in particular was in a position to benefit from the instruction, because he was abysmally ignorant about the most fundamental aspects of firing range procedures. Finally, he might well have tried much more strenuously to compensate for what he knew to be the debilitating effects of the beer that the members of the group had consumed before the test at time B. We are not in a position to know, given only this information, which of these possible explanations allows us to understand the somewhat paradoxical results produced by officer C. But again we can see how extremely important it is to be forever vigilant when mounting investigations which on their face appear to be straightforward and rather simply accomplished.

Selection

Another means by which untoward circumstances can distort the outcome of the best-meant experimental design is found in the process by which participants in two different groups are selected: one group to be used for experimental purposes and the second for the purpose of comparison.

The general point can be illustrated by a particularly obvious kind of example. Suppose we are interested in measuring the effectiveness of a special kind of parole program in keeping offenders released from prison from committing additional crimes. The program that we are establishing involves the payment of unemployment compensation funds to each of the parolees for a period of several months after release. The program is based upon the assumption that many paroled inmates, being without funds during a crucial period, turn to crime in order to support themselves.

In classic experimental form, we establish two groups for comparison purposes. Members of one group are to receive the unemployment monies, while those in the other group are not. We select the group rosters from different parts of the state, because we do not want the persons involved in the experiment to tell each other about what we are doing; that might create anger and jealousy within the group that is not to receive funds. Before we choose our sites we take some pains, of course, to ascertain that the geographical areas are fairly similar. It would not do to have a group in one place where there is, say, high unemployment and another in a setting where jobs are easy to get and salaries very high, since this condition might have an extraneous impact upon what we are trying to determine.

But it could prove to be the case that we have not been careful enough. Suppose it turned out that 80 percent of the persons in the experimental group but only 10 percent of those in the other group had been narcotics addicts. It could well happen that the former narcotics addicts in the experimental group used the funds that they received from the research program for the purchase of drugs and showed a very high relapse rate. We might learn, by careful later analysis of our data, that such a program as ours ought to begin with exclusion of persons with a history of narcotics use. But we would have been frustrated in our attempt to determine fairly how the payment of unemployment benefits serves the cause of reducing the crime committed by persons who receive the funds. Our failure is traceable to a selection fault; we neglected to make certain that the members of the groups involved in the research program were similar in all important respects.

A vastly more subtle selection problem lies in a phenomenon called *regression toward the mean*. Regression toward the mean is likely to manifest itself whenever people are chosen for a particular research or evaluation investigation on the basis of scores that differ considerably from the mean.

We can illustrate the operation of this particular phenomenon by returning to the instance of training in target shooting for police officers. Suppose a test of shooting ability is given to all members of a law enforcement agency. After the test, the 25 officers who obtained the highest scores are selected for special attention as part of a research effort. If these 25 officers are later given the very same test that they had before being selected, it is virtually certain that their average score will be lower the second time. Similarly, if the 25 officers with the lowest score were selected and then retested, it is virtually certain that their average score would be higher on the second test than it was on the original one. The phenomenon is called *regression toward the mean* because those selected on the basis of their high scores tend to drift downward on the second testing while those with low scores tend to drift upward on the second testing; in both cases the drift is toward the mean.

The phenomenon results from the fact that the score assigned to any individual contains a component stemming from the error of measurement. And the more the score deviates from the mean, the larger the error component it probably contains. If the deviation is on the high side, the chance or error component is most likely in a strongly positive direction. Thus, on a retest we would expect the chance or error component to be less positive, so that the individual high scorer will tend to have a lower score the second time. Another way of looking at the matter is that people who tend to have high scores on a given administration of a test are more likely than others to have luck on their side, at least to some extent, and it is not reasonable to expect the same degree of luck to remain with them the second time around.

Here is a good example of the operation of regression toward the mean and the resulting danger of misinterpreting data. Some years ago, it was suggested that giving glutamic acid to children would raise their IQs. An experiment was conducted in which children were given intelligence tests, and those with very low IQs were selected for a treatment which involved the administration over a period of time of dosages of glutamic acid. After a lengthy treatment regimen, these children were reexamined with an intelligence test similar to the first one. When it was found that the average IQ of the group had risen considerably, the investigators concluded that the hypothesis that dosages of glutamic acid raise IQs was supported. But the logic leading to the conclusion was flawed. The investigators had failed to rule out the alternative plausible hypothesis that the increase in IQs between the first and second testing was because of the process of regression toward the mean. When the regression factor was controlled in a later experiment, incidentally, no effect due to glutamic acid was observed.

Investigational mortality provides the third example of problems that may arise in the selection of subjects. The term refers to the loss of subjects during the course of an experimental program. The loss may be due to illness or death, unwillingness to participate, departure from the area of the investigation, lack or loss of interest, or perhaps time constraints.

The field of criminal justice is rife with experimental conclusions that might well be incorrect because of investigational mortality. A common experimental method, for instance, is to mail questionnaires to a sample of persons in order to try to determine how they feel or how they act (or, rather, how they say they act) under specified conditions. Return rates may be as low as 20 percent and are rarely as high as 80 percent. (In Soviet-bloc countries, we are told, response rates are much nearer 100 percent; whether such rates provide better insight into the subjects or merely testify to fear of the authorities remains another experimental question.) With a response rate on the order of 20 or 30 percent, or even more, you have to assume a difference between persons who returned the questionnaires and the full group to whom the questionnaires were sent.

Illustrations of the problems that might be created for criminal justice research by investigational mortality are easy to imagine. Suppose we want to determine the self-reported amount of crime committed by a random sample of the population. We send out 100 questionnaires, asking each person how often within the last year (six months might be better, because memories fade with stunning rapidity) he or she committed a larceny of more than $50, an armed robbery, an act of vandalism, or any of an array of other illegal behaviors. It does not seem far-fetched to imagine that persons who committed the greatest number of these acts will be least likely to respond to the inquiry. For one thing, they might fear the consequences of their truthful reporting. Researchers who guarantee anonymity have been known to mark questionnaires with invisible ink so they they could identify respondents, or even to put code numbers underneath the stamp on the return envelopes—practices which are highly unethical and might well be illegal invasions of privacy. In addition, persons who have committed the most crimes, we might hypothesize, are those who are the least likely to participate voluntarily in the kind of social behavior involved in filling out and returning questionnaires. They might also be more transient, so that they are overrepresented among the questionnaires which are returned to the headquarters of the survey group marked "undeliverable" by the post office.

The problems associated with investigational mortality become even more pesky when there is an intervention and difficulties arise in regard to obtaining responses from all members of the original sample after the intervention has been completed. Suppose, for example, we are trying to demonstrate that training in secretarial skills will reduce prostitution offenses among a group of women who have had five or more previous arrests for solicitation for the purpose of prostitution. We enroll 20 women in the course, which lasts for two months. Each is paid $100 a week to participate and guaranteed a well-paying job upon successful completion of the course. Four months later we find 12 of the original group still in the jobs in which they had been placed—several, in fact, have been promoted to better positions within the organizations. But we are unable to locate the other 8 women. A criminal justice researcher who is not sufficiently wary might conclude that the sample consisted only of those 12 persons who were available for testing both before and after the intervention. In such a case, the program would be acclaimed a total success in terms of what it had sought to achieve. But some suspicion might exist that the remaining 8 women were not available at the later point because they had returned to illegal activity; and this would provide a somewhat different picture of the overall success of the effort. However, this conclusion is not necessarily accurate either. It may be that some or all of the 8 who could not be located had found even better jobs in the business world, using the new skills, but had decided that they would try to conceal their past by assuming new names or otherwise eradicating as best they could means by which they could be traced. Or perhaps they had married and because they were using their married names, were now difficult for the research worker to trace.

The last illustration indicates that the selection factor of investigational mortality may work in any direction in influencing results, so that it cannot automatically be assumed that the worst or the best has happened to those persons who disappeared from the experimental effort—or, indeed, that anything different has taken place with them.

PITFALLS IN MEASUREMENT METHODS

The method by which data is collected can distort the behavior of subjects and thereby render the results inaccurate. This kind of measurement problem exists in virtually all research probes in criminal justice in which the subject knows or suspects that an experiment is being conducted. The problem also appears in research in which the very method of data collection influences the nature of the material that is gathered. The reactive effect of the experiment in criminal justice is a behavioral equivalent of the so-called *Heisenberg principle* in physics. This principle was named after the German scientist Werner Heisenberg, who won the Nobel Prize in 1932. Heisenberg enunciated the principle of indeterminacy, which holds that it is impossible to determine at the same time both the position and the velocity of an electron. Heisenberg stressed that a physical event is changed by the very process of measuring it.

Reactivity

One kind of measurement difficulty of this nature has been called the *reactive effect of measurement* (Campbell, 1957), or the *reactivity of measurement* (Campbell and Stanley, 1966). The effect grows out of awareness on the part of subjects that they are being observed or tested and their desire to make a good (or significant) impression. In this regard it is also a "center of attention" effect and could have been discussed under that heading.

For example, placing observers in a police station to record the actions of officers will almost certainly produce many responses that would not have occurred if the observers had not been present. And the difference will probably be even more dramatic if the investigation is being conducted by the chief of police and the city manager, who stand about the squad room writing things down in a conspicuous manner on a check-sheet.

Here is an example of a study that did not handle the problem of reactivity as a source of alternative plausible hypotheses. The health department of Fresno, California, wished to determine the extent of alcohol use by adolescents. Toward that end, the department surveyed 769 junior and senior high school students. On the basis of the results, the department concluded that 27 percent of the students surveyed were "heavy" or "moderate to heavy" drinkers and that 23 percent were "moderate to light" drinkers. We would be rather suspicious of these conclusions. Errors can operate in both directions. Many students, wary about who might see these results, will significantly understate their level of use. Others, who might feel compelled to brag or to reach what they believe to be the "average" level of use, will overstate.

It is true that sometimes measurement methods appear to have a negligible effect, particularly if they are unobtrusive or long-lasting. Criminal justice research workers often note that when they tape-record interviews, the subjects at first are reticent and choose their words and ideas with considerable care. But after a while they often appear to relax and to provide spontaneous and accurate information, almost as if they had become forgetful of the recording device.

Note, for instance, the experiences of Robert Reiner (1978:14) during his study of the attitudes of police officers in the United Kingdom toward various facets of unionization:

> I was keen to use the tapes for various reasons. Firstly, I wished to preserve as much detail as possible of the men's reasoning as it informed their replies, so that the meaning *they* attached to responses could be ascertained. Secondly, though it is debatable, the taping allowed for greater *rapport* once the discussion had got under way. There was frequently initial resistance to being taped, which I overcame by saying I would be prepared to switch off at any point if requested. This never occurred. In my initial discussions. . . I had experimented with various recording methods. Usually I tried to recall what had occurred, without any record being kept at the time. This, of course, meant a considerable loss of material. When I attempted to take notes with a pen in these discussions, the conversation immediately became punctuated with the injunction: "Now this is strictly off the record," even in the case of apparently insignificant items. In the pilot interviews I had also felt that the constantly visible taking of notes was off-putting and prevented deeper discussion of any item. With taping, however, after a few minutes of hesitation, discussion ran smoothly and the recording device did not seem inhibiting.

Similarly, during the work of the President's Commission on Law Enforcement and Administration of Justice in the late 1960s, a number of law students were given the assignment of riding in police cars on routine patrols. It was anticipated that the students would be able to observe only a minimum amount of "unacceptable" behavior by the officers, who would be at their best because of the strangers in the squad car. The students were to determine how the officers exercised discretion—that is, under what conditions they issued warnings, when they made arrests, and similar matters. These actions, too, of course, were undoubtedly influenced by the presence of the onlookers. But what was particularly surprising was that the officers occasionally used brutality against persons with whom they were dealing and that they sometimes (though infrequently) used the squad car for sexual activities with willing females encountered in the course of their work. The students had not expected such uninhibited actions while they were present. These activities were not reported by the commission, in large part because they were not the prime matter under study, and also— an interesting sidelight on issues of criminal justice research—because it was believed that such reports would have been inflammatory and diversionary, drawing attention away from what were believed to be more important general concerns associated with law enforcement work.

Pretesting Effect

Under certain conditions, the effect of a method of measurement may be delayed, in the sense that it shows up when the method is used a second time rather than at the first use. This effect occurs most clearly when various kinds of tests, such as attitude and intelligence tests, are used, and it is commonly called the *pretesting effect*. It has been known for generations that people do far better on the second administration of intelligence tests than they did initially. This is hardly surprising. It is obvious that during the first administration they learned some of the questions on the test. Afterwards, they may have looked up correct answers or discussed them with other persons.

Other examples of the pretesting effect are more subtle. Even when the material on the second testing is different from that on the first, subjects may show a carry-over effect resulting from an attitudinal change induced by the first testing. They may also learn to pace themselves, to answer questions with high point values first, or to leave an especially difficult question quickly rather than agonize about it. Such attitudes would be especially useful if the test material takes longer than the time alloted for completing it. This is part of a "learning to learn" phenomenon, in which practice on the first testing can provide the subject with methods and cues for more efficient performance the second time around. Two testings that require the memorization of words or syllables or concepts, though the material may be different on the two occasions, would provide the right context for the operation of this phenomenon.

The power of subconscious forces and alerting mechanisms should never be underestimated in criminal justice research. By giving one test we put into the subconscious the whole range of words, ideas, responses, and similar material associated with a particular topic. Over time ideas form, even though the person might not be thinking directly about the subject matter of the test. It is the kind of process which suddenly leads so many people to realize that they have resolved a problem that has been bothering them for a long time, though they are not at the moment consciously thinking about it. Similarly, the very idea of being tested or observed can make a person more alert and thus lead to much better performance than would occur under "normal" circumstances. At the same time, as we all know, being under scrutiny or pressure can so disturb other persons that they do not do as well as they might have done under less stressful conditions. All these matters need to be considered in conducting criminal justice research which is seeking to get material that is not contaminated by measurement flaws.

Response Set

Another effect that stems from the method of measurement is the *response set*, which has been described most thoroughly by Cronbach (1946). It refers to the tendency for response to be determined by the form rather than the content of a question or similar data-gathering item. It has been found, for example, that subjects are more likely to agree with the statement, "There is life on at least one other planet," than to disagree with the statement, "There is life on no other planet."

A particularly interesting illustration of the difficulties involved in the manner in which questions are put emerged from the work on the sex history of individuals conducted by Kinsey and his associates (1948). Kinsey found that respondents were especially nervous about revealing information regarding their sexual behavior and that such nervousness increased greatly if they believed that the interviewer might be shocked or disapproving. Among the different tactics that were developed to minimize this matter was an approach which always put the question in a way that assumed that the respondent had engaged in the behavior, rather than allowing the person being interviewed to deny readily the matter being discussed. Instead of asking, for instance, "Did you ever masturbate?" or "Did you ever commit adultery?", and perhaps getting quick "No's" as answers, the matter was put in this way: "When was the last time that you masturbated?" or "When did you last commit adultery?" The form of the question also conveyed an impression that the person doing the interview would not be surprised or shocked by a positive answer.

In police interrogations, of course, the usual impulse of guilty persons is to deny allegations that might lead to serious consequences. In order to ease admissions by suspects, the interrogators will employ less emotional and loaded terms in their inquiries. They do not ask, for example, "Did you kill the victim?" but rather employ more euphemistic language, such as, "Did you pull the trigger of the gun?" or similar kinds of more "acceptable" phrasing.

Certain classes of response set may also be noted. First, there is response acquiescence or "yea-saying," which represents the tendency to respond in an affirmative or agreeing manner as long as the content of the question is not incriminating or embarrassing (as in the illustrations above). This tendency probably stems from cultural conditioning: it is considered nicer or more polite to say yes than no.

Second, there is a tendency in response for persons to grasp at the last of a series of items put to them. Uncertain how to respond, they might ask the research worker for some suggestions regarding what it is that he or she is looking for. "Well," the researcher might try to say blandly, "it might be two times, or perhaps seven, or maybe five." The respondent is quite likely, given such prompting, to grab at the last of the series: "Yeah, five, that's right," will be the quick response. It is essential not to lead a person during the course of criminal justice research.

And third, there is the set to answer in an uncommon direction or unusual manner no matter what the content of the question. This phenomenon often lies at the basis of false confessions, a not unusual occurrence in police detective bureaus. The person being interviewed laps up the attention that is involved in the process and attempts to figure out how to prolong and intensify it. If it is granted at once that he or she was elsewhere during the events that are under review, that will be the end of the matter. But if an "interesting" or, better yet, a bizarre response is forthcoming, the expectation is that the interrogators will pay even more attention to the situation. In our relatively anonymous and self-interested society, "free" attention is a commodity that can introduce another distortion of results. It is one of the ironies of contemporary life that some persons would rather be considered suspects in a criminal investigation than ignored. Indeed, some writers believe that one of the causes of a certain amount of crime is the desire for notoriety and attention and that the newspaper headlines regarding sensational criminal activity tend to spur further episodes of the same nature. Research into airplane hijackings has generally supported the idea that when one such sensational event occurs, it is quite likely to be followed quickly by a series of similar crimes.

Changes in Measuring Instruments

Another distortion effect stemming from the measurement instrument occurs when the instrument itself changes between an initial and a later administration. The tension in a spring, for example, changes over time, and the resulting recorded weight may be accordingly affected. When long distances are measured by surveying teams using steel tapes, compensation must be made when measurements are taken under markedly different temperature conditions. The measuring tape, of course, expands as the ambient temperature increases, with resulting errors in evaluating lengths of objects that do not expand and contract at the same rate.

In criminal justice, an example is provided by the use of the homicide rate as a measure of violence. Between one decade and the next during the present century the rate of killings dropped—which would indicate a drop in violence. But that there was something wrong with the measurement method was indicated by the fact that over the same period all other crimes of violence showed an increase. Authorities were quite puzzled until they figured out that the introduction of sulpha drugs (antibiotics) was influencing the homicide rate significantly. That is, cases in which the victim might have died now resulted in only assault charges, because emergency room doctors were able to save the victim's life by use of the newly discovered drugs. Homicide rate was no longer measuring what it previously measured.

Special problems also arise when the measuring instrument is a human being. A person making judgments or evaluating certain things brings a particular set of standards by means of which he or she determines conditions. These standards are likely to change considerably over time, sometimes in ways unbeknownst to the evaluator, who thinks that everything is being done in exactly the same way as before. Anyone who has ever graded essay examinations realizes this danger. If a person grades a large number of questions, even in a single sitting, the risk of changes in the standard of evaluation is considerable. The same thing happens in law enforcement and in the sentencing of convicted offenders. As time goes by, police officers are apt to become either tougher or more lenient. They have seen a lot and they have gained some experience regarding the consequences of particular actions that they take. Judges, too, will respond to things that have happened in their own lives—perhaps even that morning at breakfast—as well as to what they have learned or come to believe during the time that they have been doing their job.

Interviewer Effect

The interviewer effect is the final problem in measurement that we will consider here. It is abundantly clear that the way we respond to another person is very much a function of the particular characteristics of that person. For example, we tend to be intimidated by certain types of people and respond to them in a cautious, anxious manner. On the other hand, we will respond to other people in a warm, friendly manner. Sometimes the determining factor is how we ourselves feel at that moment; more often, it depends on the person with whom we are interacting. The important issue often is our estimate, on the basis of what we can see and guess, of what will happen in the future.

For instance, suppose that you are a police officer in Beverly Hills, California; Grosse Point, Michigan; or Scarsdale, New York. If you see a gray-haired, elegantly tailored man walking the streets, you are likely to be quite polite when driving up to ask him the nature of his business, since persons on foot are not common in such areas. Your caution may well stem from the fact that the person might be a prominent citizen who could cause you trouble with the police chief or the mayor; indeed, it might be the mayor's brother.

Another example is the form of address used with persons falling into clear-cut categories. We are likely to use formal expressions, such as Doctor, Professor, Mr., or Mrs., with people who seem well-established but to use only first names with people who appear to be less well situated on the social ladder. It is noteworthy that interrogation officers, who are very finely attuned to the nuances of how to make people cooperate, will sometimes deliberately switch expectations in such matters, addressing prominent persons by only their first names and working-class persons quite formally as Mr. or Mrs., believing that this might unbalance them somewhat and make them tell more than they otherwise would.

There are a number of research studies which deliberately change the dress or manner of speech of persons and measure the different impacts that the varying arrangements have. Binder, McConnell, and Sjoholm (1956), as part of this work, have shown that even response patterns of which the subjects were completely unaware were affected by the sex of the interviewers.

SITUATIONAL FACTORS AS SOURCES OF ERROR

If the results of an investigation depend upon two sets of observations of the same people at different times, it is clear that many events affecting the observations can occur in the interval. For example, there may be a legislative change, so that what is a crime at time A is no longer a crime at time B, or vice versa. We will indicate some further sources of error of this nature in this section. It should be noted that intervening events that affect results can occur even when the observations are a short time, say hours, apart but their occurrence becomes all the more likely as the time period lengthens.

Suppose, for example, that a new training program is being tried with the police officers in a certain department. The officers are being trained perhaps in intervening techniques to be used with victims, a program that has been inaugurated because the city authorities believe that too many victims are dissatisfied with police performance in this area. The officers are told some of the things that we have noted in the preceding pages about interviewing techniques. They are also exposed to role-playing sessions in which one officer acts as an interrogator and a second officer plays the part of a crime victim. The other officers being trained comment on what they observe and offer suggestions. This procedure has been adopted because research work seems to demonstrate that persons are more apt to change their own behavior if they themselves make the decisions about such a change rather than if they are told in a formal manner what they ought to do.

Performance of the police before and after the new training program is evaluated by such criteria as the number of arrests, the number of complaints by citizens, and ratings by supervisors. But in the interval between the first evaluation and later evaluations, other events, entirely extraneous to the training program, may have occurred which could have some effect on the results of the experimental program. There may have been a major crime in the locale, which makes victims jumpy and likely to report everything they see as a possible criminal event. There may have been a police scandal, which heightens criticism of all officers, even those who now behave much more effectively when dealing with victims of crime. Even deteriorating economic conditions, such as increasing inflation, can abrade tempers and increase complaints, despite the real value of the training program. It is these kinds of conditions which must constantly be kept in mind when research strategies are being designed and interpreted.

EXPERIMENTERS AS SOURCES OF ERROR

The inference in regard to experimenters as sources of research error is that the experimenter somehow generates alternative plausible hypotheses without intending to do so. This process is sometimes called the *experimenter bias effect* or the *Rosenthal effect*, (1976; 1964), the latter in honor of the social psychologist who did early and extensive research on its operation.

We will use an experiment by Rosenthal and Fode (1963) to illustrate the operation of an experimenter effect. The research ostensibly involved a simple maze problem using rats as subjects. But actually the focus of experimental attention was upon two groups of undergraduate students who served as experimenters. One group of student experimenters was told that the rats were bright and should learn quickly, while the other group of student experimenters was told that the rats were dull and should show little learning. Students were assigned to both groups on an entirely random basis. Moreover, obviously without the student experimenters' knowledge, the rats assigned to the two groups of students were selected entirely randomly from a relatively homogeneous population of rats. That is, the only systematic difference between the two groups of rats was that the student experimenters were told that one group was bright and the other dull.

Experimenter biases were thus induced in the student experimenters by the actual experimenter, who was really interested in the behavior of the students rather than the behavior of the rats. The outcome supported the expectation that the biases of the experimenters can influence the data of the experiment. In this case, the students who were working with the presumably bright rats obtained data that their rats performed about 50 percent better than the rats who were presumably dull.

It should be noted in concluding that while the overall contributions of Rosenthal are widely acknowledged, details of various of his experiments have been challenged.

The work by Rosenthal warns us to be wary of the intrusion of our own biases and preferences into the research we are conducting. All of us have a large number of ideas about how things work and why they work that way, and there is an all-too-human tendency to want our ideas to be supported by research evidence. We tend to favor the groups of which we are members—sex groups, age groups, and racial and ethnic groups—and at times to derogate other kinds of persons, a process known among anthropologists as *ethnocentrism*. We believe that crime is committed by certain kinds of persons and not by others. We also have a tendency to develop a strong vested interest in having what we are doing come out "right;" other people are more likely to attend to our positive than our negative results. Under such conditions, it is absolutely essential that researchers know their own minds and their own inclinations and guard strenuously against having these biases intrude into their work. As we have seen, biases can intrude even without our conscious intent.

PROBLEMS IN CRIME STATISTICS

Much criminal justice research revolves about the use of statistics on the extent and form of criminal activity of a cohort of persons under examination. There are innumerable pitfalls in the employment of statistics regarding criminal behavior. The maxim to be remembered is that the aim of the researcher is to be able to measure as directly as possible the criminal behavior itself, not second-, third-, or fourth-hand reports of it and not official records which attend to only a small fraction of such activity. Official records will inevitably have to be employed—they sometimes will be the only information available—but the problem with them must be thoroughly appreciated and taken into account when presenting the research results.

The principal source of crime statistics now in use on a national level is the *Uniform Crime Reports* (UCR) issued annually by the Federal Bureau of Investigation (FBI). We shall discuss the shortcomings in UCR below. It should be noted that the errors they present are likely to be of a systematic nature, that is, they are likely to be of the same nature year after year, so that, though the totals may be fallacious, the trends they unveil may be more trustworthy. Thus, if it is reported that aggravated assaults have increased from 26,000 to 30,000, we might suspect that the total is far from correct, given the large number of people who do not tell the police about their experiences with assault. But at the same time it is not unlikely that the reported increase accurately reflects a larger amount of the behavior in the society.

There generally has been among scholars and laypeople conversant with the inadequacies of crime statistics a feeling that for so important a topic better public reporting is necessary. It is sometimes noted that no business operation would long remain solvent if it were as careless about keeping track of so vital an aspect of its existence as American society has been with regard to enumeration of criminal activity. Because of such discontent, Congress in 1980 authorized the establishment of a Bureau of Justice Statistics, to be located within the Department of Justice. It is the charge of the Bureau of Justice Statistics to examine all statistical reports regarding crime that are prepared in the United States and to render them more sophisticated and more useful as tools for research and for the formulation of public policy. It is presumed that this task will take as long as 10 years to accomplish. More will be said about alternatives to UCR statistics in Chapter 5.

Uniform Crime Reports

The FBI was first empowered in 1930 to collect and distribute statistics pertaining to crime in the United States. Since the compilation of the report depends on the voluntary cooperation of thousands of police agencies in the United States and their willingness and ability to transcribe local information onto the forms prescribed by the FBI, totally accurate coverage is exceedingly difficult to attain. The FBI at one time indicated in each statistical compilation issued that is was "not in a position to vouch for the validity of the reports received"; more recently it has abandoned this caution, despite its truth. Now the FBI merely warns readers against "drawing conclusions from direct comparisons of crime figures between individual communities without first considering the factors involved." This is a well-taken caveat: past reports have sometimes shown extraordinarily wide discrepancies in rates for particular crimes between adjacent cities of similar populations, discrepancies that further investigation quickly determined were a function not of different crime rates but of reporting errors.

Experience over the years has underlined the importance of approaching the Uniform Crime Reports cautiously. One of the reasons for inaccuracies is indicated by Cressey (1957:232), who notes that "the police have an obligation to protect the reputation of their cities, and when this cannot be done efficiently under existing legal and administrative machinery, it is sometimes accomplished statistically."

The UCR focuses on eight offenses, which it defines as major crimes, and uses them to calculate "index rates" of serious lawbreaking. Of these offenses, four are crimes against the person (murder, robbery, forcible rape, and aggravated assault), and four are by and large offenses against property (burglary, larceny, automobile theft, and arson). There are a number of problems with this index of serious crime in the United States. For one thing, even a slight increase in the less serious offenses, such as automobile theft, can hide significant declines in the more harmful behaviors, such as rape and murder. Thus if rape dropped from, say, 30,000 to 20,000 offenses and murder from 10,000 to 5,000—both phenomenal improvements—while automobile theft increased from 150,000 to 170,000, we would have a significant growth in the total number of serious crimes (assuming that the other offenses remained as they were). Rape would have dropped by one-third and murder by one-half, while automobile theft would have risen less than 15 percent—but that 15 percent would over-whelm the fluctuations in the originally smaller figures for crimes against the person.

In addition, as Wolfgang (1963) has pointed out, offenses such as kidnapping, and assault and battery, which do not appear on the index, may in fact involve more personal injury than other crimes listed on the index. Also, since the nation's police forces operate under differing classification systems, data must be conscientiously interpreted and redefined. The descriptive categories employed by the FBI are deliberately broad, for this purpose. *Robbery,* for example, is defined as "stealing or taking anything of value from the person by force or violence or by putting in fear, such as strong-arm robbery, stickups, robbery armed, assault to rob and attempt to rob." *Aggravated assault* is described as "assault with intent to kill or for the purpose of inflicting severe bodily injury by shooting, cutting, stabbing, maiming, poisoning, scalding, or by use of acids, explosives, or other means. Excludes simple assault, assault and battery, forgery, etc." *Larceny-theft* excludes automobile theft, embezzlement, and forgery.

A keen criminal justice researcher will be able at once to spot some of the potential difficulties even in so straightforward a set of definitions. For one thing, the concept of *attempt* in the realm of crime can be disconcerting statistically. In a study of forcible rape in Boston and Los Angeles (Chappell et al., 1977), criminal justice research workers found that the police tended to charge with "attempted rape" anyone who in any way had had physical contact with a female. This seemingly was done in order to persuade the accused offender to plead guilty to a lesser offense in order to avoid prosecution on the felony charge of attempted rape. This procedure was not followed in Boston; as a result, Boston had very different rates of "attempted rape." Undoubtedly, the different figures for Los Angeles and Boston did not accurately reflect the amount of similar activity in the two jurisdictions.

The problems involved in estimating and discussing the numerical proportions of crime accurately should by now be painfully evident. New statutes create new offenses that feed into the total amount of crime and render comparisons over time hazardous. Changing demographic charac-teristics of a population can distort the portrait of crime. The efficiency or inefficiency of the police (say a slowdown strike for a month) can change the known amount of crime without any alteration in the actual amount. Reported crime statistics must be examined with constant awareness on the part of the research worker of precisely what they purport to measure, how they are derived, and whether they are presented as gross amounts or as rates. Crime statistics contain numerous labyrinths to trap the incautious.

The importance of crime statistics in shaping attitudes and policies and for validating or disproving research hypotheses and evaluating outcomes should not be underestimated. For one thing, numerical material has a tendency to generate trustfulness; there appears to be something quite substantial in a reported figure and a calculated percentage, especially if carried to several decimal places. Public policy is more likely to be responsive to mathematics than to theory, and it is more attentive to a proclamation that "crime has increased by 7.13 percent" than to involved explanations of the deficiencies of so categoric a conclusion. It is therefore imperative that researchers learn well how to deal effectively with crime statistics and how to fashion their use of such material to the best purpose.

Unreported Crime—"The Dark Figure"

The actual number of crimes committed will always remain unknown. This point cannot be stressed too strongly. There will always be an enormous number of crimes that will not become known to any researcher by any inventory method. This is a basic problem for assessing such things as the impact of an intervention project on criminal recidivism rates for those who participated in the program.

Crimes such as carrying concealed weapons, individual narcotics transactions, or the vast range of sexual offenses that by nature are committed privately and by mutual agreement will remain beyond tabulation. In fact, since such acts do not readily fall into discrete time periods, the problem of counting them becomes extremely complex. Suppose, for example, that we were able to determine how many individuals at a given moment violate laws against carrying concealed weapons. Say that we discover that 190,000 persons in the United States carry such weapons daily. Should we list 190,000 offenses for that day, or can the offenses be divided reasonably into two or three parts for the various portions of the day? Perhaps an offense ought to be counted each time the individual emerges from a dwelling, a store, or place of business with the weapon. When the same person goes out with the same concealed weapon on the following day, is this a new offense or should it be counted as part of the old one? Such counting conundrums highlight the necessity of treating skeptically statements referring to the "total" amount of crime in a place as if this were a determinable figure.

It is possible for official statistics to show a negative effect for a given intervention when the actual effect has been positive. Suppose, for

instance, that a rape crisis center is attempting to determine the consequences of an intense lobbying effort to change court procedures in regard
to rape victims. The campaign might involve having victims witness a court
hearing on a rape case before they themselves participate in trials as the
complaining witnesses. Certain kinds of questions posed to rape victims,
particularly those inquiring into their previous sexual background, might be
banned by legislative enactment. Criminal justice researchers, trying to
determine the importance of such alterations, could well discover that the
rate of rape appears to have doubled. But closer scrutiny could show that
the reforms have encouraged women to report rape to the police much
more often, whereas in the past they had kept such information to
themselves because they assumed that the police would not be sympathetic
to them or that the prospects for convicting the offender were not
particularly promising. The researcher must think through with great care
what it is that needs to be measured and how to obtain an uncomtaminated
reading that allows the basic research issue to be adjudicated.

REFERENCES

Binder, A., McConnell, D., and Sjoholm, N. 1956 "Verbal Conditioning as a Function
of Experimental Characteristics." *Journal of Abnormal and Social Psychology* **55**:
309–314.

Campbell, D. T. 1957. "Factors Relevant to the Validity of Experiments in Social
Settings." *Psychological Bulletin* **54**:297–312.

Campbell, D. T., and Stanley, J. C. 1966. *Experimental and Quasi-Experimental
Designs for Research.* Chicago: Rand McNally.

Chappell, D., Geis, G., Schafer, S., and Siegel, L. 1977. "A Comparative Study of
Forcible Rape Offenses Known to the Police in Boston and Los Angeles." In D.
Chappell, R. Geis, and G. Geis (eds.), *Forcible Rape: The Crime, the Victim, and
the Offender* (pp. 226–244.) New York: Columbia University Press.

Cressey, D. R. 1957. "The State of Criminal Statistics." *National Probation and Parole
Journal,* **3**:230–241.

Cronbach, L. J. 1946. "Response Sets and Test Validity." *Educational and Psychological Measurement,* **6**:475–494.

Kinsey, A., Pomeroy, C. W., and Martin, C. E. 1948. *Sexual Behavior in the Human
Male.* Philadelphia: Saunders.

Orne, M. T. 1962. "On the Social Psychology of the Psychological Experiment: With
Particular Reference to Demand Characteristics and Their Implications." *American Psychologist,* **17**:776–783.

Orne, M. T., and Evane, F. J. 1965. "Social Control in the Psychological Experiment:
Antisocial Behavior and Hypnosis." *Journal of Personality and Social Psychology,*
1:189–200.

Orne, M. T., and Scheibe, K. E. 1964. "The Contribution of Nondeprivation Factors in
the Production of Sensory Deprivation Effects: The Psychology of the 'Panic
Button.'" *Journal of Abnormal and Social Psychology,* **68**:3–12.

Reiner, R. 1978. *The Blue-Coated Worker: A Sociological Study of Police Unionism.*
Cambridge: Cambridge University Press.

Roethlisberger, F. J., and Dickson, W. J. 1939. *Management and the Worker.* Cambridge, Mass.: Harvard University Press.

Rosenthal, R. 1976. *Experimenter Effects in Behavior Research.* New York: Halstead Press.

Rosenthal, R. 1964. "Experimenter Outcome-Orientation and the Results of the Psychological Experiment." *Psychological Bulletin,* **61**:405–412.

Rosenthal, R., and Fode, K. L. 1963. "The Effect of Experimenter Bias on the Performance of the Albino Rat." *Behavioral Sciences,* **8**:183–189.

Webb, E. J., Campbell, D. T., Schwartz, R. D., Sechrest, L., and Grove, J. B. 1981. *Nonreactive Measures in the Social Sciences.* Boston: Houghton Mifflin.

Winick, C. 1961. "How People Perceived the 'Mad Bomber.'" *Public Opinion Quarterly,* **25**:25–38.

Wolfgang, M. E. 1963. "Uniform Crime Reports: A Critical Appraisal." *University of Pennsylvania Law Review,* 111:708–738.

CHAPTER 5

TECHNIQUES FOR AVOIDING ERRORS

CHAPTER OUTLINE

NONREACTIVE MEASURES
  Erosion Measures
  Accretion Measures
  Physical Evidence
  Archival Data
  General Forms of Nonreactive Measures
CONTROL GROUPS
  Ethical Considerations in Using Control Groups
  Equating Treatment and Control Groups
  Placebos as Controls
DEALING WITH FLAWS IN CRIME STATISTICS
VICTIMIZATION SURVEYS
  General Considerations
  National Crime Survey (NCS)
REFERENCES

We devoted a great deal of attention in Chapter 4 to problems and pitfalls involved in criminal justice research. The considerations that can distort or destroy a research design which fails to come to grips with them need to be thoroughly understood and carefully considered when work is about to begin. The history of research is replete with cautionary tales about expensive and sophisticated research undertakings that were totally undermined because they failed to take simple precautions to assure that the results dovetailed with the questions being examined.

Once alerted, however, a research worker can take a number of steps to make certain that a task is accomplished in good order. In this chapter, we will examine a range of strategies that respond to the problems we have discussed. Research work, you will learn as you become more familiar with its features, can be enormously exciting. The investigator, led by curiosity and supported by acquired skills, comes to comprehend matters that often are known only to him or her. There is a sense of discovery, or the creation of new knowledge. But the work must be done carefully and correctly.

NONREACTIVE MEASURES

A major difficulty with a good deal of criminal justice work is that the results depend upon only one form of measurement which, like most approaches, has its particular shortcomings. A very large amount of criminal justice work, for instance, relies exclusively upon the use of questionnaires or direct interviews with those who are being studied or who are part of the experimental design. Both of these approaches, while they can uncover important information, suffer from the fact that the subjects inevitably know that they are being studied and behave somewhat differently than they would under less obtrusive conditions. A subject in research work probably believes that there is an element of evaluation involved. For some of us this will mean that we will try harder; others will react by attempting to create an image that they want to project, such as one of nonchalance, or one that they think the research worker will appreciate.

These kinds of situations produce what we earlier labeled "center of attention" effects, reactive effects of measurement, and interviewer effects. The most obvious and direct method for handling such issues is to keep the subject in the dark about the fact that he or she is involved in an experiment or under research scrutiny, to the extent that might be acceptable in terms of the ethical standards discussed in Chapter 2. But even a person who does not know exactly what is being done comprehends that *something* is being done. Most of us, under such circumstances, will try to guess at what is going on and adjust our behavior accordingly. This does not necessarily mean that the results obtained will be completely unreliable, but it does suggest that additional methods ought to be explored to check on the trustworthiness of the conclusions reached from interviews and questionnaires.

The point we would stress as strongly as possible is that research is not a cookbook type of enterprise. Certainly, as a good cook does, the researcher will have favorite recipes and a thorough basic knowledge of techniques and rules and the intricacies of induction, deduction, and logical thinking. But, in the final analysis, imagination and ingenuity can become the touchstones of the truly valuable and innovative research probe. There is a question, a problem, something that concerns or bothers you, and you ponder the most effective way to reach a solution, either through standard approaches or by some novel pathway:

> We must use all available weapons of attack, face our problems realistically and not retreat to the land of fashionable sterility, learn to sweat over our data with an admixture of judgment and intuitive rumination, and accept the usefulness of particular data even when the level of analysis available for them is markedly below that available for other data in the empirical area (Binder, 1981:329).

The foregoing quotation stands alone as Chapter 8 in a remarkable book dedicated to an exploration of inventive ways to carry out research that does not depend upon direct involvement of the subject. The book is by Eugene J. Webb and four coauthors and is titled *Nonreactive Measures in the Social Sciences*. Chapter 9 of the volume is even shorter. It is made up of seven words that constitute the epitaph on the gravestone of John Henry Newman (1801–1890): "From symbols and shadows to the truth." The earlier part of *Nonreactive Measures* is full of illustrations of clever approaches to research and will well repay careful reading. In the following sections of this chapter, we will adopt and invent specific kinds of nonreactive research approaches that appear particularly applicable to criminal justice work. While they do not consign questionnaires and interviews to the scrap heap, these approaches correspond particularly to the observation of William Prosser, a leading scholar of the legal doctrine of evidence, who noted: "There is still no man who would not accept dog tracks in the mud against the sworn testimony of a hundred eyewitnesses that no dog had passed by."

The use of nonreactive observation to produce nonreactive measures relies largely on the cleverness of the researcher in devising or discovering ways of securing information that in no way make the subject sensitive to his or her participation in a probe of any kind. The use of physical traces as research evidence is illustrated by the authors of *Nonreactive Measures* with the following story:

> The fog has probably just cleared. The singular Sherlock Holmes has been reunited with his old friend, Dr. Watson (after one of Watson's marriages), and both walked to Watson's newly-acquired office. The practice was located in a duplex of two physicians' suites, both of which had been for sale. No doubt sucking on his calabash, Holmes summarily told Watson that he had made a wise choice in purchasing the practice that he did, rather than the one on the other

side of the duplex. The data? The steps were more worn on Watson's side than on his competitor's (p. 4).

This anecdote can be used to press home a number of fundamental points about nonreactive measures. Certainly the fact that the floor on one side of the steps is more worn than on the other is suggestive, but it is far from being conclusive evidence that more patients have been visiting one set of offices than the other. The steps might have become worn down during a period before the doctor from who Watson had purchased the practice lived there. Also, the office might have been used at an earlier time as a den of assignation for prostitution, and this may account for the pattern of heavy traffic. In actual research an investigator would consider other sources to supplement the information from the steps, but the purpose of the illustration is to demonstrate the value of environmental changes in the analysis of social constructs.

There are four major types of nonreactive measures: (1) erosion measures, (2) accretion measures, (3) archival evidence, and (4) physical evidence. Police detectives must often depend on nonreactive measures for their leads and their proofs, and criminal justice research workers can learn much from an acquaintance with the skills and tactics of experienced detectives. We shall examine and illustrate the potentialities of each of these classes of nonreactive measures in the following pages.

Erosion Measures

The story about the fabled detection powers of Sherlock Holmes in deducing the richness of a medical practice from the amount of wear on the steps leading to the doctor's office is an example of what is called an *erosion* measure. An original item is examined to determine how much use it has seen, and conclusions are drawn from such observation, usually in terms of a comparison—that is, by seeing how much erosion of something else has occurred during the same period.

In the area of criminal justice such measures are sometimes employed to ascertain the likelihood that a car odometer has been turned back. The method used is to examine the amount of wear on the rubber of the accelerator pedal. Most persons who deliberately roll back odometers (and there is a lucrative trade for "spinners," the name given to persons who professionally undertake rollbacks) remember to remove stickers from the car which would indicate the true mileage at the last oil change or inspection, but they are not likely to take the trouble to replace the rubber on the accelerator pedal. Such evidence would not be conclusive in court, since drivers press variably on accelerators, but it can provide a valuable lead to an investigator and a unit of measurement for a researcher undertaking work on the crimes of used car dealers. It is also possible to locate the former owner of a car and to check with that person to determine how much mileage the vehicle registered when it was sold.

There are numerous other illustrations of erosion measures which can be helpful to research inquiries. The relationship between the way in which goods are displayed in a department store and the amount of shoplifting can be determined without any questionnaires or interviews merely by establishing a differential between legitimately sold goods and those otherwise missing under different display conditions. Indeed, some stores are said to employ the rate of shoplifting as an indication of the appeal of the goods they offer for sale. Shoplifting could, of course, be reduced to negligible proportions if all goods were kept under lock and key (as particularly valuable ones often are), but the aim is to tease and attract, and this is best done if things can readily be handled, conveying the impression that the shopper (almost) owns them. Thus, the more shoplifting, the higher sales are likely to be, other things being equal.

An erosion measure (though not in its purest form) can also be used to study the degree of honesty among junior high school students. The correlates of honesty that the researcher wants to determine may be matters such as sex, grades, and ethnic background. There are clear questions of ethics in the example that follows (indeed, it has similarities to certain of Hartshorne and May's studies, as discussed in Chapter 2), but we will omit discussion of these in this context in the interest of highlighting the use of erosion measures.

Suppose that one of the school counselors routinely interviews each student who is under his or her supervision. It could be arranged that the counselor will spend about 10 minutes in the regular interview, asking the kinds of questions and getting the kinds of information always secured— say, about the student's planned course schedule for the next year. Then the telephone will ring and the counselor will go out of the room, after having said on the phone: "Well, I guess I can see you, but I can stay only 10 minutes, because I have someone in the office with me." Then a pause, and then: "All right, but I'll have to leave the meeting in 10 minutes."

Meanwhile, a pile of coins has been left on the counselor's desk, within clear sight of the student there. The money seems to be scrambled about, making it appear likely that the counselor has no idea exactly how much the total is. Left alone, the student will be faced with a choice of not touching any of the money or perhaps taking a few coins—or perhaps even all the money. Here we would have an accurate measure of honesty, at least in that situation at that particular time. We noted earlier that this nonreactive measure is not altogether pure: for one thing, the counselor, in responding to the telephone call, is play-acting to some extent, and the student may catch on to the ruse if things are not done very carefully. But the measure is a step nearer to actual conditions than those invoked by a paper-and-pencil questionnaire about honesty. And the measure is better in some ways than such things as arrest records, for there are extremely few episodes of criminal dishonesty that ever result in any official action against an offender.

Erosion measures might be employed to determine reactions to fear of crime or fear of particular crimes in a given locality. The library collection could be examined and the rate of withdrawals of books in the 364 series (the category for books on crime under the classification system used by most libraries) could be calculated over time. It would be necessary to determine if there was any variation in the proportion of crime books in the library at one period as against another (and, in fact, this itself is a nonreactive measure of one kind of social attention to issues of crime, particularly if there is a calculation of the number of books published on crime, compared with all other kinds of fiction and nonfiction that finds its way into book form). The quantity of locks available for sale and the depletion of this stock by purchase would be another nonreactive erosion measure of fear of crime (and action stemming from such fear).

Accretion Measures

"Accretion measures" involve the accumulation or deposit of materials, with inferences drawn from observation or measurement of such deposits about the kinds of things that led to them. The use of such deposits to draw conclusions is common in police work, in both fictional and true detective cases. Dust or mud on shoes, stains on a person's clothing or fingers, poison in the digestive system, and blood on a car seat are common examples of accretion measures. Arsenic, for example, as a heavy metal which remains in the body for long periods, can be detected readily in corpses. In one notorious case, the medical examiner located arsenic in the body of a woman's husband. A check of the records indicated an unseemly number of recent deaths among her relatives and several previous mates. Their bodies were exhumed from grave sites and tested for arsenic; large quantities of the element were located. But it took meticulous laboratory and experimental work to ascertain whether the arsenic had filtered into the bodies from the ground in which they were buried or whether the arsenic could be attributed only to poisoning. The case illustrates both the value of accretion measures and the care that has to be exercised in interpreting their special meaning. In archeological research, where there is considerable dependence on drawing conclusions from things that are recovered, a society might be described as given to warfare or to more pastoral pursuits on the basis of the number of weapons and of farming and cooking implements located on a particular site. Ancient mysteries about the demise of this or that Egyptian pharoah—dating back 4000 or 5000 years—have been solved by forensic pathologists, who now are able to examine the mummified bodies to determine the cause of death, whether natural or by untoward means.

Fingerprints, too, constitute an accretion measure. Fingerprints do not change as we grow, and they cannot be erased or altered. Since their introduction at Scotland Yard in England in 1901, fingerprints have been recognized as an infallible means of personal identification. Fingerprints invisible to the human eye can be uncovered by technicians brushing powders across suspicious areas. Today, a laser-run latent-print detector can recover fingerprints that escape detection by the more traditional methods. The argon-ion laser is refracted in a mirror and onto a surface, causing amino acids in sweat to luminesce in a yellowish color.

Various kinds of research probes can be done by a shrewd criminal justice researcher who wants to take advantage of the characteristics of fingerprints as a nonreactive measure. If we have a number of individuals whose behavior we want to monitor surreptitiously, it would be possible to collect their fingerprints and thereby to determine which of them touched a particular object under conditions that had been established as part of the experimental inquiry—without intruding ourselves into the outcome measure or having had to depend upon verbal responses by the persons involved in the test.

Smudging, another accretion item, is useful to determine what books or what parts of books have received especial attention. It is often noted, for instance, that James Joyce's *Ulysses,* a difficult book at best, in most libraries is quite pristine after the first 50 or so pages, but often very soiled on the pages of the last fifth of the volume, where the erotic passages occur. Indeed, a mere count of the kinds of magazines on sale may provide a researcher with a very good indication of community acceptance of items which are sometimes alleged to be pornographic. For the courts, which take "community standards" as the measuring stick to determine which reading and viewing materials are to be deemed legal and which are not, such measures can be exceedingly important. In many court cases involving films deemed pornographic, researchers have stood outside theaters showing them and by examining clothing, age, and other indicators of demographics, have attempted to profile the segment of the community partaking of such fare.

In regard to other aspects of the field of criminal justice, there have been many amusing and informative instances of the use of accretion measures to determine things of interest. One of the better known was carried out by a newspaper columnist attempting to determine the lifestyle of J. Edgar Hoover while Hoover was serving as the director of the FBI. The columnist beat the garbage collectors to the refuse that Hoover had put out. He sifted the debris and was able to draw some quite informative conclusions about Hoover's habits: there were empty bottles of medicine which provided data about his health; reading materials, which indicated his interests; and numerous other clues of a similar nature, including his preferences in liquor. The same strategy might well be used to gather information on groups or persons of interest to a criminal justice researcher.

In the realm of drug addiction, a common accretion measure is urinalysis. The ingestion of certain drugs, most notably heroin, deposits in the body a residue which can be readily measured in the urine. The researcher thus can get a relatively determinative index of a person's opiate use from one period to the next through urinalysis. A well-known investigation into the long-term careers of one-time drug addicts, conducted by John O'Donnell (1969), involved tracking down Kentucky residents who had at one time been patients at the Public Health Service Hospital in Lexington and collecting urine samples from them. By this approach, O'Donnell was able to put to rest forever the oft-stated proposition "Once a drug addict, always a drug addict."

Like many accretion measures, particularly those in which the person involved may be in jeopardy, the use of urinalysis poses some hazards. When the government attempted to determine the level of heroin use in the army during the Vietnamese conflict, newspaper reports noted that "a GI who has enough money can slip $100 to a buddy who takes his place in the line for the urine test." The test was reported to have become something of a cat-and-mouse game, with soldiers improvising various tactics to try to defeat it. In addition, some experimenters have found that laboratories vary greatly in the accuracy of their interpretation of urinalysis results.

Among other methods that addicts sometimes use to confound urinalysis results are the following: (1) switching urines; (2) using obfuscating drugs, that is, drugs which make it difficult to assay the urine adequately for heroin; (3) removing the preservatives from the specimen bottles, so that when the urine arrives later at the laboratory it no longer can be tested satisfactorily; (4) diluting the urine with water; (5) producing specimens of insufficient quantity for chemical analysis; and (6) scheduling use of heroin around the test—that is, the addicts become knowledgeable about how long before the test they are able to use the drug and in what quantity, in order for it not to be determinable on the test. Many addicts will try to "sweat out" drugs in their system during the period immediately before they undergo urinalysis, in order to evade the consequences of a positive test. Particularly important in the area of urinalysis is that the process of taking the specimen, if it is to be done with adequate assurances of accuracy, involves intrusion into what may be regarded as the subject's privacy. The monitor has to watch carefully to ascertain that the person does not switch samples. In some cases, women addicts will insert containers with nonaddicted persons' urine into the vagina or anus and have recourse to these to defeat the test. This can be sidetracked only by close scrutiny. However, either the monitors themselves are squeamish about doing this, or they are made so by comments of the addicts who ridicule them for their close observation of the urine-collecting process. These interactions highlight the considerable difficulties that are likely to intrude into research, even using nonreactive measures, if a human element is involved.

Detective-story literature provides many examples of clever use of accretion measures that are instructive for a researcher faced with the need to construct an unobtrusive measure. In one story, detectives needed to determine where a car had come from. They did so by studying the frequencies to which the car's radio buttons were tuned. Then they triangulated the frequencies—that is, they drew lines which would intersect at the point where the car was used. Webb et al. (1981), who recount this tale, note that most novelists rely on techniques which are a good deal simpler, such as determining how fast a car was going by noting the degree to which insects are splattered on the windshield. One of the present authors saw the Illinois police employing an accretion measure when they were attempting to apprehend persons who moments before had robbed a bank. State troopers descended on a motel near the scene of the robbery and went through the parking lot feeling the hood of each car to determine if it was still warm—that is, if it had been driven very recently. Then they took down the license numbers of the warm cars and sought their owners within the motel for further questioning.

Physical Evidence

Many uses of physical evidence are similar to those employing "accretion" or "erosion" measures, since the physical evidence obviously is found—or not found—in terms of a preexisting standard and an expectation. For example, if the aim is to determine the deterrent effect of a new ordinance that makes it illegal for dog owners not to clean up on the street after their pets, it is simple enough to gauge the impact by counting dog feces in a specified area before and following the ordinance. This is physical evidence, and it also is in the nature of an accretion measure.

Other kinds of physical evidence that may be pertinent to a criminal justice researcher include an examination of the letters-to-the-editor columns of newspapers. In fact, the manner in which the media treat and display crime news can provide considerable insight, particularly if done over time, about aspects of criminal justice as they are handled by one group of opinion leaders.

A particularly fine illustration of the use of physical evidence as a nonreactive measure appears in Howard Polsky's study (1962) of the social structure of an institution for youth. Polsky decided that the authorities at the institution were largely isolated from what he regarded as its most important dynamics. Social workers, for instance, saw incarcerated boys only in their offices and then under rather sterile conditions. Polsky wanted to learn what went on in the cottages, because he believed that this was the most important segment of the operation.

Polsky moved in with the boys; but he is a very large man and was older than the boys confined to the place, so he could hardly make himself unobtrusive. In time, of course, his presence was somewhat taken for granted; boys will not perpetually adjust their behavior to an outsider if they come to believe that what the outsider sees will not in any way redound to their harm. (For a similar reaction on the part of the police, see Chapter 6.) Polsky chose to reach his important conclusions about the placement facility by noting very carefully some small but significant things that were beyond his own judgment, that is, that could not be influenced by his own biases or likes and dislikes of particular boys and were not subject to influence by the fact of his presence. For instance, he carefully watched the table interplay during the meals. He noted that the boys who were "junior" in standing to the tougher youngsters used certain language in asking that the salt be passed to them. And he observed scrupulously how long it took for them to get the salt after such a request, if they got it at all. He also noted how long it took for others to get the same service and who talked to whom and what precise words they employed. The result of this and a series of other nonreactive measures led Polsky to the conclusion that beyond the awareness and control of the authorities, the more rowdy and rougher boys were totally dominating the institution and imposing their will on the less adequate boys to the detriment of these youngsters. Polsky also provided examples of how the staff tried to equalize status and treatment but, because it only tangentially understood the basic living situation, readily fell into supporting the inequitable status quo.

There was a rule, for instance, that the first person to turn the television set on in the dormitory after the meal would be allowed to watch the program he selected until the next half-hour or hour point. In one such situation, a weaker boy picked a program but the channel was changed by a more dominant youngster. The staff came upon the scene as the altercation between the two was just beginning and immediately sided with the tougher boy, totally ignoring the rule but invoking another regulation about kinds of language and behavior. Watching, counting, and recording carefully, Polsky was able to ascertain in dramatic fashion where the real power resided within the correctional facility and how that power was exercised.

Lie detectors provide another special kind of physical evidence. They represent an attempt to neutralize the artifacts introduced by human beings when under scrutiny. To do so, they pay little heed to the literal accuracy of what a person says, but rather concentrate on his or her physiological behavior in connection with the oral response. A person may say "No" to a question about whether he or she had been outside the house on a particular evening, but the heart rate, galvanic skin response, and pulse may provide telltale signs that the answer has aroused great consternation within the person and therefore is probably not correct. It is essential, of course, that an innocent person being interrogated not know anything specific about the question being asked. That is, if the newspapers have reported a murder in the neighborhood the previous evening, everybody who knows about the event, not only its perpetrators, would respond with heightened emotion to a question about it. The key to lie detection (or polygraph work, as it is more correctly known) is to inquire about matters which only the culprit can be privy to. Thus, if the victim has reported the theft of diamonds, a polygraph operator might ask a series of questions, such as "Did you last week steal pearls?" "Did you last week steal rubies?" and "Did you last week steal diamonds?" Presumably, the guilty party would respond only to the relevant item in this sequence. And that response can be cross-checked with other special information about the event under scrutiny.

It is not unlikely that a few persons can "beat" the polygraph test, but it probably requires an extraordinary kind of mental process whereby the person being tested quickly translates one question into another in his or her mind and responds to the "new" question rather than to the original one. The essence of the test, as one operator put it, can be stated in the following terms: "The instrument does not detect lies. It detects the fear of detection—whether a person is disturbed by answering one question in comparison with other questions."

Archival Data

Archival data include actuarial records, voting records, arrest records, probation information, judicial and weather reports, budget allocations, the contents of newspapers and magazines, the total sales for different enterprises, membership lists, private diaries, reports of personnel absenteeism and turnover, annual crime statistics for diverse jurisdictions, and the contents of letters. This is a long list, but it is at best only partial, since any public or private records, issued routinely or put together for special purposes, qualify as a form of archival data.

The kinds of uses to which a criminal justice researcher may put such material are limited only by the ingenuity and the skills of the researcher. Its advantage, of course, is that it is formed and static; that is, nothing intrudes between it and the research worker. The disadvantage, equally obviously, is that the worker using archival material must be able to appreciate precisely what it means, what went into its formation, and where it might err on this or that side. A diary, for example, tells you what the person who wrote it thought, or at least what the person wanted those who read the diary to believe was uppermost in his or her mind. But what mechanisms were operating to skew or select what went into the diary? We have previously noted problems associated with crime statistics and will expand on that discussion later in this chapter. Suffice it to say that archival data, like other sources, must always be approached warily, with the strengths and shortcomings of the method and the material firmly in mind.

An excellent example of the use of archival data is provided in the research of Barbara Hanawalt (1976), a social historian at Indiana University. Hanawalt was concerned with the tough issue of determining patterns of violent death in England during the fourteenth and early fifteenth centuries, a task most certainly impossible without a complete understanding of the archival material. Hanawalt points out that a general reading of the literature of the period she is considering indicates that "the fascination with split heads, spilled brains and dismembered bodies was a dominant theme of medieval...literature" (p. 297), a condition that she notes is equally true today.

Murder provides the particular focus of Hanawalt's study because figures for illegal killings are more likely to be correct than those for events such as robbery and burglary. Deaths will be reported because they almost invariably are deemed important incidents and because their occurrence is difficult to overlook or ignore. At the same time, Hanawalt's examination of the statutes shows that the distinction between murder and manslaughter (in which there is absence of malice aforethought, defined as an intent to kill formed before the actual slaying) did not come into English law until the sixteenth century. So the records Hanawalt had to examine fail to distinguish, as they would today, between manslaughter and murder cases, except in the instances of accidental death, self-defense, and insanity on the part of the perpetrator. This makes comparison with contemporary figures a more difficult enterprise.

Hanawalt then sets forth in some detail the quality of the archival material with which she has worked. Her exposition provides a model of the manner in which a conscientious criminal justice researcher conveys to others the source of the data, so that a judgment can be reached about its values and shortcomings:

> The coroners' rolls, from which the homicide statistics for this paper are derived... are the records of inquests held by county or borough coroners over the bodies of all of those who died suddenly, violently or in suspicious circumstances. In short, the coroners investigated all deaths arising from homicide, suicide, or misadventure, i.e., accidents.
>
> When a body was discovered, the first on the scene was to raise the hue and cry, and the neighborhood or the bailiff would summon the coroner. The coroner viewed the naked body where it was found; turned it over; felt for broken bones; noted bruises and wounds on the body; and recorded the cause or instrument, the place, the date and frequently the hour of the fatality. This rather primitive post-mortem was held in the presence of a coroners' jury drawn from the free men of the neighborhood. The jurors were asked to identify the body, determine the cause and circumstances surrounding the death and, in the case of homicide, to name suspects. The coroner was to arrest the suspects, confiscate their chattels and send them to gaol. Since most felons fled as soon as they had committed a homicide, the coroner usually directed the sheriff or bailiff to make the arrest. All the information gathered at the inquest was recorded on a scrap of parchment that became part of the coroner's file: When the king's justice came to the county the coroner's clerk would copy the files onto rolls to be presented at court. The information in these rolls may be used now to study the sex ratio of victims and suspects, cyclical patterns of the deaths, relationship between victims and suspects, the weapons and motivation. Because of their erratic manners of preservation, the rolls are less reliable for arrival at the annual incidence of homicide (Hanawalt, 1976:299–300).

In the county of Northamptonshire, where she focused part of her study, Hanawalt found one of the best series of coroner's rolls, with 70 years between 1300 and 1420 available. This series listed 1307 cases: 575 homicides, 716 instances of misadventure, and 16 suicides. A difficulty in arriving at a precise statement of the homicide rate, however, lies in the fact that we still do not have adequate estimates of the populations of different parts of England in these remote periods upon which to calculate a crime rate. Hanawalt, advising caution in the matter, estimates that for London in this period, the homicide rate was in the range of 3.6 to 5.2 per 10,000 persons. She compares this with the modern British rate of about 0.05 per 10,000 population and American urban rates in the range of 1.0 to 1.5 per 10,000. "So common was violent death from homicide that in medieval London," Hanawalt (1956:302) writes, "the man in the street ran more risk of dying at the hands of a fellow citizen than he did from an accident."

General Forms of Nonreactive Measure

A nonreactive measurement category that can be designated as "observations" includes various other kinds of information-gathering enterprises in which subjects are not aware of the presence of the observers. An example of such a method is that employed in the television program *Candid Camera,* where the filming is done from behind peepholes or one-way vision mirrors, so that the people being photographed are not aware of the process. Anyone who has seen this program will understand at once that when people believe they are not being watched, they behave differently from the way they do when they know that their activities are under scrutiny. A criminal justice researcher once took advantage of this technique to determine the extent of shoplifting from the meat counter in a supermarket by watching customers from behind a one-way mirror. People, assuming that no one was looking, engaged in all sorts of personal actions, such as rearranging their clothing in intimate ways. Also, in terms of what had been anticipated, a surprising number of shoppers could be seen taking the wrapped packages of meat and hiding them under their outer garments. The ethical issue in this type of research is obvious enough.

Characteristics which may be observed and recorded unobtrusively include (1) physical features such as clothes, hairstyle, beard length, and scars and similar body marks; (2) expressive movements such as speech style; grimaces; frowns; and arm, leg, and eye movements; (3) social location, as for example, whether and how persons are clustered in groups or whether they remain in isolation; (4) language behavior, including types of words and references employed, emotional tones and overtones, and kinds of errors and word slips; and (5) the amount of time spent on various tasks. An investigator may be unobtrusive by blending in with other people in the setting as well as by being out of sight, as behind a peephole.

All the foregoing nonreactive observations may be accomplished directly by use of hidden hardware such as audio tape recorders, video tape recorders, cameras, instruments for measuring eye movements, recorders of body movements, and photoelectric cells. In addition, the nonreactive observer can intervene actively, either with or without hidden hardware, in order to increase the efficiency of data gathering. Intervention by observers is discussed more fully in Chapter 6.

All nonreactive measures are, of course, subject to error. That is why we have stressed that their strengths and weaknesses must be weighed and stated carefully, and that their most effective use is as supplementary and complementary research tools in conjunction with other techniques. Sometimes, because of the uncertainties inherent in field research (which make it susceptible to criticisms by purists), criminal justice workers have retreated to their laboratories, where control of every little artifact and aspect of their work becomes much more readily possible. But they run a risk in trying to generalize what they learn from the laboratory to real-life situations. Many would argue persuasively that the errors caused by generalizing from the laboratory situation to the actual social setting are likely to be more damaging than those that result from the possible inaccuracy of more uncontrolled measures in everyday life.

Knowledge can be accumulated to an impressive degree by successive imperfect measures. Correlatively, uncertainty about the results and their meaning are reduced as new information accumulates, despite the imperfection of each new component. Strict and total reliance on questionnaires and interviews and on laboratory work in criminal justice research will doom the research to a highly delimited range of conclusions, particularly as such conclusions bear upon important issues essential for informed policymaking. Expanding research approaches by recourse to the kinds of measures we have discussed above seem an essential aspect of sophisticated criminal justice inquiry. The issue is nicely summarized by Webb et al. (1981) in *Nonreactive Measures:*

> If no single measurement class is perfect, neither is any scientifically useless. Many studies and many novel sources of data have been mentioned in these pages. The reader may indeed have wondered which turn of the page would provide the commentary on some Ouija-board investigation. It would have been there had we known of one, and had it met some reasonable criteria of scientific worth. These "oddball" studies have been discussed because they demonstrate ways in which the investigator may shore up reactive infirmities of the interview and questionnaire. As a group these classes of measurement are themselves infirm, and individually contain more risk (more rival plausible hypotheses) than does a well-constructed interview.
>
> That does not trouble us, nor does it argue against their use, for the most fertile search for validity comes from a combined series of different measures, each with its idiosyncratic weaknesses, each pointed to a single hypothesis. When a hypothesis can survive the confrontation of a series of complementary methods of testing, it contains a degree of validity unattainable by one tested within the more constricted framework of a single method (p. 315).

It is a sharp and skillful criminal justice researcher who is able, first, to determine the standard means for reaching the results that are desired and, second, to let his or her imagination run riot and hit upon some further and nonreactive measures to extend and enrich whatever results are achieved by the usual investigative methods.

CONTROL GROUPS

The use of a control group is one of the most efficient and effective ways to make certain that research conclusions mean what the researcher had hoped they would mean. A control group consists of subjects who are exposed to precisely the same conditions as the experimental subjects except for the treatment of central concern. If differences then are obtained between control and experimental subjects, it is reasonably certain that the differences result from that treatment and not from other variables. We use the qualifying adverb "reasonably" because it often is not possible to be absolutely sure that the members of the control group have not been "contaminated," that is, that they have not been subjected to some influence that extends beyond those bearing upon members of the experimental group.

This can be illustrated by a research probe designed to determine how paroled narcotics addicts are influenced by living in a halfway house for five months after their release from prison. Every second inmate who is released from an institution is sent to the halfway house. These persons are enrolled as the experimental group. The remaining half of the released individuals constitute the control group. The aim is to see if a halfway house accomplishes such goals as reducing subsequent crime and reducing later use of heroin or other illegal drugs. But the dynamics of the situation—the very establishment of the experimental situation—can insidiously bear upon the outcome.

For instance, it is likely that persons in the control group, since they live in the same neighborhoods as those who were assigned to the halfway house, will learn of the existence of the experimental program. They may conclude that only by sheer fortune did they escape being placed in that facility and that they ought to behave themselves more suitably in order to avoid such a fate in the future, since they much prefer being able to return to their own homes. In this case, it is quite possible that their records on the outside reflect in some part not what ordinarily would have happened but what happens under circumstances which were not meant to intrude into the investigation. The result might be avoided by having members of the control group come from a very distant neighborhood, but in that event distortion is possible from the very nature of the different neighborhoods into which the parolees are being released.

Nonetheless, using a control group is a very powerful research weapon. It can help to eliminate alternative plausible hypotheses which stem from the "center of attention" effects discussed earlier. It can go a long way toward eliminating intrusions that deflect unambiguous deduction.

Ethical Considerations in Using Control Groups

The matter of ethics poses very important considerations when control groups are employed under field conditions. Consider the ingredients of the halfway house experiment outlined above. An actual research project which followed such an outline demonstrated that the persons assigned to the halfway house developed a significantly higher rate of heroin addiction than the members of the control group (Himelson et al., 1967). Of course, the experimenter did not know that this would happen when the research was blueprinted, but that hardly makes things any better for the subjects of the probe. Compounding this was the fact that the experimental subjects felt deprived of liberty because of the constraints under which they had to live as residents of a facility run by correctional authorities. The authorities maintained that they were trying to help the residents rather than allowing them to cope unaided with their drug problems, but this did nothing to alleviate the subjective feelings of deprivation among parolees. Their feelings, of course, were heightened when it turned out that the well-meaning effort had failed to achieve its goal.

The question becomes: What right does an experimenter have to withhold things from one group that are granted to another group and thereby to inflict an injury, or even to bring about unhappiness or discomfort? As with most ethical issues, the answer is difficult to formulate. The mitigating or excusing circumstance has to be that the potential negative consequences were deemed, in the best judgment available at the time, likely to be small compared with longer-range gains. The harm must, in addition, be temporary and unavoidable.

Equating Treatment and Control Groups

It is essential, as we noted, that experimental and control groups be handled identically except for the treatment of immediate interest, so that differences that are later noted between the groups at the end of the study could have resulted only from that treatment. This implies, of course, that there must be no difference between the experimental and control subjects before the start of experimentation.

Matching is one method for equating experimental and control groups. To accomplish matching in a satisfactory manner, the research worker has to know enough about the subject matter to determine in advance of experimentation just what differences between persons could affect the measurement variables. The most common way of matching groups is to make certain that members of both are alike in terms of such things as age, sex, racial or ethnic background, education, and socioeconomic status. The assumption is that if there are notable variations in any of these characteristics, the variation will be a powerful explanation of the outcome. The underlying idea, of course, is that each of the items has a strong influence on how human beings behave. Certainly, the striking variations in crime rates for offenses such as homicide, burglary, and robbery between men and women indicate how essential sex matching is if the experiment has anything to do with these offenses.

Matching can be done on a person-to-person basis, so that each person in the treatment group is like one person in the control group in terms of the matching variable or variables. That is, if an individual in the treatment group has an IQ of 118, is in the age range 18 to 20, and is from a working-class family, then that person is matched with someone in the control group with the same characteristics. Since this matching is one to one, there clearly will be the same number of persons in the treatment and control groups.

Matching can also be done in regard to overall group characteristics. If IQ is the matching variable and the average IQ of the treatment group is 118, this would lead to choosing the control group so that its average IQ is 118. This method is easier and sometimes suitable enough for the work contemplated. But it raises the usual difficulties with averages or means, most particularly because there may be wide variations in the components that go to make up the mean. Thus, two persons with IQs of 119 and 117 will have an average IQ of 118. So will two persons whose IQs are 84 and 152.

One of the major problems with use of matching techniques is that it is difficult to be certain that important variables have not been overlooked. That is, matching may have been done in terms of sex, IQ, and educational achievement, but not in terms of motivational level, and motivational level may be what will affect the variable of central interest most powerfully and thus account for an alternative plausible hypothesis. In addition, person-by-person matching can produce a negative impact upon the overall sensitivity of analysis if the relationship between matching variables and the central variable is not strong enough to compensate for an increase in base error.

The technique of *randomization* avoids the necessity of specifying and using all the variables that could generate alternative hypotheses. With randomization, the research worker assigns people to treatment and control groups in a fashion that makes it equally likely for any given individual to fall into either group. It may be accomplished by the toss of a coin—if a tail comes up, the individual is assigned to the treatment group; if a head, to the control group. More elaborate randomization techniques include the use of a table of random numbers, which is a series of numbers generated by the operation of chance. The persons to be in the experiment are each assigned a number, and then those numbers which correspond to, say, the first 50 in the table of random numbers are placed in one group; those corresponding to the next 50 in the control group. (The use of a table of random numbers is fully discussed in Chapter 11). What must be avoided in any randomization is a technique which introduces a bias that makes it more likely that certain individuals will fall into one group rather than the other.

A classic randomization error would be to alphabetize the total universe of persons to take part in the experiment and then to select the first 100 for the treatment group and the next 100 for the control group. In doing this, you skew the populations, because persons of particular ethnic groups tend to be unevenly distributed in regard to the first initials of their last names (note, for instance, the disproportionate number of Irish and Scottish people whose last names begin with Mc or Mac). Besides, it is not unlikely that persons whose last names are at the beginning of the alphabet come to differ in some ways from those with names appearing at the end of the alphabet. Schoolteachers, for instance, have the habit of calling on students in alphabetical order, and many other of life's activities follow the same procedure. It is debatable whether this selection ultimately has a bearing upon the people whose names are called earliest and most often by teachers and others, but it certainly is possible that this is so. And the aim of randomization most particularly is to avoid all possible contamination.

Adequate randomization eliminates systematic biasing by ensuring that people with certain characteristics will not appear in one group more often than (or rather than) in another group. Whether the subject is tall or short, has a high or a low IQ, is a college graduate or a high school dropout, has high or low socioeconomic status, or whatever, there is an equal chance of being assigned to treatment or control groups.

It is not possible, of course, to be perfectly certain that this random assignment will result in a full balancing of the variables between treatment and control groups. The toss of a coin, for instance, should produce an equal number of heads and tails over a long series of tosses, assuming that the coin is not unevenly weighted and the toss is done without a biasing twist. But all of us know of instances in which a head will come up 5 or even 10 times in a row in a particular trial. The likelihood of true balancing increases as the size of the sampling increases, however. The process can be illustrated more precisely in the following way: If four persons, two with high IQs and two with low IQs, are to be assigned randomly to two groups, there is a high probability—the exact probability is one out of three chances—that the two persons with high IQs will wind up in one group and the two with low IQs in the other. But if there are 20 people, 10 with high IQs and 10 with low IQs, it is very unlikely that you will get all the high IQs in one of the experimental groups and all the low IQs in the other. The likelihood of equivalence increases as the number of people available for assignment grows to 100, to 1000, and to 10,000.

A further method of equating treatment and control groups is referred to as *using subjects as their own controls.*This process involves employing the *same* individuals for both treatment and control conditions. For example, the memory or perceptual ability of a group of people may be measured under stable conditions in an experiment which is seeking to learn how reliable eyewitness testimony about criminal events is under specified circumstances. This situation constitutes the control condition. Treatment might take the form of having the persons drink alcoholic beverages to the point where their blood-alcohol levels reached 0.08 percent. Determining the memory and the perceptual ability of these people again, after the ingestion of alcohol, constitutes the measurement for the treatment condition. The same subjects therefore contribute to both treatment and control data and provide in some senses the ultimate in matching. Clearly, however, the criminal justice research worker must be assured that biological or psychological changes in the subjects between the control and treatment measurements do not generate alternative plausible hypotheses.

The emphasis so far has been on the comparability of the people who are placed in treatment and control groups. The principles also apply generally if there are two different treatment groups rather than one treatment group and one control group. For example, subjects in a treatment group might be given a certain dosage of a barbiturate (a drug such as Nembutal and Seconal—a "downer" in the vernacular) in order to see how it affects the performance of certain tasks. Members of another treatment group might be given a dosage twice that administered to the first treatment group and the same performance measures would then be made.

Placebos as Controls

The *placebo effect* is a phenomenon often found in medical contexts: patients may improve when they think they are being treated, even though in fact they are not being treated (good discussions of the effect occur in Shapiro, 1960, and Grunbaum, 1981). If patients who come to a clinic with a throat infection are given colored sugar pills, pills that have no medical value whatsoever, a substantial number of them will improve. Pharmacologically inert substances, substances incapable of eliciting a response when prescribed in reasonable quantities (such as sugar pills and injections of salt water), are known as *placebos*. The term *placebo* derives from the Latin for "I shall please." A number of proprietary drugs on the market for colds, headaches, backaches, and similar conditions work on the placebo principle. Their essential ingredient is an analgesic—a pain reliever—but there is no curative agent in the drugs. They operate by easing the discomfort of the illness and making the patient believe that curative powers are at work. They may highlight one of the rare positive values of advertising: it heightens the placebo effect by conditioning the public to believe wholeheartedly in the fictional strength of powerless products.

According to one review of placebo effects, about 35 percent of patients will respond to a placebo for a large range of medical ailments. These include chronic headache, angina pectoris, rheumatoid arthritis, cough, peptic ulcer, hay fever and essential hypertension. Some scholars also argue (see, for example, Binder, 1976) that psychotherapy works because of the faith of the patient in the process rather than because the therapist behaves in a specific way on the basis of a guiding theory.

As far as the individual patient or subject is concerned, it may make little or no difference whether improvement has resulted from specific effects of an agent or of a process, as opposed to the results of faith. But in many cases of criminal justice research, the hypothesis of an effect that has been produced because of this or that specified agent or process is critically different from the hypothesis of an effect that has come about because of the faith of the subject. For the researcher who must disentangle the hypothesis of specific effect (such as a certain kind of biochemical action) from the hypothesis of placebo-induced effect, it is essential to use the specific agent (for example, the drug) with one group of subjects and a similar but neutral agent with the other. If equivalent changes take place in both groups of subjects (that is, if the placebo produces as much effect as the specific agent), then one can reasonably conclude that the agent is no more effective than raw faith. Using a placebo in this way is called a *placebo control approach,* and the group that gets the placebo rather than the specific agent is referred to as the *placebo control group.* A placebo control group is useful whenever there may be alternative plausible hypotheses stemming from "center of attention" effects or reactive effects of measurement.

There are some hints in the experimental literature about the role that placebos play, with their curious ability to induce cures. Biochemists suggest that faith in the curative abilities of a drug actually produces a response in the cerebral cortex, triggered by a brain function, and that the body's own opiates are called into action to produce the reduction in pain that is recorded. Another explanation is that the patient's confidence in a physician goes a long way toward helping the patient, whatever the mechanism by which this operates may be. In one instance it was discovered that a medication later found to be of no value at all proved effective among about 80 percent of the patients of physicians who expressed enthusiasm about the remedy. With doctors in whom the patients had little confidence, and whose relationship with patients was otherwise flawed, the same drug was reported to have produced unpleasant effects, including nausea, dizziness, and pain.

Placebos arouse some ethical concerns that the criminal justice researcher should take into account. Sissela Bok (1978) argues that the deception involved in their use is likely to encourage other kinds of ruses and the withholding of information from patients and research subjects. She believes (as do others discussed in Chapter 2) that persons involved in experiments should not be lied to and that all their questions should be answered honestly, practices that might well render the use of placebos impossible if the aim is to produce pure experimental conditions. For physicians, placebos (it is suggested) are sometimes a weapon. It was found in one study that the majority of physicians provided placebos to patients they dislike, consider difficult, or suspect of exaggerating pain. When such patients reported relief, the physicians incorrectly took that as proof of malingering. This illustrates the kind of faulty interpretive logic that should devoutly be avoided by criminal justice researchers intent upon doing acceptable work.

One method used to make certain that placebo experiments are not themselves contaminated by other influences is to conduct *double-blind* experiments, where the administrator does not know which subjects get drugs and which placebos. Without such controls, it is possible that the person who knows that a placebo is being used conveys the knowledge to the subject either directly or, more likely, in some subtle manner. It then may be the attitude of the administrator rather than the drug itself that produces the results that later are discovered. In some instances, it does not appear necessary to use the double-blind procedure, since the experimenter apparently has no likely influence upon the outcome. If only subjects are kept ignorant as to the type of treatment or placebo, the experiment is said to be *blind*.

DEALING WITH FLAWS IN CRIME STATISTICS

Another problem that often taxes the mind of the criminal justice researcher is the need to deal with matters that undermine the integrity of general counts of crime, counts that were described and discussed in Chapter 4.

The first necessary step is to exercise caution in the use of such material, to appreciate yourself and to let others know the shortcomings of the figures that are being employed. A second step is liberal use of common sense and analytical thinking. If nothing of significance appears to have changed that will have an effect on the accuracy of official reports of criminal activity of certain kinds, then it is not unreasonable to regard such reports as measuring the direction of criminal activity, that is, its increase or decrease.

What might be some of the factors that ought to be scrutinized before arriving at a determination that nothing unusual has influenced the quality of the statistical information this year or this period as compared with another one? First, do the officials have any particular reason for fudging the statistics? Some law enforcement agencies like to see sharp rises in crime rates, because they can use these to inflate their budgetary demands. Others prefer decreases, because they can point to these as indicators of a job well done. Second, are there any social factors that might warp the accuracy of the crime reports? A given jurisdiction might have had one murderer who accounted for 27 killings, and while in truth the rate of homicide grew tremendously because of this, the figures hardly indicate a pervasive crime wave. Similarly, an influx of transients at a particular moment may distort crime figures, since these figures usually are calculated in terms of the resident population, as rates per 100,000 persons living in the jurisdiction. Third, attention might be paid to places with similar kinds of characteristics, such as city size, ethnic mix, and age structure. If these places show relatively constant crime rates and the site you are studying shows a striking decrease in crime rates, you are going to have to look very closely to determine why this discrepancy occurred, and whether it is really a true indicator of crime in your area.

All in all, it may be better to do some intensive sampling within the jurisdiction that you are concerned with, in order to try to determine for yourself the nature and the amount of crime rather than to rely on official reports by agencies which are not so closely concerned with your research. If you want to see whether a particular program (say, having citizens engrave their social security numbers on property such as television sets) has an impact on the robbery rate, it may be best to sample personally citizens' reports of robberies both before and after the intervention rather than to depend on the official tallies. For one thing, in this example, the fact that people have their numbers on their property may encourage them to report offenses that they might otherwise have ignored. Because of this, it might turn out that reliance only on official reports rather than on your own inquiry would show an increase in the amount of theft where none actually had taken place.

VICTIMIZATION SURVEYS

The material above provides a prelude to a review of the surveys that have been carried out among the general population in order to determine victimizations that are not necessarily reported to law enforcement agencies. A thorough understanding of these materials is essential for a criminal justice researcher, who must often rely upon such sources as indices of the amount of crime.

General Considerations

The deficiencies of the *Uniform Crime Reports* (UCR) led in 1966 to the first attempt in the United States (and, indeed, in the world) to measure the amount of crime by asking a large random sample of residents throughout the country about their personal experiences as crime victims (Ennis, 1967: Biderman et al., 1967; Reiss, 1967). The surveys showed, not unexpectedly, that persons told interviewers about a good deal more crime committed against them than they had reported to law enforcement authorities. Burglaries were 10 times as high as the UCR figures indicated, aggravated assaults more than twice as high, and robberies 50 percent above the UCR figures, according to the victimization surveys. Only vehicle thefts were reported to be lower, by a small though puzzling amount. It was believed that people probably report cars as stolen to the police and then find that they themselves had misplaced the cars or that someone else had perhaps borrowed them. Philip Ennis, who conducted the first victimization survey, suggested that persons "may either forget the incident when interviewed or be too embarrassed to mention it" (1967:37).

The failure of individuals to report accurately their personal victimization experiences and those of other members of their household is one of the fundamental flaws in victimization inventories as measures of the amount of criminal activity in a jurisdiction. Research workers have at times run what they call "reverse record checks," in which they examine all reports of crime recorded in the police station and then interview the victims who filed these reports. One such study is summarized in Table 2. The table shows that in investigations conducted in Washington, D.C.; Baltimore; and San Jose, California, there were 982 victims determined from police files and interviewed by census workers. When these respondents were asked whether they had been victimized during a specified number of months preceding the interview, more than 70 percent reported their known victimizations to the interviewer in regard to assault, robbery, rape, burglary, and larceny. As can be seen in Table 2, the proportion of known victims who told the interviewers about their victimization varied substantially, depending upon the type of crime. Nearly 9 out of 10 burglary victims but fewer than half the assault victims mentioned to the census interviewer the victimization that had been reported to the police (Garofalo and Hindelang, 1977:13–14).

Two explanations seem to account for this dropoff rate. First, there is simple forgetting. The longer ago an event took place (and this need be but a few months), the more likely it is to go unmentioned. Second, there is some indication that in face-to-face personal crimes, victimizations committed by persons known to the victim are less likely to be mentioned to survey interviewers than those perpetrated by strangers.

Victims of crime may also have difficulty when it comes to defining certain things that have happened to them as *crimes*. Wife-beating is a notorious illustration of this phenomenon. Wife-beating is believed to be extremely common in the United States, but it is not likely either to be reported to the police or to be mentioned to an interviewer who is seeking information about victims of criminal assault. The wife may not want to jeopardize her relationship with her husband, particularly if she is economically dependent on him. She may be fearful that any disclosure will bring further physical abuse. But most likely she does not make the connection in her mind between what happened to her and what might be prosecutable in a criminal court under the law.

Conversely, there are some things which would never hold up in a courtroom or survive screening at the police station but which will be called *crimes* by the person being interviewed as part of a victimization survey. In many instances, the problem lies in the difficulty of proof: private events, such as rape, present considerable problems since there is often no corroboration of the offense, and a trial is likely to become a contest

TABLE 2

PROPORTION OF KNOWN VICTIMS SAMPLED FROM POLICE FILES
(Who Reported the Sampled Crime to Survey Interviewers: Washington, D.C., Baltimore, and San Jose)

	Washington, D.C.			Baltimore			San Jose			Three-city total		
	Number of completed interviews	Offenses reported to interviewers		Number of completed interviews	Offenses reported to interviewers		Number of completed interviews	Offenses reported to interviewers		Number of completed interviews	Offenses reported to interviewers	
		Number	Percent		Number	Percent		Number	Percent		Number	Percent
Assault	54	35	65	99	36	36	81	39	48	234	94	47
Robbery	57	52	91	103	78	76	80	61	76	240	191	80
Rape	—	—	—	—	—	—	45	30	67	45	30	67
Burglary	68	60	88	77	66	66	104	94	90	249	220	88
Larceny	47	36	77	83	62	75	84	68	81	214	166	78
Total crimes	226	183	81	362	242	67	394	292	74	982	701	71

Source: Garofalo and Hindelang, 1977:13–14.

between the accused, who claims consensual behavior, and the victim, who claims force or coercion. Since the offender gets the benefit of a juridical presumption of innocence and the need to prove the offense "beyond a reasonable doubt" the offender may prevail despite the fact that the law actually had been violated. Such events may pose fewer problems numerically than those in which the victim defines as criminal something that in fact did not come up to the legal criteria specified to render the act illegal. Matters that we think should be crimes, or that arguably might be crimes, are likely to be translated into actual crimes when we are asked by an interviewer to detail our victimization experiences. The mere fact of being asked the question tends to place the respondent in a position where he or she wants to be helpful and provide the kinds of information that the interviewer obviously desires to obtain (a "center of attention" effect).

National Crime Survey (NCS)

The National Crime Survey (NCS), based upon earlier victimization surveys, was begun in 1972 under the sponsorship of the Law Enforcement Assistance Administration (LEAA) and is now carried out by the Bureau of the Census. The NCS has been described as "the most important innovation in the area of crime statistics since the 1930's" (Fienberg, 1977:4). NCS interviews include individuals in approximately 65,000 households through the United States. At first, they also included interviews conducted with managers of commercial establishments, in order to inventory their victimization by crimes such as burglary and shoplifting, but because of the expense and the generally lower yield of this work, it has been abandoned.

Panels of respondents are used in the NCS work—that is, the same persons are interviewed every six months—in order to eliminate some of the recall problems or what is called *telescoping*. Telescoping is defined in a National Research Council report that examined crime surveys in the following terms:

> Incorrect placement of the time of occurrence of an event as reported by a respondent. Reporting the event as more recent than actual occurrence is forward telescoping, and reporting an event as earlier in time than actual occurrence is backward telescoping (Penick and Owens, 1976:234).

Use of panels makes it possible to check on previous interviews to be certain that the material offered has not been reported before. The Census Bureau, however, because of insufficient resources, has failed to date to do this kind of checking to make certain that duplicative reports are not tallied.

The NCS questionnaires also tap attitudes regarding fear of crime and views about the decline or improvement in the neighborhood in regard to crime as these changes are perceived by the respondent. Information is also gathered about what steps a respondent or members of his or her family might have taken to protect against victimization, such as installing new and better locks on doors or windows.

Location of the victimization interviewing in the Census Bureau has permitted some relatively sophisticated revisions of the NCS approach through the years, since the technique is a good deal more flexible than that which constitutes the basis for the UCR reports, which merely rely on information furnished by local law enforcement agencies. For example, in the earlier stages of victimization research respondents were asked whether they had undergone any surgery because of criminal victimization. It was found that the number of affirmative responses increased notably when the wording of the question was changed: instead of using the word *surgery*, interviewers asked respondents whether "anyone has cut on you" during the previous months. This is but another illustration of the subtlety of information gathering in criminal justice—and of the need to try to counteract matters which distort the accuracy of the information being sought.

Recently, a thorough reexamination has been made of crime statistics in the United States as part of a program to bring together the UCR and the NCS reports into a single inventory. Among the matters that were considered in regard to improvement of the NCS (matters which provide a criminal justice researcher with a good idea of the kinds of questions that need to be asked of all statistical reporting approaches) were the following: (1) inclusion of offenses other than those covered, offenses such as vandalism and fraud; (2) more thorough determination of the harm suffered as a consequence of crime; (3) determination through questions of the characteristics that make some victimization experiences very memorable and others less so; (4) extension of interviewing to cover groups now not part of the survey, in order to learn if their omission significantly distorts the NCS (such groups include persons living in military barracks, children under the age of 12, and institutionalized persons, such as prison inmates and individuals confined to mental hospitals); (5) examination of the relationship between lifestyle and victimization, especially in regard to things which might be changed or about which suitable cautionary advice might be offered; (6) more intense and thorough determination of the fear of crime, including the relationship between fear and presentations of crime in the news media; (7) attempts to see if persons interviewed might, with suitable guarantees of anonymity, provide information about their own criminal activity; (8) gathering of facts about victims' experiences with the criminal justice system and their reactions to those experiences; (9) inclusion of questions about experiences as a bystander or a witness of a criminal event (Biderman, 1978).

There also have been discussions regarding the possibility of using telephone survey techniques, such as random digit dialing (which overcomes the problem of unlisted numbers but has difficulties of its own, particularly in relation to telephones which are not answered and those for business establishments rather than households). The issue with telephone surveys involves the quality of information that will be secured in tandem with the cost savings and the possibility of improved sampling. Another consideration—one that is important but tends to be understated in criminal justice research—is danger. Household surveys expose an interviewer to risks of personal harm that would be eliminated if a telephone approach were employed.

It is notable the NCS data tend to remain relatively stable—that is, the rises and declines in the amount of reported criminal victimization are much less dramatic than those that appear in the UCR reports. However, over the years that both have been issued, the UCR and NCS have almost invariably reflected changes in the same direction in the amount of criminal activity taking place in the United States. When one report notes an increase, the other is likely to do so too, however disparate their precise figures are for the rates for a particular individual criminal activity. This reinforces the view that both measures are relatively reliable indicators of trends in lawbreaking (O'Brien et al., 1980).

For the criminal justice researcher the NCS survey provides an opportunity to take advantage of finely honed questions that have been pretested, tested, and refined over the past decade. The survey has not been employed adequately to date as an evaluative instrument—that is, as a determiner of changes in rates of crime as measured before and following an intervention—but it assuredly has this potential.

Copies of the NCS questionnaire should be put on file in any organization that conducts criminal justice research. In fact, one of the most important initial steps that any person contemplating doing criminal justice research ought to take is to establish a good personal file of questionnaires that have been employed in criminal justice research projects. Construction of such questionnaires is a very complicated, expensive, and time-consuming endeavor, and the work can be reduced by the employment of questionnaires that have been put together by other persons or organizations, if you first secure permission for such use. The results from surveys conducted previously with the same questionnaire also allow a comparison to be drawn between some of your own findings and those of earlier workers, a comparison which may well render your conclusions that much more meaningful and informative.

REFERENCES

Biderman, A. D. (ed.) 1978. *Toward an Agenda for Research on National Victimization Survey Statistics.* Washington, D.C.: Bureau of Social Science Research.

Biderman, A. D., Johnson, L. A., McIntyre, J., and Weir, A. 1967. *Report on a Pilot Study in the District of Columbia on Victimization and Attitudes Toward Law*

Enforcement. Washington, D.C.: President's Commission on Law Enforcement and Administration of Justice.

Biderman, A. D., and Reiss, A. J., Jr., 1967. "On Exploring the 'Dark Figure' of Crime." *Annals of the American Academy of Political and Social Science*, **374**:1–15.

Binder, A. 1981. "A Statistician on Method." In E. J. Webb, D. T. Campbell, R. D. Schwartz, L. Sechrist, and J. B. Grove. *Nonreactive Measures in the Social Sciences*. Boston: Houghton Mifflin.

Binder, A. 1976. "Cultural and Scientific Perspectives on Therapy." In Binder, V. L., Binder, A., and Rimland, B. (eds.), *Modern Therapies* (pp. 3–16). Englewood Cliffs, N.J.: Prentice-Hall.

Bok, S. 1978. *Lying: Moral Choice in Public and Private Life*. New York: Pantheon.

Ennis, P. 1967. *Criminal Victimization in the United States: A Report of a National Survey*. Washington, D.C.: President's Commission on Law Enforcement and Administration of Justice.

Fienberg, S. E. 1977. "Testimony." In *Suspension of the National Crime Survey* (pp. 3–23). Hearing before the Subcommittee on Crime of the Committee on the Judiciary. U.S. House of Representatives, 95th Cong., 1st Sess., Washington, D.C.: Government Printing Office.

Garofalo, J., and Hindelang, M. J. 1977. *An Introduction to the National Crime Survey*. Washington, D.C.: National Criminal Justice Information and Statistics Service, Law Enforcement Assistance Administration, U.S. Department of Justice.

Grunbaum, A. 1981. "The Placebo Concept." *Behavior Research and Therapy*, **19**:157–167.

Hanawalt, B. A. 1976. "Violent Death in Fourteenth- and Early Fifteenth-Century England." *Comparative Studies in Society and History*, **18**:297–320.

Himelson, A. N., Miller, D. E., and Geis, G. 1967. "The East Los Angeles Halfway House for Felon Addicts." *International Journal of the Addictions*, **2**:305–311.

McMullan, P. S., Collins, J. J., Jr., Gandossy, R., and Lenski, J. G. 1978. *Analysis of the Utility and Benefits of the National Crime Survey (NCS)*. Washington, D.C.: Office of Planning and Management, Law Enforcement Assistance Administration, U.S. Department of Justice.

O'Brien, R. M., Shichor, D., and Decker, D. L. 1980. "An Empirical Assessment of the Validity of the UCR and NCS Crime Rates." *Sociological Quarterly*, **21**:391–401.

O'Donnell, J. A. 1969. *Narcotic Addicts in Kentucky*. Chevy Chase, Md.: National Institute of Mental Health, Department of Health, Education, and Welfare.

Penick, B.K.E., and Owens III, M.E.B. 1976. *Surveying Crime: Panel for the Evaluation of Crime Surveys*. Washington, D.C.: National Academy of Sciences.

Polsky, H. W. 1962. *Cottage Six*. New York: Russell Sage Foundation.

Prosser, W. L. 1964. *Handbook of the Law of Torts*, 3d ed. St. Paul: West.

Reiss, A. J., Jr., 1967. *Studies in Crime and Law Enforcement in Major Metropolitan Areas*. Washington, D.C.: President's Commission on Law Enforcement and Administration of Justice.

Shapiro, A. K. 1960. "A Contribution to a History of the Placebo Effect." *Behavioral Science*, **5**:109–135.

Webb, E. J., Campbell, D. T., Schwartz, R. D., Sechrest, L., and Grove, J. B. 1981. *Nonreactive Measures in the Social Sciences*. Boston: Houghton Mifflin.

CHAPTER 6

STANDARD APPROACHES TO RESEARCH

CHAPTER OUTLINE

WAYS OF CLASSIFYING RESEARCH
   Classification by Purpose
   Statistical Classification
   Temporal Classification
   Classification by Control over Variables
CONTROL AND ADVANCEMENT OF KNOWLEDGE
SYSTEMATIC OBSERVATION
   Naturalistic Observation
      The observer's role
      External validity of naturalistic observation
      Unstructured and structured observation
      Naturalistic observation: Some problems and limitations
   Surveys: Questionnaires and Interviews
   Physical Traces and Archival Records
   Sociometry
EXPERIMENTATION
   The "True" Experiment
   The Nonlaboratory Experiment
REFERENCES

WAYS OF CLASSIFYING RESEARCH

There are a large number of different ways to conduct research. The diversity of these approaches has led to attempts to achieve order among them by arranging them into classifications in terms of their major characteristics. In this way, further refinements and an overall perspective can more readily be achieved.

Classification by Purpose

One classificatory scheme focuses upon the *purpose* of the research. It categorizes approaches according to whether they involve (1) exploration, (2) description, or (3) explanation.

Exploratory research (or *pilot research,* as it often is called) is a type of work that is generally carried out at minimum expense and with little planning. The goal most often is to attain some familiarity with the mechanisms and interrelationships that exist in a new domain of concern. The criminal justice researcher may, for instance, want to understand the means by which directives of the chief of a large police department are transmitted through the ranks and down to the patrol officers who are responsible for executing them. It seems desirable, in terms of the nature of the problem and the research resources available, to begin by conducting informal observations and interviews throughout the department. On the basis of this work, it may be decided to proceed with a more formal and systematic approach; or it may prove that what can be found out by this method satisfies for the moment the need for information in the chief's office. These informal observations and interviews constitute a form of exploratory research.

To illustrate the use of the concept of exploratory or pilot research in practice, we have the following selection from a report in the *Justice Assistance News,* issued by the federal Department of Justice (1981):

> Do youth offenders get a sentencing break as they move from juvenile to adult criminal courts? Lenient sentences for some young adult offenders have raised concerns that the protection of juvenile court records from use in adult proceedings may allow youngsters with extensive criminal records to be treated as first offenders.
>
> Exploratory research in three jurisdictions suggests that young offenders did receive lighter sentences in courts where juvenile records were not used. But the researchers conclude that factors other than the youngster's criminal history exert a significant influence on the sanctioning decision.
>
> The analysis of data from [the] small, pilot effort is necessarily tentative, reflecting the initial exploration of a complex issue (p. 13).

Descriptive research and explanatory research involve more systematic planning than takes place in exploratory work. The words *descriptive* and *explanatory* are employed because the purpose of the former is to describe situations and events, while the aim of the latter is to explain them. The difficulties that arise when an attempt is made to pigeonhole forms of research into neat classificatory schemes can be seen in the fact that exploratory research can involve a considerable degree of description. Also, while description and explanation differ in the degree of generality of the relationships which are expressed, they also include at times the same level and form of work.

Statistical Classification

Another method of classification is in terms of the kind of statistics employed in assembling and analyzing data. Perhaps the most common reference in this domain is to *correlational analysis*. Typically, the goal in distinctions of this nature is to differentiate between attempts to discover relationships and attempts to discover causes. The issues involved in such a dichotomy are taken up more fully in Chapter 9, under the heading "Correlation and Causation." In many regards, the distinction between research aimed at discovering relationships—that is, correlational research—and research aimed at examining and determining causation is like the distinction between descriptive and explanatory research. The differentiation does serve to highlight various kinds of emphases, but because of overlap, such labels are not particularly helpful in truly establishing fundamental categories of research that tell important things about the nature of the work.

Temporal Classification

A third method of classifying and thinking about research rests on time dimensions. In this area, we have, for example, *cross-sectional studies* and *longitudinal studies*. Cross-sectional studies are conducted at a specific time only or over a short period of time. Longitudinal studies, on the other hand, are conducted over an extended period, often years or decades. Some of the classic studies in juvenile delinquency involve efforts to locate people who had gotten into trouble as youngsters and to determine how they were making out as adults (see, for instance, Robins and O'Neal, 1958; Glueck, 1952). In a well-known longitudinal study, Hathaway and Monachesi (1954) administered a personality test to more than 4000 ninth-grade boys and girls in the city of Minneapolis. Their hypothesis was that certain personality characteristics in children tend to lead to later delinquent behavior. Two years after they had given the test and established personality configurations for the individuals tested, the investigators made a rigorous check of the official records to determine who had been adjudicated as delinquent. They found that 22 percent of the boys and 8 percent of the girls whom they had originally tested were listed in the official files as having committed acts of delinquency. It was discovered that some personality items were slightly related to later delinquency but that overall, contrary to their expectations, personality configurations—at least those which they had established—did not provide a sound basis for predicting juvenile delinquency.

The research is regarded as longitudinal in that the same subjects were traced over a long period of time, two years in this particular instance. Generally speaking, people use a special designation for longitudinal research studies because of their uniqueness, but they do not often employ the other component of the classification—cross-sectional studies— because the vast majority of investigations fall into this class.

Classification by Control over Variables

The method of classifying research that has been adopted for this chapter is based upon the degree of control exercised over variables, both variables that are central to the research and those that are potentially intrusive in regard to the findings. This chapter, then, discusses research that is oriented toward the general refinement of knowledge with finer classification based upon the degree of control used in the research.

The objective of this chapter and Chapter 7 is not to provide the precise details necessary to guide a reader through the complex task of conducting a research project from start to finish, although we take up the underlying principles involved in such work. Fundamentally, our aim is to offer for the novice in research methodology a pattern of thought in terms of the spectrum of research approaches, acquainting him or her with the essential features of various forms of research. For those who require, or who will at some time require, detailed treatments aimed at developing particular expertise, we will offer appropriate references to comprehensive treatises on individual subjects. Indeed, it might be noted, as can be seen from the references, that an entire book may be devoted to the presentation of the methods for carrying out any one of the various types of research that we will be discussing.

CONTROL AND THE ADVANCEMENT OF KNOWLEDGE

Research methods vary to a great degree in terms of the amount of control exercised by researchers over the material with which they work. At one end, very little control is exerted. Research workers become absorbed in the study and employ whatever skills they possess to discover what is interesting or appears to be important. Obviously, such discoveries have to be made in terms of some preexisting ideas, some predetermined set of assumptions about relevance. But in such work there is no true attempt to do any more than suggest that a relationship exists between one thing and another on the basis of a hunch, a suspicion, or some commonsense views of possible linkages.

But there are perils in such efforts. A story is told of a tribe which believed that eclipses are caused when an angry demon cuts off the sunshine. This demon was said to be frightened by loud noises. Whenever an eclipse took place, the tribespeople gathered their kitchenware and banged loudly upon it. The eclipse ended, confirming their original belief. An outside observer who merely described what had gone on might well be impelled to accept the validity of the assumed cause of and alleged cure for eclipses. This is one of the dangers of uncontrolled observations.

Anthropologists have often developed field studies based upon such uncontrolled observation to a high degree of sophistication, and what we learn from them can have profound value. One of the most famous contributions was Margaret Mead's conclusion (1928) that among tribes which she studied there was no period of adolescent discomfort. On the basis of this field observation she was able to shatter the prevalent conviction in western societies that the malaise often accompanying the period of adolescence has some inevitable cause, such as an unresolved Oedipus conflict or a biological set of events.

Note, too, Mead's observational finding (1972) that puts into much finer perspective our own ideas about deviance. She discovered in the Arapesh tribal group individuals who were capable of good clear thinking and who could perform extremely well on our intelligence tests. These persons, however, proved to be the "deviant" individuals in Arapesh society, because, as Mead points out, they "had difficulty in dealing with the soft, uncertain outlines of the culture, in which no one did skilled work, no one could interpret accurately a shouted signal." These kinds of uncontrolled field notations immensely enrich scientific work, perhaps more so in many regards than many rigidly monitored experimental investigations.

A further illustration of the valuable insights that can be gathered from observational data is provided in the work of Karen Blixen (1980), a highly perceptive writer who spent almost two decades living among the native peoples of Kenya. Blixen offers the following material on ideas of right and wrong in her own culture—she was from Denmark—and the culture in which she found herself half a century ago. A researcher committed to gathering information by more rigidly controlled methods might speculate on how the hypotheses herein suggested could further be tested. But it would also have to be granted that the ideas that Blixen generates could hardly have been arrived at without some initial unstructured observation in which a keen mind examined what went on and reached some conclusions about matters that were important:

> The ideas of justice in Europe and Africa are not the same and those of the one world are unbearable to the other. To the African there is but one way of counterbalancing the catastrophes of existence; it shall be done by replacement; he does not look for the motive of the action. Whether you lie in wait for your enemy and cut his throat in the dark; or you fell a tree, and a thoughtless stranger passes by and is killed; so far as punishment goes,...it is the same thing. A loss has been brought upon the community and must be made up for, somewhere, by somebody....In those days this went against my ideas of justice (pp. 93–94).

These illustrations stand at one end of the continuum of approaches to research classified on the basis of control; they involve virtually no control. At the other end stand projects such as those in which a laboratory psychologist studies such things as the classical conditioning of eye-blinks to puffs of air applied systematically to subjects strapped in head-harnesses.

Fieldwork in the manner of anthropologists and ethologists is generally called *naturalistic observation*. At the other end of the continuum, where we have the true experiment, the researcher enjoys full control of the investigative context. Between these two extreme points on the spectrum there are many situations where the researcher can exercise some, much, or a good deal of control over the subject matter, though, of course, less than the full control made possible by laboratory conditions.

Important advances of knowledge occur at all points along the continuum, from naturalistic observations through partial control to full control. It is sometimes argued that all approaches to knowledge short of experimentation must remain approximations to truth, since only an experiment can provide critical proof or disproof of a hypothesis. In actuality, not even an experiment proves a hypothesis: the only difference between experimentation and the approaches having less control is that fuller control makes it possible to rule out alternative plausible hypotheses more convincingly. Because of this, the central hypothesis of interest remains in a stronger position at the end of the work. Since it is never possible to rule out completely all conceivable alternative hypotheses (and thus the central hypothesis cannot be proven), the difference between experimentation and the other approaches is purely one of degree.

This is a matter whose import must be thoroughly appreciated by the newcomer to scientific research. Older hands are apt to be keenly aware of its significance; but there appears to us to be a tendency among more newly arrived research workers, who, perhaps because they are somewhat less secure in their places, believe that the most tightly controlled experiment is necessarily the best or even the only type of acceptable work. With experience, it may be that a person comes to appreciate the relative strengths and weaknesses of all approaches to knowledge and gains a certain tolerance and ecumenical appreciation for a variety of kinds of searches for insight and truth. The novelist John Fowles, perhaps one of the keenest minds at work today, has perceptively noted that the more control and precision intrude into experimental work, the more it becomes essential to use somewhat arbitrary and shorthand symbols for the vast variety of the subject matter. "Our fallacy," Fowles writes, "lies in supposing that the limiting nature of scientific method corresponds to the nature of ordinary experience." It is a wise point, worth keeping in mind. The matter has been particularly well expressed by Percy Bridgman, a winner of the Nobel Prize and a physicist with a deep understanding of the strengths and weaknesses of each of the methods of deriving knowledge:

I like to say that there is no scientific method as such, but that the most vital feature of the scientist's procedure has been merely to do his utmost with his mind, *no holds barred.* This means in particular that no special privileges are accorded to authority or to tradition, that personal prejudices and predictions are carefully guarded against, that one makes continued check to assure oneself that one is not making mistakes, and that any line of inquiry will be followed that appears at all promising (Bridgman, 1950, 370).

It is essential to think of acquiring knowledge as a slow, grinding process. Each set of observations, each comparison, each analysis takes us one small step forward. A step may involve rejecting a clearly inadequate central hypothesis or accepting the central hypothesis in the sense of specifying that it has received support under a unique or novel set of conditions.

One must fully appreciate that the gain in internal validity that comes with experimentation may be accompanied by a marked loss in external validity. That is, the results of the experiment may be perfectly accurate for the time and place and persons and situation involved in that experiment but may not have much that is appropriate or relevant for anything even slightly removed from that particular set of circumstances. Take the experimenter we discussed earlier who employs a set of cards in a laboratory to try to determine with some precision when police officers will make an arrest. The experimental situation, with the "scientific" control through the use of the prearranged cards, may provide a relatively "clean" and controlled experimental technique. Such control may aid greatly in eliminating a number of alternative hypotheses which might otherwise explain the officers' choices. But the experiment may well have much less than adequate success in predicting what an officer will actually do under field conditions. Another investigator who has done nothing else but observe police officers at work day after day for months on end might be able to do better in predicting than the card sorter. The latter kind of work may be regarded as "sloppy" in the sense that it involves minimum control and many alternative hypotheses, but at the same time it probably comes nearer than the neater experimental inquiry to providing information relevant to important policy issues.

Thus, to summarize in terms of the categories set out earlier, we can observe that exploratory research necessarily has minimum control and explanatory research must have considerable control. Less control is possible in a longitudinal study, particularly one over many years, than in a study completed in a short period of time.

SYSTEMATIC OBSERVATION

For all of us, observation obviously constitutes an important personal technique for survival on a day-to-day basis. We could not get across streets safely or interact in any satisfactory way with other persons if we did not look around us and reach conclusions about what has happened, what is now occurring, and what is likely to take place. Such observation becomes a research method and is referred to as *systematic* when the process itself and the mode of recording it follow a certain regularity. That regularity is generally the result of abiding by a set of rules in regard to the way observation is to be conducted. The rules impose a certain degree of regularity upon the process of observation and thereby allow replication (that is, they allow others to undertake the same kind of effort according to the same game plan). The rules also permit the application of general principles of scientific inference to the materials that are derived from the observational process.

Systematic observation includes the following procedures: (1) naturalistic observation, in which the observer notes the activities of people in their natural environments; (2) surveys, which include questionnaires and interviews; (3) observation of physical traces and archival records; and (4) sociometric studies of group interactions.

Naturalistic Observation

The Observer's Role   A central issue in naturalistic observation is the degree of openness of the observer's role in the setting—that is, how much the group or person being observed is allowed to become aware of the investigative procedure. Gold (1966) has distinguished four different roles that may be taken by field observers: (1) complete participant, (2) participant as observer, (3) observer as participant, and (4) complete observer.

The complete participant conceals his or her identity and purpose from those being observed and participates as a functioning member in the activities at hand. Whether the subject of study is as innocent as a Saturday night social visit or as illegal as terrorism or drug smuggling, the complete participant occupies a fully operational position in the proceedings. Obviously, there are difficult legal and ethical issues involved in complete participation when the activity is illegal. Also, at times what seems to be no more than a routine research endeavor may turn dangerous as the group becomes restless or is challenged (say, by a rival gang). Even when the naturalistic setting encompasses perfectly legal and moral activities, there is the ethical issue of deception when the true identity of the research worker is concealed, a matter discussed in Chapter 2.

The participant as observer cooperates fully with the group being observed but makes the group aware of his or her role as a researcher. While the ethical issue of deception is handled satisfactorily in this case, the issue of legality of activity may remain. Beyond that (and this is also a problem with the role of complete participant), there is the danger of becoming overidentified with the interests and viewpoints of those being observed and thereby losing an important degree of research objectivity. As many investigators in the field of police work have found, overidentification may lead to their becoming "more cop than researcher."

The observer as participant is one who identifies himself or herself as an observer and interacts with participants only sporadically and formally. There is no attempt at actual participation.

The complete observer is at the opposite extreme from the complete participant. The complete observer is detached and removed, observing the process without becoming part of it.

In this chapter, the complete participant is illustrated by Humphreys's research on homosexual behavior (1970), the participant as observer by Rubinstein's research on the police (1973), and the observer as participant by Reiss's research (1971), also on the police. The complete observer is illustrated by the observational portion of a field experiment by Robertson et al. (1972), in which people were assigned to observe under actual traffic conditions whether or not seat belts were being used. There was no interaction in this work between observers and the occupants of the cars that were observed.

External Validity of Naturalistic Observation   As noted earlier, naturalistic observation has advantages over more controlled methods with regard to external validity. If the observations are unobtrusive, the investigators are able to note and record events and interactions as they actually take place, with or without the observers' presence. But as the observer becomes more obvious to the participants being watched, generalizability to the same context without the presence of the observer becomes more chancy. It then becomes necessary to establish the extent to which the observer influenced the observed results. Sometimes this may be done on the basis of ideas from other kinds of studies which were conducted both with and without identifiable observers (say, in the latter case, by use of a one-way mirror). These kinds of studies give us at least some idea of the influence of an outsider upon other people's behavior. The considerable impact that outsiders may have upon behavior is amusingly illustrated by observations (using first an obtrusive measure, then an unobtrusive one) which indicated that a man is much more likely to wash his hands after urinating in a public restroom if there is another man present than if he believes he is alone and unobserved. In this case, the outside observer induced a certain degree of what can be taken as conformity to informal norms; in some cases, the outsider can induce displays of anger, or passivity, or any of a host of behaviors that otherwise would not have occurred.

Unstructured and Structured Observation   Naturalistic observations vary along a dimension ranging from instances in which the observer exercises great freedom and flexibility in terms of what is observed and noted to instances in which only very specific kinds of actions are recorded and counted. In the unstructured situations, the observer might watch sequences of events and actions in accordance with some very broad guidelines and may alter the focus of observations as the situation unfolds. That is, the emphasis may at first be upon what people are saying, but it may appear more reasonable after a while to pay closer heed to what movements they make when they are talking or what facial expressions they adopt.

Field comments, whether recorded as events and behavior unfold or written down subsequently, are central to later analysis. Many persons trained in observation are able to hold in their minds the kinds of things that concern them, but all agree that the sooner observations are committed to some kind of permanent form, the better the results are likely to be. Obviously, there are certain limitations when the researcher is a complete participant or even a participant as observer. Many field observers will carry a tape recorder in a briefcase and as soon as what they have seen is concluded, will hasten to a convenient isolated spot and dictate into the machine the things that they want to be able to call back when they do their later analyses. It is essential, whatever technique is used, that the material be recorded as quickly as possible after it occurs. The human memory is highly fallible, and the more removed in time the recording is, the less likely it is to be accurate and thorough. Systematic recording usually includes such things as the date and place of the observation; descriptions of participants, contexts, events, behaviors, and interactions; and their ordering. Anecdotes are widely used to describe and report the behaviors and interactions that have been observed. Such anecdotes add life to a report. But the essential integrity must not be sacrificed for a good anecdote: the illustrations should accurately portray the sense of what occurred.

One of the best-known examples of the unstructured observational approach in criminal justice research is found in the study by Laud Humphreys (1970) of homosexual encounters in public park restrooms—or "tearooms," as their habitués call them. Humphreys, who did the research for his doctoral dissertation at Washington University in St. Louis, would enter the tearooms and volunteer to serve as a "watchqueen," a person who stands as a lookout at the window of the facility while other persons there engage in homosexual activity. He did not reveal his research identity and was therefore a complete participant. Humphreys presumably entered upon the study with only general ideas of what might be the most significant aspects of the behavior that he was examining. He obviously wanted to note who did what to whom, in terms of the relative ages of the participants and the roles that they adopted in the homosexual activity. He ultimately concluded that the most significant aspect of the homosexual behavior was the fact that the persons involved did not exchange any words, a finding that is reflected in the subtitle of Humphreys's book: "Impersonal Sex in Public Places." (See the related discussion in Chapter 2.)

Once the generalization was adequately confirmed by a continuing series of observations in which the essential finding proved true, Humphreys was obligated to try to explain this key finding. He used a number of suggestive ideas, including the belief that the participants did not want to identify themselves to each other and did not want to change a routinized transaction into anything more personal.

A highly unstructured observational approach entails major difficulties because it depends so strongly on results that may be affected by irrelevant biases of the observer. That is, the observer may enter the field with a set of ideas of what ought to occur or a fixed opinion of what, from all that takes place, is most important to record. Such kinds of biases might blind an observer to contradictory materials or to more important elements of the situation. And, of course, anecdotal material cannot be tested statistically, unless certain aspects of it are converted to quantifiable form by a counting process.

Structuring the observations reduces some of these difficulties by allowing researchers to focus on restricted aspects of the behavior under review. Observers then take care to be certain to note the presence, absence, or degree of specified behaviors or behavioral interactions rather than allowing themselves total freedom to determine what to observe. Use of the structured approach requires adequate knowledge of the phenomena to be studied, so that appropriate checklists and other recording documents can be set up in advance. For certain tastes in research, the gain in reliability and the reduction of the influence of irrelevant personal biases by the use of structured observation is had at the expense of the "richness" that is associated at times with less restricted observations and anecdotal reporting. Some researchers try to combine the best of these worlds by using unstructured observation when they first enter the field and thereafter determining from their initial loose observations what it is that should be put under more systematic scrutiny in later work. Then they focus on matters that they have come to believe are particularly important.

Reliability in research refers to the consistency of repeated data from a single observer as well as agreement among observers. The level of reliability in observational work can be raised by the proper training of observers, by having observers compare their results under pilot or exploratory conditions, and by having more than one observer for each recording session. It is preferable, of course, that pilot work not contaminate the research that constitutes the study. In Humphreys's research, for instance, it would seem best to have done any preliminary work at a site different from the one later used, on the assumption that as unobtrusive as the role of "watchqueen" may have been, it still could have influenced the kinds of persons who continued to come to the park. Had that population been thinned out by pilot work, then the sample being observed would have been rendered unnecessarily more selective.

Different degrees of structuring in naturalistic observation may be most directly illustrated by contrasting the approach of Rubinstein with that of Reiss to the study of everyday police work. Despite the considerable difference in approaches, both contributed immeasurably to our understanding of police performance.

Jonathan Rubinstein (1973) entered training as a recruit in the Philadelphia police department and subsequently was assigned to a squad car as an active officer. His identity as a researcher was known to the other officers and he was, therefore, a participant as observer. He observed carefully his own behavior and that of other officers and drew upon his sharp intelligence to arrive at a number of important conclusions about the nature of police work. There are, for instance, findings about the effect of the hierarchy of values held by commanding officers on the work of officers making arrests. (Later in the chapter we will illustrate an experimental design which sought to check by more stringent means possible discrepancies between a chief's views and officers' views).

> There is absolutely no doubt in the mind of the district patrolman about how seriously vice arrests, particularly for gambling, are regarded by his superiors. He may not know what other value they have, since the more experience he acquires in making vice arrests, the clearer it becomes to him that gambling is not deterred by them; he does understand that the department wants a lot of them (p. 52).

Rubinstein relates how the emphasis on vice arrests influences a wide range of other departmental procedures, including some bending of the law in order to "justify" searches without warrants.

There also is admiration for the police (mixed at some points with condemnation of certain aspects of their behavior) in Rubinstein's observational report:

> A policeman rarely fails to make an effort to save a victim from death when he is presented with an opportunity to do so. The principal way a patrolman can directly prevent a murder is by getting a grievously wounded person to medical treatment.as quickly as possible. Regardless of how he feels about a person, the patrolman does not hesitate to get himself covered with another person's blood and gore or to assume the risks involved in driving quickly through the crowded streets of the city. The patrolman does not receive accolades from anyone for doing these things (although his failure to do them might be noted and censured); it is part of his job (p. 342).

When you are finished with Rubinstein's study, you know a good deal more about the elements of police work than might have been gained from a more rigidly monitored experimental effort and certainly more than from one conducted under aseptic laboratory conditions. On the other hand, you are not certain how the researcher's own emotional beliefs and commitments influenced what he saw and what he reports, which topics he chose to address and which he did not consider.

The study of the police by Reiss (1970, 1971) shows a good deal more structuring, though it is still naturalistic observation. He investigated the use of excessive force by police officers in the cities of Boston, Chicago, and Washington. The goal of the observation was to determine the validity of arguments by citizens, especially blacks, about brutal behavior on the part of the police. A total of 36 observers were used. They worked seven days a week during a seven-week period one summer. Among their other tasks, the observers sat in patrol cars, watched bookings at police stations, and noted the lockup procedures that occurred in high-crime areas in the cities where the research work was carried on.

Clearly, this was not nonreactive observation, but certain features of the study seemed to minimize the presence of the observers. First, full cooperation had been obtained from the top police administrators, who were guaranteed that their cities would not be identified individually in the final study. The officers in the police forces had been told that the primary interest of the observers was in the way citizens react to the police. In addition, the observers generally were sympathetic to the police and able to develop relationships of trust with them, a not uncommon experience when outsiders come to participate deeply in the work of other people and begin to see that work as the people performing it do. When this occurs, as noted above, it becomes particularly important to guard against allowing such empathy to compromise the integrity of the observational process.

The observers participating in Reiss's study—they were primarily students in law schools or criminal justice or criminology majors—noted in particular that an officer involved in a dispute seemed to forget entirely that the observer was present. That the presence of observers might not have had much importance in conditioning the behavior of the officers is suggested by the fact that at times the officers used severe, brutal, and unnecessary force against citizens. Of course, they might have done this more often if unobserved, but the suspicion was that this was not so—that they in time came to view the observers as part of the regular job scenery.

The following are examples of the kinds of observations that were made during the course of Reiss's study (1970):

> On a Friday in the middle of July, the observer arrived for the 4 to 12 midnight watch. The beat car that had been randomly chosen carried two white patrolmen—one with 14 years of experience in the precinct, the other with three.
>
> The watch began rather routinely as the policemen cruised the district. Their first radio dispatch came about 5:30 p.m. They were told to investigate two drunks in a cemetery. On arriving they found two white men "sleeping one off." Without questioning the men, the older policeman began to search one of the men, ripping his shirt and hitting him in the groin with a nightstick. The younger policeman, as he searched the second, ripped away the seat of his trousers, exposing his buttocks. The policemen then prodded the men toward the cemetery fence and forced them to climb it, laughing at the plight of the drunk with the exposed buttocks (p. 58).
>
> Cases where the offender resists an arrest provide perhaps the most difficulty in judging the legitimacy of the force applied. An encounter that began as a dispatch to a disturbance at a private residence was one case about which there could be honest difference in judgment. On arrival, the policemen—one white, the other black—met a white woman who claimed that her husband, who was in the backyard and drunk, had beaten her. She asked the policemen to "take him in." The observer reported that the police found the man in the house. When they attempted to take him, he resisted by placing his hands between the door jamb. Both policemen then grabbed him. The black policeman said, "We're going to have trouble, so let's finish it right here." He grabbed the offender and

knocked him down. Both policemen then wrestled with the man, handcuffed him and took him to the station. As they did so, one of the policemen remarked, "These sons of bitches want to fight, so you have to break them quick" (p. 60).

The summary conclusions of this inquiry provide a sense of the kinds of information that can be secured by this type of structured approach (in contrast to that of Rubinstein). Undue force (as defined by the observers) was recorded in 37 of the 3826 encounters observed between police officers and citizens. The rate of undue use of force was found to be 5.9 per 1000 in encounters between the police officers and white citizens and 2.8 per 1000 in encounters between the police and black citizens. While the evidence pointed to the fact that undue force was used more often against whites than against blacks, it also showed that the most likely victim of police brutality was a lower-class male of either race. "Open defiance" on the part of the person with whom the officer was dealing was the condition most likely to precipitate an arrest by the officer. In this context, *defiance* referred to the perception of the officer about the manner in which the person was behaving, not to any objective evaluation by an outsider. In almost half the cases in which undue force was deemed to have been employed, the officers indicated that they believed that the persons involved had defied their authority or had resisted an arrest procedure.

We also find in Reiss's report (1971) conclusions like the following. During the course of the study period there were "5,360 mobilizations of police, of which 28 percent failed to produce any transactions with citizens. Eighty-one percent originated with citizens telephoning the police for service, 14 percent with police patrol, 5 percent with citizen's mobilizing the police in a field setting." The modal tour of duty of a police officer was found to result in no arrests, and Reiss, commenting on the numerical tabulation of his inventory of how time is spent by the police, notes that "the police overload with noncriminal matters develops out of the organization's success in making it relatively easy for citizens to penetrate its boundaries with demands for services." It is interesting that on the basis of his fieldwork with the police, Reiss (1971) is moved to make policy recommendations as well as to present the numerical findings of his counts of police operations. On relationships between the police and civilians, for instance, he remarks:

> Training in human relations, in my judgment, seems at best misguided. It is not uncommon in such programs to try to train the police to accept incivility with indifference. I submit that in a civil society no one should be trained or paid to accept incivility; to accept invectives that begin with "mother" or animal names. That is not to say that the police cannot be disciplined to deal in a civil fashion with citizens who behave with incivility (pp. 184, 185).

Naturalistic Observation: Some Problems and Limitations   Despite its usefulness in the drawing of conclusions about the everyday world and even suggesting policy implications, it is clear that naturalistic observation is not a fine-tuned approach for discriminating among alternative hypotheses. But, as we have indicated before, the accumulation of knowledge and the concomitant focusing on more delimiting hypotheses is a gradual process. Valuable information pointing toward that end can be gained by good observational procedures. And, as we have repeatedly emphasized, research rarely entails a critical study or a perfect experiment but rather is made up of a process of chipping away at the rock of ignorance. It is often the case that the next step after naturalistic observation is a process of zeroing in with more precision on a hypothesis through recourse to procedures that involve more control. That phase may be marked by use of an experimental or a quasi-experimental design.

We might, for example, pursue the hypothesis that the police are more likely to use undue force with lower-class and "defiant" people by setting up experimental and control conditions. We could, for instance, use actors in scenarios where the police do not realize they are dealing with actors, though there obviously is considerable personal risk in this type of approach. The actors might attempt to behave in the same manner with each officer they encounter, in order to determine how different officers respond to similar stimuli. How the actor would behave could have been determined by the information gathered during the earlier observation. Or the actors might try a repertoire of different behaviors to attempt to learn at what point most officers define what is happening as unacceptable enough that they feel obliged to take forcible action against it.

While naturalistic observation at first glance appears to involve routine skills that are possessed by every human being, an unplanned casual approach can prove to be extremely inefficient. It is useful to determine the purposes of the study as carefully as possible before collecting data and to plan what is to be observed in at least a general way. Knowledge of the subject matter will prove to be extremely valuable for this planning exercise. Planning should include specifications of what is being sought. Actions most often are rapid and complex, and it is utterly impossible to record more than a small portion of them (except on film or tape—but then the film must be viewed in order to isolate important components). The categories should be defined clearly enough so that observers can be trained to discriminate among them adequately. In this regard, it would undoubtedly prove instructive if the reader and some friends or classmates were to observe a staged interaction during a class session and to attempt to record what happened in terms of a prearranged plan for gathering data. The errors and differences in the results among you would provide some indication of the complexity of skilled observation.

Recording may vary from notes in longhand or shorthand to systematic checking of predetermined categories that have been set up as lists upon which the observer need only check the appropriate column or box when the event occurs. If there is a question about whether recording on the scene or later recording will be the most suitable procedure, it is a good idea to pretest these alternatives before starting the actual gathering of research information. Reiss (1971, p. 15) reached the following conclusion in regard to recording during the study that he conducted:

> Despite some experience and advice that one should not record in the presence of police, in our police-observation studies pretesting disclosed that observers could keep an incident log during the period of observation.... It was possible to do so because not uncommonly officers perform similar tasks in the field.

Another criminal justice researcher, attempting to obtain the views of executives of multinational corporations in regard to criminal laws which bear upon their businesses, found that for the most part he could record behavior and responses during the interview without unduly alarming respondents. But he learned that it was essential not to tip his hand—not to reveal what he regarded as significant—to the person with whom the work was being conducted. Sometimes he would wait half a minute or more and put down an earlier remark as if it were the one that had just been uttered. Keeping things in mind as the observation and conversation proceeds is, however, a tiring task, and it requires some earlier training and much practice before it can be done adeptly. It can prove particularly useful to have two persons conduct interviews so that one can maintain the flow of conversation while the other writes.

Continuous observation is seldom possible, and might not be the most fruitful use of the researcher's time, so part of the planning ought to include the selection of adequate time samples. Time samples should be selected in such a manner that there is no bias which will produce distortion in generalizing from the samples to the events. It would not ordinarily do, for instance, to observe police interactions exclusively between noon and four o'clock in the afternoon on Tuesdays and Wednesdays, since the periods of greatest tension and most frenzied activity are on weekend evenings.

Reiss (1971) presents the following example of the types of problems that may be encountered in selecting proper time samples in observational studies:

> In one of our observation studies we were interested in transactions between police and citizens. No single frame of such transactions existed in the police jurisdictions selected for study. Transactions were recorded separately for different divisions of the police department, and no official record was kept for many of them. At the outset we decided to limit our search for a satisfactory frame to patrol divisions where the largest volume of transactions with the public occurred. Although the police department recorded all calls for police service from citizens, it would have been impractical to sample them at the time received and to dispatch an observer to be present when the transaction took place. Moreover, that sampling frame would have excluded all transactions the police developed on their initiative. The foot and car beats in precincts were chosen as the sampling frame (pp. 9–10).

More detailed information on systematic approaches to naturalistic observation may be found in Sackett (1978a; 1978b), Bickman and Henchy (1972), and McCall and Simmons (1969).

Surveys: Questionnaires and Interviews

Naturalistic observation is oriented toward events and behaviors as they occur. Surveys, on the other hand, are observational approaches which aim at determining people's attitudes, values, perceptions, feelings, beliefs, future expectations, and past experiences—indeed, any personal construct that can be inferred from answers to questions. If the questions are in printed form and the subject indicates his or her answers by writing or by marks, the survey is said to be a *questionnaire*. If the questions are presented orally to the subject and the answers are recorded by the person asking the questions, the survey is called an *interview*.

The issue that arises immediately is how seriously the answers to questionnaires or interviews can be taken in terms of revealing actual attitudes and values or the other kinds of information requested. Just because persons state, in answer to a question, that they have no prejudice against members of minority groups does not necessarily mean that they indeed are unprejudiced. Not only are there the usual "center of attention" effects, but subjects may be unaware of their feelings or unable to remember accurately a past occurrence. Moreover, many people find it difficult to express personal values or feelings in the verbal form required as answers to questions.

Despite these limitations, surveys are widely used for research work. This is in part because some of their shortcomings can be overcome through the mode of administration and in part because they possess many advantages that more than compensate for the liabilities.

A questionnaire was used by Toch, Grant, and Galvin (1975), for instance, to evaluate the street behavior of officers in the Oakland, California, police department. The items consisted of descriptions of common street situations which were taken from actual experiences. The response to each item was one of several alternative solutions. Two samples follow (pp. 370–372):

Incident 1
Time: 2100 [9 P.M.]
Location: 23rd Avenue & E. 24th Street
Subject: MN [male Negro] 30
Appearance and Activity: Officer approaches scene and hears sound of argument. Officer knocks. Argument stops. Door opened by subject wearing T-shirt. Officer asks if police needed. Subject says, "No, pig!" and slams door in officer's face.

Do you think you should take further action?

If *yes*, do you think you'd make an arrest?

If you think you'd take action *other than arrest*, what would you be most likely to do?

Incident 5
Time: 0100 [1 A.M.]
Location: 85th E. 14th, IFO 85 Club
Subject: 4 Vehicles double parked, all attended. About 20 MN&FN's in front of club.
Appearance and Activity: Officer drives by slowly and is obviously seen by drivers of double-parked cars. Officer continues on and notes in rear view mirror that vehicles are not being moved.

Do you think you would take further action?

If *yes,* do you think you would make an arrest or issue a citation?

If you think you'd take action *other than arrest,* what would you most be likely to do?

One of the goals of the full questionnaire, which included a total of 12 incidents, was to determine the degree of conformity between the responses of the officers and the answers supplied by the chief of police. To illustrate the kinds of results that are obtainable by this technique, we can note that for incident 1 the chief stated that the situation required no further action. But only 45 percent of the officers, less than half, agreed. Almost one-fourth of the officers (24 percent) said that they would attempt to gain entry to the premises.

On the other hand, almost all officers (93 percent) agreed with the chief that some action was required in incident 5. Moreover, 70 percent responded in the same manner as the chief, replying that they would ticket the car, though some said that they would give a ticket only if a warning was not heeded.

Table 3 compares questionnaires and interviews in terms of their respective advantages and disadvantages in regard to matters such as cost, skill required for administration, and some ingredients of the techniques themselves.

Interviews and questionnaires may be fully structured so that both the questions and the range of possible answers are determined beforehand. A most elementary form of question would be this:

1 Have you ever been arrested? Yes_____ No_____.

But even so simple a question can be treacherous, which is one of the compelling reasons why it is essential that questionnaires always be pretested to make certain that the questions asked truly get at the kinds of information you want to obtain. For instance, respondent A may reply that he has never been arrested, while respondent B says that she has been arrested. Both may have been detained temporarily by the police on suspicion of being involved in gang activity, and then released. But respondent A did not consider this an arrest, since he knew he was innocent of any involvement and fully expected to be set free. Respondent B, on the other hand, may have interpreted the question as asking only if she had ever been held against her will by a law enforcement officer because of activity

TABLE 3
COMPARISON OF QUESTIONNAIRES AND INTERVIEWS

Questionnaires		Interviews	
Advantages	Disadvantages	Advantages	Disadvantages
Relatively inexpensive	Fixed wording does not allow correction of possible misinterpretation or lack of understanding.	Interviewer may amplify where necessary and correct misunderstandings.	Tends to be expensive and time-consuming.
No skill required in administering—may even be mailed or handed out with printed instructions.			Considerable skill necessary in administering.
Greater feeling of anonymity on part of respondent.	In mailed surveys, typical response rates are frequently in the range 10–20%, and hardly ever above 50%	May be used whenever language is understood; no reading required.	
Respondent may feel less pressured for immediate response.	Literacy problems make even simple questionnaires inappropriate for many people; complicated questionnaires may be understandable only to the well-educated.	High rates of cooperation are possible to obtain. Further probing possible for sensitive or complex topics.	

believed to be against the law. To be certain that we have both respondents answering the question in the terms that we want, we will have to stipulate clearly what definitions we are operating with.

Besides fully structured inquiries, both interviews and questionnaires may also use some predetermined questions that are open-ended in terms of the responses that may be elicited. Here is an example:

> **2** What is your general feeling about the use of deadly force by the police in this city?

Such a question is likely to provide a richer context of responses, because the persons being queried are not constrained either by a simple yes-no choice or a set of categories to which they must adjust their beliefs. At the same time, the answers to such an open-ended question are likely to cover a wide range of emotional and factual territory, and any effort to make numerical sense out of them could be a perplexing enterprise. Nonetheless, such answers could convey more important overtones and information than would be acquired from set responses. What strategy will be used by the researcher depends in considerable measure on what is desired.

Finally, as may be seen in the examples we set out earlier from the work of Toch and his colleagues, surveys may be made up of predetermined questions with a mixture of fixed-alternative and open-ended patterns of response.

Interviews (though not questionnaires) also may be less structured in that neither the questions nor the alternative possible answers are fully predetermined. Typically, many questions are decided upon before the interview; in some cases the categories of answers have been established as well. At the same time, the interviewer can be free to move to other kinds of questions as the interaction develops and interesting and productive lines of response are opened up. Reiss (1971) notes that interviews of this sort can prove extremely useful for augmenting naturalistic observations.

Ethics becomes a concern with interviews and questionnaires when there is a potential invasion of privacy. Surveys, for example, have been known to include questions such as: "Have you had a homosexual encounter?" or "Have you ever been unfaithful to your spouse?" Anonymity is the minimum requirement with this type of intrusive questioning; but even then, there is the lingering uncertainty about the lasting effects upon the person who gives positive responses to such questions. Clearly the consequences are likely to be greater in the case of an interview than in the case of the more impersonal questionnaire.

Concerns also arise in surveys that ask youngsters to report their violations of the law. These surveys are often used to supplement official counts of delinquency, which clearly represent but a small portion of the actual number of delinquent acts. Since many (probably most) episodes of juvenile delinquency remain unobserved or unreported, it is only through a self-reporting approach by means of an interview or a questionnaire that a research worker can obtain an indication of the actual extent of juvenile crime. A good deal has been written on this subject by Gold (1966, 1970), Erikson (1972), and a number of other scholars. This issue is closely related to the distinction between crime reported in the UCR and that found in both self-reports and victimization surveys, as discussed in Chapter 5.

Is it ethical to ask young persons to reveal earlier illegal acts? It would seem that there is no problem if there is vigorous anonymity and the questioning is sufficiently general. The detachment associated with a questionnaire would appear to make it preferable to an interview. But too-specific questions can awaken memories that produce anxiety in the context of a potentially different and more mature value system that may now characterize the person who is questioned. In reporting the data, virtually all criminal justice researchers use aggregate means by which the rates for groups of persons are presented so that individual responses remain hidden in the overall data.

Further details about questionnaires and interviews as methods that can be employed to good purpose by persons working in the field of criminal justice research are presented in Selltiz, Wrightsman, and Cook (1976).

Physical Traces and Archival Records

Physical and archival records are also targets of the observational method. These were discussed in Chapter 5 in the context of unobtrusive measures. Just as with the other methods of systematic observation, searches for physical traces and of archival records are guided by plans based on knowledge. You should have some idea what it is that you are looking for; otherwise you are likely to flounder about aimlessly. It is one thing to read newspapers looking for some ideas (and it may be a reasonable first step), but it is a move forward to have a knowledge-based plan. Thus, for example, you might wish to determine the biases expressed in the newspapers of a large city toward the "deadly force" policy of the local police department. One method would be to study the stories and editorials dealing with individual cases and the subject in general over a period of time in one or several of the large-circulation dailies. Or it might be that the aim is to determine how different papers handle the same story. In that case, suburban papers, papers directed to the residents of the minority communities, and metropolitan dailies could be examined for the treatment of particular stories on the issue of concern. And, rather than searching through all issues of the newspapers, it might be more fruitful to select issues on the basis of events which seem likely to produce stories reflecting different opinions and biases.

Most writing about the uses of physical traces and archival records in research merely lists and describes examples of such work (as, for instance, in Webb, et al., 1981). But some beginning analysis of the technique may be found in Smith (1981).

Sociometry

Sociometry is concerned with the social interaction among members of a group, including their social choices and the patterns of communication. This method started with the work of Jacob Moreno in the early 1930s. Moreno used what he called *sociograms* to show the preference and dominance relationships in groups.

For example, choices in a group of four persons (A, B, C, and D) may be shown sociometrically as in Figure 2. Figure 2 is interpreted in this fashion: it indicates that A and B both have said that their favorite person is the other; A has chosen B, and B has chosen A. (Sometimes the choice of a "favorite" is put in specific terms, such as "the person I would most like to sit next to in class" or "the person I would most like to share squad-car duty with in a dangerous police situation" or "the person I most respect.") Person B was

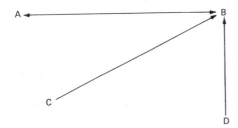

FIGURE 2
Choices in a group of four as shown
sociometrically.

also selected by C and D. No one selected either C or D, however. The diagram may be interpreted as demonstrating the considerable support within this group for person B; it also seems reasonable to assume that A would be B's lieutenant, since the unanimously selected leader has designated A as his or her first choice.

To increase the likelihood of sincere responses to the question that is put to the respondents in a sociometric study, whenever feasible the subjects are told that the investigator will comply with their requests as far as possible. And, of course, if this promise is made by the researcher, all efforts should be made to see that it is honored. Sociometric analyses may also be based on direct observation of who sits next to whom, who eats lunch with whom, who votes the same way as whom, and so forth.

The resulting data can be used to form constructs regarding the relative positions of individuals in a group, types of subgroups that exist, and the relative desirability of individuals as well as the cohesiveness of the group. Moreno (1934) used the technique to measure attraction by establishing a ratio of number of choices—that is, the number of times a person was selected—to number of choices plus number of rejections entered against that person.

Jennings (1934) used sociometric techniques to study the stated preferences for others among girls living in a state training school for delinquents. The girls were asked who they would want to live with in the dormitories, who they would prefer to work with, and which others they would not want as companions. On the basis of the data that were gathered by this technique, the residents were classified as *overchosen, average-chosen,* or *underchosen.* It was found that the category of choice that characterized the girls was closely related to their leadership roles in the school community. Examination of the reasons that were given for the sociometric choices and rejections provided explanatory constructs about the kinds of characteristics that eventuate in positions of leadership in this kind of situation. Such leadership, it was found, was not based on special personality traits or combinations of such traits; rather, it was based on the contribution made interpersonally in a given group.

EXPERIMENTATION

The "True" Experiment

The true experiment and naturalistic observation are at opposite ends of the continuum that goes from maximum to minimum control. Control takes the form of changing or manipulating certain features of the environment as well as maintaining the other relevant features of that environment within known and acceptable bounds. We all are familiar with the temperature-regulated and soundproof room, the sterilized equipment, and the face masks and rubber gloves of the medical scientist. These items are meant to control extraneous factors, such as incidental noises or airborne bacteria, that could have undesired effects on the results of the work.

The medical scientist doing the true experiment also controls which subjects receive what treatment and at what time they receive it. The first control is over extraneous factors; the second is over the independent variable. But in its broadest sense, control refers to any procedure to eliminate the threat to valid conclusions that comes from alternative plausible hypotheses. While controlling aspects of the environment, the experimenter records outcome measures that are of interest.

The contextual features that are manipulated or varied by the experimenter are called *independent variables* or *treatments*. The outcome measures are called *dependent variables* or *outcomes*.

All experiments include, as a minimum, an independent variable, a dependent variable, controlled variables, and units of assignment, such as people, groups, departments, and neighborhoods. The true experiment has two additional features: (1) There is full control or almost full control of variables known at the time to be sources of alternative plausible hypotheses. (2) The assignment of units for the purposes of assessing treatment effects is done on a random basis. Both full control and randomization are highly desirable in the effort to rule out most alternative possible explanations.

It must be stressed, however, that no procedure, including randomization, can assure the experimenter that the obtained differences in the experiment were not brought about by some initial difference between the groups (or by some difference developed otherwise than by the treatment). Nevertheless, randomization, while less than perfect, is clearly the best way to proceed in the attempt to equalize groups.

Because of the amount of control necessary in a true experiment, it is usually best conducted in a laboratory. This point might indeed be put more forcefully (though more abstrusely) by noting that the amount of control necessary over variables in an experiment defines a laboratory.

Full—or almost full—control is not possible in many research designs that have other features of an experiment. This is true in most field situations. Similarly, in some contexts, randomization is not possible. It may be necessary, for example, to use nonequivalent groups that differ in ways other than merely manner of treatment in the experiment. Where randomization is not used we have what is called a *quasi experiment*.

In many experiments, both independent and dependent variables are in numerical form, but it is important to note that this is not always the case. The independent variable could be the type of drug administered to subjects, where the number of values of the independent variable (or number of levels of treatment) is identical to the number of drugs. The array of possible experimental designs is vast indeed—and entire books have been devoted to the different types and their statistical analyses. See, for example, Kirk (1969) and Myers (1972). We shall present only a few of these forms to illustrate certain basic common features.

An elementary design is one in which units are randomly assigned to an experimental or to a control group, then the experimental treatment is introduced, and finally both groups are evaluated or measured on the dependent variable. There are no measurements before the treatment, which is applied only to the experimental group.

This design is often diagrammed in the following fashion:

Experimental group:	R	T	O_2^E
Control group:	R		O_2^C

where R indicates random assignment of units, T stands for the application of treatment, and O_2^E indicates an outcome measure for the experimental group and O_2^C an outcome measure for the control group.

If outcomes O_2^E and O_2^C differ, we can conclude that the treatment was effective in producing a result. Random assignment of subjects to experimental and control groups was expected to guard against relevant differences between the groups prior to the experiment.

We can use our earlier illustration of a halfway house for drug addicts to demonstrate briefly how this form of experiment operates. We might have 100 persons randomly assigned to the experimental group and 100 placed in the control group. The experimental group lives in the halfway house. The outcome measure is return to drugs after an 18-month period. The O_2^E results show that routine urinalysis resulted in the detection of 23 persons from the halfway house group under the influence of heroin or other addictive drugs. The O_2^C measure indicates that 56 persons in the control group had returned to drugs, as detected by the same kind of urinalysis procedures. We are inclined to conclude that the halfway house has produced the kinds of results which were claimed would come about when it was established.

A slightly more complex design occurs when both groups are evaluated or measured before as well as following the experimental treatment. Diagramming this process produces the following schema:

Experimental group:	R	O_1^E	T	O_2^E
Control group:	R	O_1^C		O_2^C

where O_1^E and O_1^C represent initial measures for the experimental and control groups respectively. Frequently, change scores are used in the analysis of the results of this design, so that the difference between O_2^E and O_1^E is compared with the difference between O_2^C and O_1^C. As before, units are randomly assigned, but the R preceding O_1^E and O_1^C does not mean that the randomization must occur before these initial measures are taken. In fact, one can use this design to select people for subsequent random assignment on the basis of the value of the initial measurement. For example, a technique for improving police officers' target shooting may be potentially useful only with officers who initially are below a certain ability level in that skill. The first measurement allows the investigator to choose these officers for the subsequent experiment.

"Before" measures also allow the investigator to determine how well the randomization process equated the groups. We may find, purely by chance, that members of the control group had prior scores averaging 84 while those in the experimental group had a 93 average. On the basis of this information, we can better interpret the results as changes from the earlier to the later position rather than, as in the previous design, having to use only outcomes of two supposedly equivalent groups of persons. As we have noted earlier, random assignment depends on the working of probability for equating groups, and it can produce undesirable results in a given case, particularly where the sample sizes are small.

Comparing changes for the two groups in the "before-after" measurement sequence—that is, comparing $(O_2^E - O_1^E)$ with $(O_2^C - O_1^C)$—provides an evaluation of the effects of the treatment even where the randomization did not make the groups equivalent. But there remains the danger in this design, as opposed to the previous one, the "after only" design, that there will be a pretesting effect. That is, the first measurement may have an effect on the second one. In the example above, for instance, the effort to secure ratings based on a pretest condition might have afforded some of the persons enough practice in target shooting to contaminate the measure of instruction. But if this effect is direct—that is, if it bears equally on all persons—it can be ruled out as an alternative plausible hypothesis, because it would affect the control group as well as the experimental group.

More complex designs—indeed, vastly more complex designs (see, e.g., Winer, 1971)—are used to accomplish more esoteric types of control. We will illustrate such increased complexity by an experimental design that combines the features of the "before-after" design with the "after only" design aimed at attaining the advantages of the former while controlling for any pretesting effects (reactive effect of measurement). The design is known as the *Solomon four-group design* and may be diagrammed as follows:

Experimental group I:	R	$O_1^{E_I}$	T	$O_2^{E_I}$
Control group I:	R	$O_1^{C_I}$		$O_2^{C_I}$
Experimental group II:	R		T	$O_2^{E_{II}}$
Control group II:	R			$O_2^{C_{II}}$

Both experimental group I and experimental group II receive the same experimental treatments, but only group I is evaluated before treatment (giving O_1^{EI}). Of the two control groups, control group I is evaluated initially—at the same time as experimental group II—producing the measurement O_1^{CI}. Control group II is not evaluated initially. All four groups are measured after treatments are administered to experimental groups I and II, giving the measurements O_2^{EI}, O_2^{CI}, O_2^{EII}, and O_2^{CII}.

The effect of the treatment is shown in four comparisons:

$$(O_2^{EI} - O_1^{EI})$$

$$(O_2^{EI} - O_2^{CI})$$

$$(O_2^{EII} - O_2^{CII})$$

and $$(O_2^{EII} - O_1^{CI})$$

Comparing $(O_2^{CII} - O_1^{CI})$ with $(O_2^{CI} - O_1^{CI})$ gives us any effects of pretesting, since control group II was not evaluated initially but control group I was. If $(O_2^{CII} - O_1^{CI})$ and $(O_2^{CI} - O_1^{CI})$ are of the same magnitude, there is no basis for inferring a pretesting effect.

Another gain from this design is the possibility of comparing treatment effect from a "before-after" design, on the one hand, with that from an "after only" design, on the other. The former treatment effect is the difference between $(O_2^{EI} - O_1^{EI})$ and $(O_2^{CI} - O_1^{CI})$, and the latter is the simple difference between O_2^{EII} and O_2^{CII}.

While this approach is illustrative of the increasing complexity possible in experimental design, with corresponding increases in information-giving potential, the cost of using twice as many groups as the two preceding designs makes it economical principally when there are strong indications of a pretesting effect that the investigator desires to measure.

The Nonlaboratory Experiment

The true experiment, as we noted above, requires full or a rather substantial degree of control over the variables as well as random assignment of the experimental units. In many field situations it is possible to exert enough control over independent and extraneous variables to satisfy the broad criteria that define an experiment, but this usually occurs at a considerably lower level than is possible in a laboratory. In such situations, moreover, it typically is not possible to assign units randomly to conditions and to keep the assignment satisfactorily uncontaminated by extraneous matters.

For obvious reasons, experiments of this sort, involving less control, are frequently referred to as *field experiments*. They are also sometimes called *quasi experiments*, though this particular expression has taken on a somewhat different, though closely related, meaning in recent years. In the latest usage, quasi experiments are simply experiments that do not involve random assignments of units for comparisons of change. On the basis of this newer definition, it is possible to be in a situation where there is full control of independent and relevant variables in a laboratory but to have a quasi experiment rather than a true experiment because of nonrandom assignment of units.

It is important to reemphasize that when less than full experimentation is used, the loss in accuracy for applied decision making may be more apparent than real. It is often the case that the introduction of full laboratory control so distorts the nature and relationships of variables of interest that the error in generalizing from laboratory to real life far exceeds the error inherent in the lessened control of field experimentation.

An example of a field experiment involving control groups and randomization is provided in research by Robertson et al. (1974), who examined the effectiveness of television messages in encouraging the use of seat belts in automobiles. Persons concerned with traffic safety decided on the basis of statistical analyses of accidents that injury and death are considerably less when people wear seat belts than when they do not. The aim was to determine how best to get them to take these self-protective steps. One method would be to manufacture cars which will not move unless the seat belt is fastened; but this would run into great resistance from consumers in a society of individualists such as the United States. A law that required car manufacturers to interconnect circuits so that the starter could be activated only if front seat belts were connected lasted on the books only one year. Besides, in a nation of tinkerers it is likely that as soon as a "foolproof" device was invented, someone would find a way to circumvent it—that is, to get a car going without fastening the operator's and riders' seat belts. Another approach, which has been adopted by some nations, would be to make it a criminal offense, entailing a fine or loss of license, if a driver is apprehended without his or her seat belt fastened.

The aim for Robertson and his coworkers was to determine if some less stringent measure might accomplish the desired goal. It was known from research that though lap belts have been standard equipment for the front seats of American-made cars since 1964 and though a 1968 federal law required both lap and torso belts in front seats and lap belts in rear seats of all automobiles manufactured for sale in the United States, between 80 and 90 percent of all automobile drivers did not use seat belts.

The goal of the research by Robertson and his colleagues was to determine whether television and radio campaigns which alert and, in many cases, attempt to frighten nonusers into conformity were having any effect.

The experimental analysis was well-designed and well-executed. First, six television messages were produced in collaboration with an advertising agency. The content of each was based on an earlier analysis of the factors influencing the use and nonuse of seat belts. The following describes one of the messages (Robertson et al., 1974):

A father is shown lifting his teenaged son from a wheel chair into a car. As they ride along, safety belts obviously fastened, the father's thoughts are voiced off-camera intermixed with the son's on-camera expressions of excitement at going to a football game. The father expresses guilt for not having encouraged his son to use safety belts before the crash in which he was injured. The analogy to the protections that the son wore when he played football is drawn (p. 1073).

The messages were shown at times and in connection with television programs that would draw the audience deemed most appropriate. The message quoted above, for example, was shown during football games. To establish a control and an experimental group, a community was chosen that had a dual cable television system that had been designed to carry out marketing studies. There were 6400 households on cable E, on which the messages were released, and 7400 on cable C, which served as the control. No messages were transmitted on cable C. The two cables were distributed in haphazard fashion throughout the community; there were no differences between the two sets of households in terms of demographic characteristics.

The messages were shown for nine consecutive months. For one month before the television campaign and until the end of it, automobiles were observed in traffic to determine whether drivers were using safety belts. Observation sites were chosen in order to maximize the anticipated likelihood of observing automobiles from homes connected to one of the cables. Consistency and regularity were maintained for the conditions of observation.

The experiment operated on a "double-blind" design. The television viewers did not know that they were being studied, and the persons who carried out the observations were not aware of the purpose of the study. License plate numbers were used to trace the ownership of the cars through the state department of motor vehicles. The name of the car owner could be compared with the roster of households on cables C and E.

Thus, though this study was not a laboratory experiment (the subjects went about their business in the community with almost no restrictions on their behavior), it did involve a control group, a double-blind procedure, randomization, and careful structuring of the observational procedures. It therefore qualifies as an experiment, though it was carried out in the field.

Though the results of the experiment are not pertinent to our discussion of its design, it seems only fair to note them. It was found that the television messages had no effect on the use of safety belts. The percentage of use of safety belts for cable E drivers was just about identical to that for cable C drivers. Clearly, this does not indicate that it is not possible to increase use of safety belts by means of advertising campaigns on television, but it does indicate that this will take some additional planning and new tactics— assuming that it is possible to do it at all.

In their book on quasi experimentation, Cook and Campbell (1979) distinguished between two major categories: *nonequivalent group designs* and *interrupted time-series designs*.

In nonequivalent group designs, randomization is not possible and the comparisons are made between groups that differ from each other not only in treatment received but also in other ways. The investigator, therefore, must be able to rule out, by some means, alternative plausible hypotheses that may result from the additional differences which were not or could not be taken care of by random assignment.

An example of a quasi experiment with nonequivalent groups is the "Kansas City preventive patrol experiment" (Kelling et al., 1974). The experiment was aimed at testing the impact that routine preventive patrol has on crime rates and on the public's fear of crime. The experimental area consisted of 15 beats covering 32 square miles. The beats were matched as closely as possible by computer in groups of three on the basis of their crime rates, calls for service, ethnic composition, and socioeconomic factors. That is, each grouping of three beats (there were five such groupings) had roughly similar units on the matched variables as a result of the computer process.

In each matched group of three, one beat was designated as *reactive,* one as *proactive,* and one as a *control.* In the reactive beats (a total of five), there was no patrol; police vehicles assigned to those beats entered them only in response to calls for service. In the proactive beats (again five in all), the Kansas City Police Department increased the visibility of patrols by two to three times the level before the experiment. Finally, in the five control beats, conditions were maintained at the usual level, which actually involved one car per beat.

Thus, there were three levels of treatment—that is, three different arrangements for patrol: high visibility of police vehicles in the proactive areas; the usual visibility in the control area; and low visibility in the reactive areas, where the cars were seen only while going to and from calls. No random assignment was made of police officers involved in the experiment. The officers involved were those who had been patroling each area before the inauguration of the experiment, a condition creating uncontrolled differences over beats.

Dependent variables were measured for periods before the experiment and during the experimental period to produce what we have discussed as a "before-after" design (sometimes formally called "untreated control group design with pretest and posttest.")

The results of the experiment indicated that differing visibility of patrols, over the range studied, brought about no differential effects on crime rates or on citizens' fear of crime. To illustrate: Out of a total of 51 comparisons among reactive, proactive, and control beats on reported crime, only one was large enough to be noteworthy.

In interrupted time-series designs, repeated measures are made on a group at certain time intervals before a treatment is applied and then at equivalent time intervals after the treatment. The time intervals may be hours, days, weeks, months, or whatever is desired.

An excellent example of an interrupted time-series design is the experimental study of the effects of a 1975 gun control law in Massachusetts (Deutsch and Alt, 1977; Hay and McCleary, 1977). Guns are involved in a large proportion of homicides in the United States, and some people believe that tighter control on their ownership and sale would reduce both the rate of murder and manslaughter and the number of crimes, such as robbery, which often are committed with guns. Others believe that the problem and its solution are best explained by other things: the National Rifle Association, for example, proclaims that "people kill, not guns." Some people also point out that in Switzerland there is a very high level of ownership of weapons, since all citizens as part of their military obligations are required to keep guns in their homes, but the rate of crimes of violence and crimes against property is low. Therefore, they argue, ownership of guns need not be related to crimes committed with guns.

The Massachusetts law mandates a minimum one-year sentence for any person convicted of carrying a gun without proper authorization. There is no possibility of receiving a suspended sentence for the offense, nor is the convicted person eligible for parole before having served one year in jail.

The research sought to determine the deterrent effect of the gun control law. Toward this end, criminal offenses in the city of Boston which involved the use of a gun (specifically homicide, assault with a gun, and armed robbery) were tallied on a monthly basis for a time period before the law was enacted and for six months after it went into operation. There could, of course, be no randomization in this experiment. The independent variable was the status of the gun control law, with two levels or values: nonexistent (that is, the law had not yet been put into operation) and operative (the bill had been signed into law). The dependent variables were the sequences of crime rates for the three designated offenses.

Table 4 shows the monthly occurrences of the offense of assault with a gun for the six months before and the six months after the law was enacted. The researchers concluded that the law had reduced the number of assaults with a gun. The same conclusion was reached for armed robbery but not for

TABLE 4
ASSAULTS WITH A GUN BEFORE AND AFTER THE MASSACHUSETTS GUN CONTROL LAW OF 1975

Before April 1975		After April 1975	
Month	Number	Month	Number
October 1974	68	May 1975	51
November 1974	56	June 1975	40
December 1974	57	July 1975	50
January 1975	53	August 1975	40
February 1975	53	September 1975	47
March 1975	69	October 1975	52

homicide. For that offense, it was concluded (Deutsch and Alt, 1977:565) that "because of the large proportion of residential homicides, any future impact of gun control on homicide in general may not show up for several years, if ever."

There has been some dispute about the validity of these conclusions with regard to statistical techniques (Hay and McCleary, 1979). Such arguments are too esoteric to pursue in the present context. It is the experimental approach and its potentialities that we want to highlight.

REFERENCES

Bickman, L., and Henchy, T. 1972. *Beyond the Laboratory: Field Research in Social Psychology.* New York: McGraw-Hill.

Blixen, K. 1980. *Out of Africa.* Harmondsworth: Penguin Books.

Bridgman, P. 1950. *Reflections of a Physicist.* New York: Philosophical Library.

Cook, T. D., and Campbell, D. T. 1979. *Quasi-Experimentation: Design and Analysis Issues for Field Settings.* Chicago: Rand-McNally.

Deutsch, S. J., and Alt, F. B. 1977. "The Effect of Massachusetts' Gun Control Law on Gun-Related Crimes in the City of Boston." *Evaluation Quarterly,* 1:543–568.

Erickson, M. L. 1972. "The Changing Relationship Between Official and Self-Reported Measures of Delinquency: An Exploratory Predictive Study." *Journal of Criminal Law, Criminology, and Police Science,* 3:388–395.

Glueck, S., and Glueck, E. 1952. *Delinquents in the Making: Paths to Prevention.* New York: Harper.

Gold, M. 1970. *Delinquent Behavior in an American City.* Belmont, Calif.: Brooks/Cole.

Gold, M. 1966. "Undetected Delinquent Behavior." *Journal of Research in Crime and Delinquency,* 3:27–46.

Hathaway, S., and Monachesi, E. D. (eds.). 1953. *Analyzing and Predicting Juvenile Delinquency With the Minnesota Multiphasic Inventory.* Minneapolis: University of Minnesota Press.

Hay, R. A., Jr., and McCleary, R. 1979. "Box-Tiao Time Series Models for Impact Assessment: A Comment on the Recent Work of Deutsch and Alt," *Evaluation Quarterly,* 3:277–314.

Hay, L. R., Nelson, R. O., and Hay, W. M. 1980. "Methodological Problems in the Use of Participant Observers." *Journal of Applied Behavior Analysis,* 13:501–504.

Humphreys, L. 1970. *Tearoom Trade: Impersonal Sex in Public Places.* Chicago: Aldine.

Jennings, H. 1943. *Leadership and Isolation.* New York: Longmans.

Kelling, G. L., Pate, T., Dieckman, D., and Browne, C. E. 1974. *The Kansas City Preventive Patrol Experiment: A Technical Report.* Washington, D.C.: Police Foundation.

Kirk, R. E. 1968. *Experimental Design Procedure for the Behavioral Sciences,* Belmont, Calif.: Brooks/Cole.

McCall, G. J., and Simmons, J. L. 1969. *Issues in Participant Observation.* Reading, Mass.: Addison-Wesley.

Mead, M. 1972. *Blackberry Winter: My Earliest Years.* New York: Morrow.

Mead, M. 1928. *Coming of Age in Samoa.* New York: Morrow.

Moreno, J. L. 1934. *Who Shall Survive?* New York: Nervous and Mental Disease Publishing Co.

Myers, J. L. 1972. *Fundamentals of Experimental Design* (2d ed.). Boston: Allyn and Bacon.

Reiss, A. J., Jr. 1970. "Police Brutality." In N. Johnston, L. Savitz, and M. E. Wolfgang (eds.), *The Sociology of Punishment and Correction* (2d ed.). New York: Wiley.

Reiss, A. J., Jr. 1971. *The Police and the Public.* New Haven: Yale University Press.

Robertson, L. S., Kelley, A. B., O'Neill, B., Wixon, C. W., Eisworth, R. S., and Haddon, W., Jr., 1974. "A Controlled Study of the Effect of Television Messages on Safety Belt Use," *American Journal of Public Health,* **64**:1071–1080.

Robins, L. N., and O'Neal, P. 1958. "Mortality, Mobility, and Crime: Problem Children Thirty Years Later." *American Sociological Review,* 23:162–171.

Rubinstein, J. 1973. *Urban Police.* New York: Farrar, Straus and Giroux.

Sackett, G. P. 1978a. *Observing Behavior, Volume 1: Theory and Application in Mental Retardation.* Baltimore: University Press.

Sackett, G. P. 1978b. *Observing Behavior, vol. 2, Data Collection and Analysis Methods.* Baltimore: University Press.

Selltiz, C. Wrightsman, L. S., and Cook, S. W. 1976. *Research Methods in Social Relations* (3rd ed.). New York: Holt, Rinehart and Winston.

Smith, H. W. 1981. *Strategies of Social Research: The Methodological Imagination* (2d ed.). Englewood Cliffs, N.J.: Prentice-Hall.

Toch, H., Grant, J. D., and Galvin, R. T. 1975. *Agents of Change: A Study in Police Reform.* New York: Wiley.

Webb, E. J., Campbell, D. T., Schwartz, R. D., Sechrest, L. and Grove, J. B. 1981. *Nonreactive Measures in the Social Sciences.* Boston: Houghton Mifflin.

Woner, B. J. 1971. *Statistical Principles in Experimental Design* (2d ed.). New York: McGraw-Hill.

CHAPTER 7

PROGRAM EVALUATION

CHAPTER OUTLINE

WHAT IS PROGRAM EVALUATION?

AN EXAMPLE: EVALUATING "SCARED STRAIGHT"
    The Program
    The Finckenauer Reports

EVALUATOR AS ADVOCATE

ISSUES OF GENERALIZABILITY

ASSESSING PROCESS AND ASSESSING IMPACT
    Process Assessment
        Participation of target populations
        Monitoring delivery of services
        The Kansas City "preventive patrol" experiment:
          An example of process assessment
        In conclusion: Process assessment
    Impact Assessment

ISSUES OF ECONOMICS

CONCLUSIONS

REFERENCES

WHAT IS PROGRAM EVALUATION?

Program evaluation seeks to determine how effectively different kinds of arrangements work out in practice. The term *how effectively* conceals a number of very complicated questions, most of which can be subsumed under the heading "criteria of success." An able criminal justice researcher must devote a great deal of thought and intelligent planning to determining those outcomes which signal effectiveness and success. It may be that saving money or decreasing crime or increasing morale is a particularly important goal—or perhaps a combination of these.

Evaluation research can be carried out with almost any kind of program to determine whether it is achieving those things claimed for it or, more generally, to determine what its consequences are. The program in question may be one which inaugurates a four-day work week in a police or probation department or one which sends juvenile offenders to a community mental health agency, where they are examined before they go to juvenile court or are placed on probation. Or we might be interested in determining the outcome of the introduction of a program in transactional analysis in a maximum security prison, or the enlistment of community residents in an effort to provide various kinds of support services for the local police department.

Among the questions toward which the evaluation might be directed are these: Is the program more effective in achieving certain specified goals than an alternative program or than no program at all? What parts of the program are most effective? This last inquiry is one that tends to be neglected by even the best evaluators, who merely try to discover whether a program "works" overall and fail to appreciate that different parts of it might be producing contradictory results that cancel out any overall effect.

Another question might be: With which types of clients is the program most effective? Again, a program that shows no particular positive result may, when scrutinized more closely, be found to be strikingly effective with one kind of client and counterproductive with another kind. If so, blueprints for future programs can readily be drawn up which concentrate only on those kinds of persons with whom the program worked. In such an instance, however, there probably is some need for continuing evaluative monitoring of the program. The reason for this is quite subtle, and might well be appreciated only by a person highly experienced in evaluation research. When you begin the second program, enrolling only those kinds of persons with whom the first program appeared to work, you now have a different mix of clientele and that mix may be conducive to a different outcome than had been anticipated.

Take this illustration to show the logic of the preceding point. Suppose there are 20 juvenile delinquents participating in a program of group therapy. Ten are determined to be "weak and passive" and the other ten to be "strong and forceful." Evaluation shows that the ten weaker youngsters do much better in this program than they did in others that have been evaluated, while the stronger ones do less well. On this basis, we might decide to include only youngsters deemed weak and passive in the next phase of the program. But don't be surprised if the failure rate rises dramatically, because it may be that the weaker youngsters succeed only when they are mixed in with stronger ones. This may be because when we have only weak youngsters, the stronger ones among them take on the "tough" roles that could be tied to failure in the program.

It will be appreciated that all this is speculative, meant only to show that it is not always possible to take the results of one evaluative effort and to assume without testing that such results can be used as a basis for a subsequent successful enterprise. Continuous monitoring should be the order of the day, until it is demonstrably clear that further probes will add little information or that their expense is not commensurate with the value of the information that will be gleaned. This issue of cost-effectiveness has become a particularly important element of evaluation research as inflation continues to plague the country and the matter of expenditures for social programs become increasingly controversial.

Another issue that must constantly be checked in evaluative work is whether the services outlined for a particular program truly are being delivered in the manner proclaimed and are going to the intended participants. It sometimes is the case that what the program blueprint says the effort is all about bears precious little relationship to the reality. A program supposedly testing the value of bilingual education in a prison setting may on closer scrutiny turn out to offer but a few hours a month of such education and then only to a very limited group of inmates.

Modern evaluation research consists of applying the principles of research methodology (systematic decision making) to the task of securing answers to the kinds of questions and solutions to the kinds of problems that we have set out in the foregoing paragraphs. Throughout recorded history, persons and institutions have sought to discover the effect of what they have been doing and thereby to learn something from the inquiry. Otherwise, we would be doomed to repeating incessantly the errors of our ancestors. But before the application of the methods of sophisticated evaluation research emerged, information about outcomes was subject to the various kinds of errors endemic in all areas of human decision making that is undertaken without clear-cut rules and rigid logic. We have discussed throughout this book different kinds of tactics for minimizing such human biases and errors. The same principles apply, of course, to all forms of evaluation research in which the aim is to assess the consequences of social programs. In this chapter, we will expand upon the array of research methods to include unique considerations involved with evaluation efforts.

AN EXAMPLE: EVALUATING "SCARED STRAIGHT"

The Program

Let us turn to a dramatic example to emphasize the differences between everyday informal judgment about the effectiveness of programs and the use of evaluation as a form of systematic decision making. We will focus on "Scared Straight," a program that was designed to reduce the incidence of juvenile crime (see U.S. Congress, 1980).

No one questions that the phenomenon of delinquency constitutes a serious problem in the United States. Crimes of violence are committed by youths to an extraordinarily greater degree than by adults; so, too, are offenses against property. In the United States, delinquency is regarded as particularly disturbing because the country historically has tended to look on its youth with hope and concern.

Juvenile delinquency constitutes an impressively high proportion of serious crime in the United States. Youths between the ages of 15 and 18 make up about 8 percent of the population, but they account for about 16 percent of the total number of arrests for crimes of violence. In addition, delinquents have a tendency to continue in criminal careers when they reach adulthood. It has been observed that virtually every adult prison inmate has a record of delinquency. (On the other hand, the chain of logic is less than complete, since it is also true that many delinquents do not graduate to adult crime, and an unknown percentage of the law-abiding population represents products of the juvenile justice system).

Delinquency has always aroused a zeal for corrective programs, in large part because of the abiding faith of Americans that young persons can be reformed if they are turned in the correct direction before they move beyond an impressionable age. Given these conditions, when a new and seemingly innovative program comes along that appears to be effective in reducing delinquency, it can arouse bubbling, if uncritical, enthusiasm among the public.

Such was the case with a program initiated at the Rahway State Prison in New Jersey. In this program, youngsters who presumably have committed criminal offenses face inmates (identified as "lifers") who are in prison for acts such as murder and forcible rape. As part of the program, the prisoners shout at the youngsters, lecture them about the dismal nature of life inside the walls, threaten them with bodily harm, describe vividly the continuous violence and the sexual exploitation of "punks" (young prisoners), and deliberately use brutally frank and obscene language.

The aim is to make bluntly clear to the youngsters the ultimate consequences of a life of crime, to frighten them so thoroughly that they will change their ways and never again engage in delinquent or criminal behavior.

The method was dramatized in a film that was titled, appropriately enough, *Scared Straight!* It was shown on television stations throughout the country. A report on the screening conveys a sense of the contents of the film and audience reaction to it:

> *Scared Straight!* played to a large and enthusiastic audience. There had probably never been a television documentary like it: the obscene language, the descriptions of violence and sodomy, the passionate intensity of the prisoners, the resonating steel sounds of cell doors slamming shut. "Please don't make me hurt you," a lifer spits in the face of a teenage boy, "because if I have to break your face to get my point across, I'll do it, you little dummy. You're here for two hours, you belong to us for two hours." One after another, the prisoners berate, rant, strut, and menace. "I'm bad, you see me boy, I'm bad," snarls another "You see them pretty blue eyes of yours? I'll take one out of your face and squish it in front of you." In prison, "the big eat the little."

The 17 youngsters who were shown in the film as the recipients of this barrage certainly seemed duly terrified. Following the experience, they claimed, not surprisingly, that they now were reformed, completely cured of any previous inclination toward violating the law. This testimony, which in evaluation work is often dubbed *anecdotal evidence* (and given only minimum credence), was supplemented by informal claims by proponents of the "Scared Straight" program that there was a "success rate" of between 80 and 90 percent among those youngsters who had been involved in the program. It was said that some 8000 juveniles had participated in a "Scared Straight" experience and that 16 of the 17 boys shown in the television film had turned their backs on delinquency. Peter Falk, the actor who narrated the television show, solemnly conveyed the information about the impact of the program that was being depicted.

Everything was in place for authorities and the lay public to conclude that a miraculous method had at last been discovered for eradicating or, at least, substantially reducing the amount of juvenile crime in the United States. First, the process possessed a considerable degree of *face validity*; that is, at a first glance it had obvious appeal and seemed to make sense. There was logic to this: when people are sufficiently frightened about the consequences of some behavior they will adjust their actions to avoid those fearful consequences. What reasonable middle- or upper-class person, seeing the television film, would not think: What an awful existence prison life is? I've got to be law-abiding or those terrible things could happen to me.

In addition, the arguments by the narrator were being delivered by a distinguished actor who had played the part of an astute and discriminating, though kindly, detective in a television series that had achieved a very wide audience throughout the country. Research work indicates clearly that audiences listen more attentively to a person they respect and "know" than they do to a person with whom they are unfamiliar and who lacks status.

Episodes have been staged in which precisely the same message is conveyed by a high-status person and a low-status person, with the views of the listeners checked afterward. Despite the fact that exactly the same thing has been said, listeners tend to align their views with that of the prestigious speaker and to reject the opinions of the déclassé speaker.

Furthermore, as we noted above, the dramatic presentation of the "Scared Straight" program on television indicated that the method portrayed worked. The youngsters obviously seemed to be quite frightened, and they said that they had been reformed by the experience they had undergone in the prison.

Finally, a major industrial organization, the Signal Companies, had underwritten the presentation of the film and during the television screening the company's president, Forrest Shumway, spoke glowingly of the results that the Rahway program had produced. Shumway, in fact, argued that merely watching the program on television would modify criminal behavior. The third sentence of the following excerpt conveys Shumway's conviction that the program would have an effect upon wayward members of the viewing audience. The quotation is from a San Francisco newspaper.

> For me, there is only one measure of the worth of this program. It was set forth with eloquent directness in the remark of one chastened young delinquent, all his bravado gone as he left Rahway: "I think it will change my life." I hope and believe that a lot of lost youngsters will feel that way after watching Scared Straight! We'll all be winners if they do.

The television program also prompted response in the political arena, which perhaps testifies to the longing legislators have for uncomplicated solutions which permit them to enact laws putting an end to social difficulties. In California, for instance, a state senator introduced a measure that would have mandated the busing of thousands of youngsters to prisons, over long distances, for appropriate "scaring." Apparently moved by a similar motivation, the Maryland legislature enacted a bill which allows judges in certain counties to sentence adolescent offenders to adult jails. The youngsters could be kept in these facilities for no more than two weeks, by which time, presumably, they would have been sufficiently intimidated and terrorized to mend their ways.

Amidst such hullaballoo there appeared two formal evaluation reports which put a considerable damper on the enthusiasm that accompanied the television screening of Scared Straight! These reports were Finckenauer and Storti (1979) and Finckenauer (1979).

The Finckenauer Reports

The work by Finckenauer and his colleague represented an attempt to demonstrate—or to disprove—a conclusion that had been reached on the basis of anecdotal evidence and what seemed to be commonsense observation. This is what science is all about—the effort to adjudicate matters in a systematic and irrefutable way rather than to rely on unsystematic reports and testimony by persons who sometimes are taken at their word because they seem to know what they are talking about, because they look authoritative, or because they convey a strong sense of self-assurance.

Finckenauer employed a quasi-experimental design to try to determine the effects of the "Scared Straight" program. He formed an experimental group of 46 youngsters. These youngsters attended the project sessions during which they were exposed to the lessons that constituted the essential ingredient of the televised program: they were hectored, put down, provided with dire predictions of their fate if they did not mend their ways, and otherwise intimidated. There was also a control group of 35 youngsters who did not take part in the project sessions. The experimental and control subjects were selected at random from youngsters who had been referred by different agencies which deal with youths involved in what are deemed delinquent lifestyles. The sponsoring agencies had also been selected at random, from a list of all the New Jersey groups that had sent youngsters to be exposed to the "Scared Straight" experience at Rahway.

An initial finding was that relatively few of those youngsters who were being referred to the program were delinquency-prone. Using a scale that predicted the likelihood of future delinquent behavior, the investigators found that 72 percent of the 81 youngsters involved in the evaluation study had a low probability of committing delinquent acts, 20 percent had a medium probability, and only 8 percent had a high probability. There were no differences between the youngsters in the experimental group and those in the control group in terms of their likelihood of delinquent behavior as determined by the test scale. In short, it did not appear that hard-core youths who presumably required the resounding "scares" were the ones who were being referred to the project. Examining what they had found, Finckenauer and Storti (1979, p. 15) raised the following questions:

> Why do these particular kids need to attend the Project? Why are referring agencies not sending more high probability juveniles who might be more in need of deterrence? If the low probability of delinquency juveniles in fact do not become delinquent, can the JAPH [Juvenile Awareness Project Help—the formal name of the Rahway project] claim credit?

The evaluators thus suggest the likelihood that, with or without exposure to "Scared Straight," very many of the youngsters involved would not have gone on to delinquent behavior, that the program was claiming credit for reforming youths who were not going to get into trouble anyway.

No difference was found by Finckenauer and Storti (1979) in regard to changes in attitudes among those youngsters who were exposed and those who were not exposed to the Rahway experience. The attitudes that were investigated included those toward law, justice, punishment, self, and the police. The youths who visited the prisons appeared to have become more negative in their attitude toward crime, but the magnitude of the difference proved to be very small. There is, thus, no evidence that the experimentals were scared into a different set of attitudes.

In terms of recidivism, which is the crucial variable, Finckenauer's study (1979) found that "a significantly higher proportion of the juveniles who did *not* attend the Project did better in terms of subsequent offenses than did the group which attended" (p. 9). The recidivism figures were based on juvenile court records and covered a minimum of six months of follow-up. They showed that 58.7 percent of the experimental group and 51.8 percent of the control group had some experience with the juvenile court in the six months after exposure to the "Scared Straight" program. An interesting finding was that 6 of the 19 youths in the experimental group who had no previous records of delinquency turned up with subsequent court records. This compared with only 1 of the 21 in the control group (that is, 21 youngsters in the control group had no previous records, and afterwards only one had a juvenile court record).

It would be hypothesized (though the experimental work is hardly adequate to prove the point) that the "Scared Straight" program has a tendency to encourage delinquency rather than to discourage it. This might be brought about by familiarizing the youngsters with prison life. Perhaps the toughest kids among those exposed to the program get the idea that they really can thrive in a prison setting and get some pleasure out of pushing others about. Other possible explanations also suggest themselves, but fundamentally it would require careful testing to determine why the program apparently does not produce the kinds of results its advocates maintain it will and precisely what kinds of results it does bring about.

It becomes clear, then, that evaluation research methods raised great doubts about the informal claims and judgments. Details concerning the "Scared Straight" effort and its evaluations are still being debated. For our purposes, the lesson is that emotional crusades created by intuitive judgments ought to be carefully and thoroughly checked out before they become the basis for social policy.

EVALUATOR AS ADVOCATE

For the criminal justice evaluator who is concerned about the results of what he or she has investigated, an important issue becomes the advisability of moving from an objective investigative role into a position of advocacy. The advocate is one who does more than set forth a conclusion based upon research. The advocate pushes for a policy that seems to follow from the material that has been gathered in the evaluation. This generally involves something other than impartial scientific work.

A notable illustration of advocacy by an evaluator is found in the work of Chein and his associates (1964). They recounted dispassionately the dynamics of heroin addiction in the New York slums. Then, that portion of their work completed, they turned to a passionate plea for what they believed to be a more decent and considerate public policy in regard to heroin users. The essence of their position lay far afield in most respects from their findings. It was based on the view that heroin addiction often is an adaptation to intolerable social conditions and that it was cruel beyond understanding to allow such social conditions to prevail and then to victimize further the addict who takes one of the few means available to escape the tyranny of his or her social position.

This viewpoint, obviously, is debatable, and there are very many persons who would strongly disagree with it on any number of grounds. Most certainly the position cannot be supported (or rebutted) by the conclusions reached during the evaluation work. Should the evaluator therefore refrain from moving beyond that work in the direction of advocacy?

The subject of the scientist as advocate was thoroughly debated as an aftermath of the use of the hydrogen bomb against Japan near the end of the Second World War. There were some atomic physicists who said that their job was to discover the scientific information that allowed nuclear weapons (as well as peaceful use of nuclear energy) to be developed—and that was all their job involved. Others, however, said that because they knew more than anybody else about the nuclear products and because of the kind of work they were doing, they felt obligated to take a stand regarding the "proper" use and safeguards surrounding the use of the materials which their work had led them to put together.

Note, in this connection, the strong feelings of one researcher about involvement in policy debate:

> It has been claimed that no question of scientists' responsibility for application of their work arises because applications cannot be foreseen or planned, and anyway are not in the hands of the scientists. This argument is simply silly. Although it is true that the applications of fundamental research cannot be forecast in any detail, the general areas of possible application to which the fundamental work is contributing are likely to be clear. And for scientists to wash their hands of the problem by claiming that responsibility lies in the hands of others is to attempt to escape from the responsibilities all people have for their actions which might affect other people adversely, whether these actions are scientific, artistic or anything else (Belsey, 1980:429).

While it is true that no one is likely to be as thoroughly versed in the nuances of a matter as the person who carried out the evaluation, it is also true that, unlike evaluators, politicians, as policymakers, have constituencies—those who elected them—to whom they ultimately are responsible. It is also true that once evaluators enter the public arena to press for policy, the objectivity of their evaluation work is likely to come under suspicion: their evaluations are likely to be regarded thereafter as partisan rather than impartial.

If evaluators do decide to debate—say, about whether "Scared Straight" ought to be expanded or dropped as a program—they must use care to distinguish between what they have found and what they believe on the basis of less-than-scientific evidence. The evaluation of "Scared Straight," for example, only suggests that the program might not be valuable for reducing recidivism; it does not prove the matter. It may be that some attitudes that were not examined undergo considerable change for the better on the basis of exposure to the program. It may also be that recidivism changes dramatically when the period during which it is measured is extended from six months to as long as two years. Neither of these outcomes seems likely, but for the moment there is no evidence available to disprove them. The evaluator discussing policy, therefore, must make certain that the limits of science are clearly noted. And the evaluator ought to guard against succumbing to the all-too-human tendency to believe that competence in one area is widely generalizable, in the manner of motion picture and television stars who pontificate about matters of foreign policy, the morality of the young, and other matters on which neither acting ability nor good looks provides satisfactory expertise.

ISSUES OF GENERALIZABILITY

There are a number of logical pitfalls that tend to waylay unwary evaluators. Important issues of generalizability inevitably arise when evaluators examine phenomena. We can pass along the following cautionary tale, related to one of the authors during his own experience in a research class:

> A farmer, the class was informed, had obtained a bumper crop of potatoes when he used 12 pounds of nitrate fertilizer. He did even better when he doubled that amount. A further increment of fertilizer, however, resulted in the total destruction of the crop. The lesson pressed home to us in the gentle drawl of our professor was: "Don't extrapolate beyond the data."

Problems in logic also occur if an evaluator bases a recommendation for change on what is found to have resulted from a naturally arising event. The fact that "good" or "bad" results, by specified standards, ensued when place A decriminalized possession of small amounts of marijuana does not mean that there will be similar outcomes in place B, even if the second place seems to be much the same as the first. The satisfactory outcome in A may have been brought about by precisely those conditions that originally led to the change in the law. The conditions that delayed the change in B might also frustrate expectations if the change is instituted on the basis of the experience of place A.

This point is emphasized by consideration of an evaluation that showed that a spontaneously occurring dispersion of inner-city delinquents to the suburbs was accompanied by a significant decline in their lawbreaking. To put it simply: when they left the ghettos, they apparently stopped breaking the law. This does *not* signify that a housing policy that forces dispersion to the suburbs will produce the same results, or, even if it does, that those results are the consequence of a similar process. The first dispersion might well have been the result of attitudes held by parents that led to their quest for a safer environment for their children. Without such attitudes, a forced geographic exodus might not produce equivalent outcomes. Indeed, it could so anger and annoy the youths that their rate of delinquency would increase dramatically.

ASSESSING PROCESS AND ASSESSING IMPACT

There are two components of program evaluation that are particularly important: *process assessment* and *impact assessment*.

Process assessment is directed at determining the kinds of services being delivered and the amounts and appropriateness of the services. It also deals with the persons and groups of people who are receiving the services and the appropriateness of these target units. Impact assessment (or goal assessment) is aimed at determining a program's effectiveness in achieving intended—and clearly stated—results.

Process Assessment

Rossi and his colleagues (1979) have considered process assessment from two perspectives: *participation of target populations* and *monitoring delivery of services*.

Participation of Target Populations   Social programs are organized to provide services to a certain group of people. These people form the target population. They may be the victims of violent crimes, juvenile offenders, released prison inmates, or all the residents in a city served by a particular police department.

The precise nature and the extent of involvement of the target population are matters that an evaluator can determine with some specificity. A program aimed at providing psychological services to police officers who kill citizens in the line of duty could not be effective if officers who had used deadly force did not participate. A skilled evaluator will make certain that the precise nature of the target group is set forth and that all persons who meet such requirements, or a suitable sample, are involved in the evaluation probe. At the same time, it is essential to specify the services—the interventions—that will be delivered. Oftentimes, as we noted earlier, the blueprint may not be followed. For instance, a program may be designed to employ guided group interaction, a form of group therapy, for prison guards. But the evaluator might discover that the interaction occupies no more than a few hours every other week and then most of the guards who are supposed to be enrolled are absent, because they deliberately stay away, forget to attend, or are ill or on vacation. The evaluation of such an effort would be likely (though not certain) to show results quite different from those of a program that took 30 hours a week of the targeted groups' time and showed 100 percent attendance rates for all sessions.

There is bias in a program when only a subgroup of the target population survives the entire length of the effort. Biasing may also come about through differential selection at the entry point to program services or through differences in dropout rates over subgroups.

To illustrate: A program of community-based counseling services for juvenile offenders may have as its target population all youngsters arrested by members of a police department and alleged to have committed status offenses or nonassaultive criminal offenses. The targeted youngsters also are specified as those who do not have more than two previous arrests on their records. The counseling session is voluntary. An evaluator may discover that only young offenders whose families are affluent enough to have the necessary transportation and time to bring them in for counseling are attending each of the scheduled sessions. This is an example of selective bias.

Participation of target populations may be assessed by the use of surveys or by the analysis of program records. In many instances, it is desirable to compare the characteristics of those who participate with those who drop out and with those who are eligible but do not participate. Some of the most awful illustrations of poor evaluation research involve failure to take account of the dropouts and what might be their special characteristics. In one such effort, an evaluator maintained that the program he was examining had proved to be a total success. All members of the organization being studied who had completed the course of instruction proved to be drug free, he announced. There were, he said, some 120 persons who fell into this category.

Later review of the findings disclosed, however, that the organization in question defined a person as a member only if he or she had completed the indoctrination course. That course, lasting 16 weeks, involved twice-weekly urinalysis in order to discover any return to drug use. By the end of the course, almost by definition, each "member" was drug-free, the aim of the effort. But it was noted in the report that only 35 percent of those who began the course lasted long enough to achieve "membership." Seen in this different light, the achievement is a good deal less exemplary.

Monitoring Delivery of Services Monitoring delivery of services is aimed at determining whether or not services are being delivered in the fashion stated in the initial planning documents. It is possible that services are being delivered in an unsatisfactory manner or, indeed, that they are not being delivered at all. It is also quite possible that services other than those intended are being given. It often happens that there is so much variability in delivered services that only certain recipients get what can be considered adequate attention, and then only at certain times. This inconsistency makes it very difficult to pinpoint the elements that contributed to the ultimate success or failure of a program. It is impossible to say, for instance, that a program of training did or did not work if the program was almost totally erratic.

This type of monitoring requires clear specification by program implementers and evaluators of the services that are going to be involved. As Larson and his colleagues (1979) reported in a recent analysis of criminal justice evaluation, such specification often is not present. They noted their conclusions about a number of programs examined:

> The best descriptions seemed either to include a detailed outline of procedures for the implementation of the program or to go beyond a generalized or idealized version and supplement the picture of the total program with specific examples of program activities.
>
> In contrast, many program descriptions were very brief. This was the most frequently cited problem...
>
> At times evaluations went into considerable depth in discussing some aspects of the program while barely mentioning the most critical features (p. 40).

The delivery of services may differ from that intended for reasons over which operators have no control. Often supervisors will demand a change in program structure, sometimes on the basis of unfavorable publicity, sometimes as a result of surprise visits or shifts in their own priorities. At times, actual sabotage may alter the elements of the blueprint. The latter is particularly likely to occur when a program is foisted upon a staff over its direct or hidden opposition. The research on prisons is replete with stories of the attempts of new wardens to inaugurate what they regarded as more kindly efforts to aid prisoners, efforts which were subverted by long-term custodial officers who saw them as dangerous, mindless, and counterproductive. Similarly, a program aimed at increasing the number of women in a police department may be thwarted in terms of its actual operation because of failure to win the implementing officers over to the project before its inauguration.

Another example of inadvertent failure to execute programs appropriately can occur if it proves impossible to recruit an adequate staff. A project designed to deal with psychological stress among police officers may operate differently from the plan because the desired team of licensed, Ph.D.-level clinical psychologists cannot be obtained and M.A.-level psychologists have to be used.

Monitoring delivery of services may be accomplished by: (1) use of records detailing delivery; (2) observation by staff of the evaluation team; (3) information obtained from providers of service, by interviews, narrative reports, or questionnaires; (4) information from recipients of services or from those associated with the recipients. Combinations of these approaches are recommended so that there can be a cross-check on the accuracy of the material gathered.

Care needs to be exercised so that such material is gathered systematically and so that as many data sources as possible are tapped, not only those most readily available or most comforting to the evaluator. It is often useful to have participants in the program provide, either in writing or through tape recordings, their impressions of what is going on and the details of the delivery of services. This can be undertaken at regular intervals so that the evaluator achieves an understanding of changes in the program.

Relentless, on-site monitoring also may turn up discrepancies between the stated and the actual ethos of a service program. In one halfway house for men who were former heroin addicts, for instance (Miller et al., 1967), the program was supposed to conform to the design of a "therapeutic community." It was said that the men were responsible for their own fates and, therefore, were expected to take action to arrange their lives. When two of the residents came home late from work and found that the meat for their supper had been stolen, probably by one of the residents who had taken it home to his family, the staff turned an indifferent ear to the complaints. "It's your house, you live here, settle your own business," the men were told. When the hungry men did nothing more than sulk, staff members interpreted this as additional evidence that they were not yet sufficiently mature to assume the responsibilities of the therapeutic community. The evaluator's interviews, however, indicated that the men regarded the staff as clearly posturing. "That's so much junk about us managing our own affairs," they would say. "When it's something important to them, they always make the decisions and take action." Indeed, only a week before, the house manager's remark that the place "looks like a pigsty," but "if you guys want to live like this that's your business," had quickly been altered when it was learned that the feisty director of the State Department of Corrections was due for a visit. Work crews were asembled, bucket-and-mop squads were put to work, and the laissez-faire attitude was abruptly terminated. It could be said in truth that it was by no means a "pure" therapeutic community that was being subjected to evaluation, but something quite different, with overtones of "therapeutic community" attitudes and an admixture of a great many other considerations.

The Kansas City "Preventive Patrol" Experiment: An Example of Process Assessment   Earlier we discussed the Kansas City "preventive patrol" experiment (Kelling et al., 1974), which essentially involved an evaluation of the effectiveness of routine preventive police patrol. We can employ the same experiment to illustrate some of the issues involved in process assessment.

The target population in this instance was the community of residents in the 15-beat experimental area. When a targeted group is a community rather than a more narrowly defined population (such as police officers under stress or arrested juvenile offenders), the only practical way to determine that the intended group is reached is by a survey of sampled target units.

In the Kansas City experiment the evaluators used such an approach by selecting random samples of households for evaluation before the experiment began and after the experiment was finished. There were 1203 households in the "before" probe, which came to about 80 in each beat area; and 1201 in the "after" probe, made after the program had been in operation for a year. Of the 1201 households in the "after" survey, 553 had also been in the "before" survey and 648 were newly chosen. The former group is referred to as the repeated sample and the latter as the non-repeated sample. The advantage of a repeated sample is that it possesses precisely the same characteristics as the original group, since, of course, it *is* the same group. (See the discussion on control in Chapter 5.) The disadvantage is that sometimes there is a memory factor at work, so that the respondents recall what they had said earlier and their subsequent answers are somewhat influenced by their previous responses rather than by the situation which is being evaluated.

The survey items that most closely reflected services to the target population were those that dealt with citizens' perceptions of the effectiveness of the police and their satisfaction with police service. Some results are presented below:

Neighborhood Police Effectiveness

When asked how good a job neighborhood officers were doing fighting crime, citizens in the repeated sample indicated a little less than "moderately good job" on the average. Perceptions of neighborhood police effectiveness varied significantly by police strategy...

Residents of control and proactive [when the police seek out matters rather than responding or reacting to complaints] beats believed neighborhood officers had improved in fighting crime. Residents of reactive beats perceived neighborhood police officers as being less effective in fighting crime (p. 364).

Satisfaction with Police Service

Only the responses from the nonrepeated sample are presented, due to the small number of persons from the repeated sample who called the police both years. Residents in reactive beats who called the police during the experiment appeared to be less satisfied with police service than those who called the police before the experiment. At the same time, proactive and control beat citizens who called the police during the experiment were more satisfied with the police service than those who called before the experiment....On the whole, citizens were "moderately satisfied" with the police services regardless of experimental condition or year.

More detailed questions about the incident which prompted citizens to call the police were also asked. A few more citizens in the proactive beats in 1973 made calls about juvenile disturbances than did 1972 respondents. Reactive and control beat respondents in 1973 made fewer calls about juveniles than did the 1972 respondents (p. 379).

In the Kansas City experiment, monitoring delivery of services was accomplished by observers (technically, they were observers as participants). The observers had backgrounds in disciplines such as sociology, psychology, or public administration, and they were given one week of training in methods of field observation. They rode with officers in the police cars, with the expectation that they "would be useful monitors of unanticipated consequences of the preventive patrol experiment and could help the task force answer questions concerning those duties police officers actually perform on patrol" (p. 31). A central task of the observers was focusing on interactions between the police and citizens. In that process they recorded on tape cassettes 997 incidents of such interaction and prepared detailed written descriptions of the interactions. Observations were made during all three police watches and over the 15 beats. A total of 48 officers were observed for a total observation time of some 4500 hours.

The observers also filled out survey questionnaires after encounters between officers and citizens. Separate questionnaires were used for encounters that were initiated by officers and those that were initiated by citizens. Similar survey instruments were used with the officers and with the citizens involved in each of the episodes. The following illustrates findings based upon the work of the observers:

> The official disposition of the transaction did not vary significantly by officer assignment (p. 474).
> The observers evaluated the officers in the reactive beats as having the most positive "character" during the encounters (p. 456).

In Conclusion: Process Assessment   It must be appreciated that virtually all criminal justice interventions are unique phenomena and that their results come from a variety of interacting elements. "Program testing," as Edward A. Suchman (1967, p. 77) has noted, "has almost no generalizability, being applicable solely to the specific programs being evaluated." This is a bit of an overstatement, since quite shrewd guesses can be made about the transferability of one program to a second site, but Suchman's observation, from a scientific point of view, is literally true.

This being so, it is important that persons trying to understand satisfactorily what was involved in any program be provided with a thorough portrait of the procedures and processes involved, including many of the nuances and some anecdotal material that can be conveyed only by an evaluator with observational skills, a person who is able to determine what is important and to describe with accuracy and grace the nature of such matters.

Impact Assessment

Impact assessment, as noted earlier, is aimed at determining the effectiveness of the program in terms of achievement of its stated goals. A central goal of the Rahway program, for instance, was to reduce the recidivism of delinquents—to "scare them straight." The evaluation determined that the goal was not achieved during the period in which the program was scrutinized (Finckenauer, 1979).

Measures of outcome are of critical concern in impact assessment. The evaluator must determine an outcome or a series of outcomes that are measurable and that reflect the intended goal of the program. Recidivism is an obvious outcome measure in the Rahway program. But there are often other kinds of measures that can be important in determining the value of a program. The Rahway program, thus, might have had no use whatsoever in terms of straightening out the delinquents to whom it was directed. But it could have proved extremely valuable in keeping the prisoners who transmitted the lesson on a law-abiding course after their release from prison. That is, they could well have proved to have been their own best audience, rather than the youngsters to whom they thought they were directing their message. These kinds of unusual possible outcomes—things not commonly thought of—can be found in virtually all programs. Many group therapy programs in prisons, for example, have been shown by astute evaluation not to have much effect upon prisoners' behavior, but to be extraordinarily useful to the prison administrators as a source of information about discontents and other issues of prison management.

The concept of outcome in the realm of evaluation implies a change or a difference over time. *Change* refers to comparison of measurements before and after the program is introduced; *difference* refers to comparison of measurements of participants in the program and comparable nonpartici-pants, that is, the control group members.

Tight evaluation designs, like all the research efforts discussed in this book, aim to rule out explanations for obtained changes or differences other than that the outcome was a product of the operation of the program in question. Such explanations are another form of the alternative plausible hypotheses that we have been warning against throughout the book. Finckenauer (1979), in evaluating the Rahway program, employed random assignment of referred youngsters to experimental and control conditions to eliminate explanations based on possible inherent differences between participants and nonparticipants in the program. If he had indeed found lower recidivism rates for participants in the program, the random assign-ment procedure would have guarded against the explanation or hypothesis that the difference resulted from some extraneous factor, such as less serious delinquency records among members of the participant group.

Similarly, in the Kansas City "preventive patrol experiment," the 15 beats in the area studied were computer-matched into five groups of three each on the basis of crime statistics, number of calls for service, ethnic and income characteristics, and the transiency of the population. Then, within each of the five groups, there was random assignment of one beat to reactive, one to control, and one to proactive patrol. The matching and random assignment made it reasonable to conclude that any differences found among the reactive, control, and proactive situations resulted from the conditions of the experiment rather than from inherent differences within the beats assigned to each of the three experimental conditions. Suppose that the beats for proactive patrol had been allowed to have fewer black residents and more wealthy families than the beats for the control and reactive patrol conditions. Then, finding that citizens' attitudes toward police officers after the experiment were more positive in the proactive area than in the control and reactive areas would have as an alternative plausible explanation the fact that blacks and the poor tend to have more negative attitudes toward the police than whites and the affluent.

ISSUES OF ECONOMICS

Program costs represent the final issue for us in this consideration of evaluation efforts. While a particular program might prove effective in reaching targeted individuals, in the actual delivery of services, and in accomplishing its stated goals, it may do so only at a prohibitive cost, or, at least, at a cost considerably higher than for competing programs that are only slightly less effective.

There is a developing field referred to as *cost-benefit analysis* that provides the conceptual framework for such considerations. Esoteric analyses of costs and benefits, or cost-effectiveness, are beyond the scope of the present discussion (if you desire to probe deeper into the matter, see Squire and van der Tak, 1975), but in many cases a simple calculation of cost per client or cost per stated benefit can be useful for purposes of comparison. Palmer, Bohnstedt, and Lewis (1978), for example, evaluated a group of diversion programs and divided average cost per project by average number of clients served. They then compared the resulting average cost per client with estimated costs of processing young offenders further into the juvenile justice system rather than diverting them out. They conclude:

> During the project year that was assessed funded expenditures for individual... diversion projects ranged from a low of $39,322 to a high of $250,000. The average expenditure was $101,957. The number of clients served ranged from 196 to 806— the average being 408. Cost per case therefore ranged from a low of $107 to a high of $600 and the average was $250....
>
> The estimated average cost per Law Enforcement arrest for ...[the] projects was $511; for probation processing it was $477: Using these figures together with actual recidivism rates for clients and comparisons in the same... projects, an average saving of $31.95 was found for each diversion client who was referred from a justice system source (pp. 186–188).

A final example of cost benefit analysis, which encompasses a sophisticated use of the technique, is found in the evaluation of a "Negligent Operator" (Neg-Op) component of the accident prevention program of the Department of Motor Vehicles in California (Brown and Marchi, 1976).

In California a "point" is assigned for each traffic conviction that involves the unsafe operation of a motor vehicle on a public road. One point is also given when an operator is involved in an accident for which he or she is responsible; two points are assigned for such major violations as drunk and reckless driving. The vehicle code defines persons as "Negligent Operators" (Neg-Ops) if their driving records show a count of four points in one year, six points in two years, or eight points in three years.

The Department of Motor Vehicles operates a four-part program for Neg-Ops. First, a warning letter is mailed when an operator accumulates three points in a year. Those drivers who subsequently pick up the additional points to become defined as Neg-Ops are required to participate in a group education meeting. Thereafter, those drivers who have taken part in the group education meeting but who continue to accumulate points are scheduled for individual hearings. As a result of that interview, at the discretion of a drivers-improvement analyst, the person may be placed on probation. If the probation is violated by the accumulation of further points, the driver is summoned to a probation-violation hearing. In most cases, this hearing leads to the suspension of the operator's driving license.

Evaluation of the Neg-Op program took advantage of the sequential nature of the program "treatment" regimen: first, warning letter; second, group education meeting; third, individual hearing; and fourth, probation violation hearing. Two random sets of drivers (license numbers were the basis for the randomization process) were used in the evaluation. One group consisted of those drivers who received all four treatments; the other was made up of drivers who were withdrawn from the Neg-Op program before receiving their next level of treatment. That is, if an operator had received no treatment, received a warning letter, engaged in a group education meeting, or received an individual hearing, and was selected for control, no further treatments were administered, regardless of the person's subsequent driving record.

To reemphasize the design: While all subsequent treatments were withheld from those selected for the control group, operators in the experimental group were allowed to proceed normally through subsequent treatments. This procedure allowed evaluation of certain components of the Neg-Op program as well as examination of the program as a whole.

The outcome measures used were subsequent accidents and subsequent convictions. The effect of the warning letter alone could be evaluated by comparison of operators who were put into the control group before receiving the warning letter with those put into the control group after receiving the warning letter. Similarly, the impact of group education meetings could be evaluated by comparison of operators who were put into the control group before being assigned to a group-education meeting with those put into the control after being assigned to a group-education meeting. Other steps could be evaluated by use of the same processes.

TABLE 5
EFFECTS OF NEG-OP TREATMENTS ON ACCIDENTS

Treatment group	Accident reduction, percent	Annual accident decrease per 1000 treatments, number
Warning letter	3.9	4.6
Group education hearing	4.2	4.6
Individual hearing	17.0	20.1
Probation-violation hearing	8.7	9.7

The results in terms of subsequent accidents are shown in Table 5. It was also found that all Neg-Op treatments were effective in reducing subsequent convictions. These ranged from a 10.7 percent reduction for the warning letter to a 22.9 percent reduction for the probation-violation hearing.

Cost-effectiveness was evaluated by comparing program costs with estimates of the monetary loss involved in subsequent accidents. The report noted: "If the monetary benefits derived from preventing one accident are greater than the costs to prevent one accident, then the program is said to be cost-beneficial" (Brown and Marchi, 1976:881). Admittedly, the estimations of accident costs were crude, especially when fatalities were taken into consideration, since there is no decent way to calculate things such as the grief and emotional loss, among other matters, that attend such accidents. But there were financial guidelines available from the experiences of the National Safety Council and the National Highway Traffic Safety Administration that the evaluators took advantage of for their work.

The warning letter was determined to be cost-effective, even though it did not reduce accidents greatly, because the cost of issuing the letter was so low. Similarly, the individual hearing and the Neg-Op Program as a whole were found to be cost-effective. But this was not true of the group education meeting or the probation-violation hearing. On the basis of this information, policymakers were better able to decide how they could most effectively allocate available resources to deal with unsafe drivers.

CONCLUSIONS

It is not necessary to evaluate each and every aspect of criminal justice programs. Indeed in some matters the evaluation itself may not prove cost-effective; it may involve more expenditure of funds than any conclusion that it might reach could save anybody, and the subject itself might not be of much importance. At the same time, when it is carried out, evaluation should be done with care and skill, because very important decisions often are made on the basis of its results. It also should be noted that when significant new work is being done, the need for careful evaluation can be crucial. Some years ago the British "Seerbohm report" (Great Britain, 1968) captured well the importance of evaluation work: "It is both wasteful and irresponsible to set experiments in motion and omit to record and analyze what happens," the report noted. "It makes no sense in terms of administrative efficiency, and, however little intended, it indicates a careless attitude toward human welfare."

REFERENCES

Belsey, A. 1980. "Scientific Research and Moral Problems." *New Universities Quarterly,* **34**:429–438.

Brown, E., and Marchi, S. A. 1976. *Post Licensing Control Reporting and Evaluation System Summary Report.* 2 vols. Sacramento, Calif.: Division of Drivers Licenses, Department of Motor Vehicles.

Chein, I., Gerard, D. L., Lee, R. S. and Rosenfeld, E. 1964. *The Road to H: Narcotics, Delinquency and Social Policy.* New York: Basic Books.

Finckenauer, J. O. 1979. *Juvenile Awareness Project. Evaluation Report No. 2.* Newark: Rutgers University School of Criminal Justice.

Finckenauer, J. O., and Storti, J. R. 1979. *Juvenile Awareness Project Help. Evaluation Report No. 1.* Newark: Rutgers University School of Criminal Justice.

Great Britain (1968). *Report of the Committee on Local Authority and Allied Personal Social Services.* Command 3703. London: Her Majesty's Stationery Office.

Kelling, G. L., Pate, T., Dieckman, D., and Brown, C. E. 1974. *The Kansas City Preventive Patrol Experiment: A Technical Report.* Washington, D.C.: Police Foundation.

Larson, R. C., Bier, V. M., Kaplan, E. H., Mattingly, C., Eckels, T. J., Reichman, N., and Berliner, L. S. 1979. *Interim Analysis of 200 Evaluations on Criminal Justice.* Cambridge, Mass.: Operations Research Center, Massachusetts Institute of Technology.

Miller, D. E., Himelson, A. N., and Geis, G. 1967. "The East Los Angeles Halfway House for Felon Addicts." *International Journal of Addictions,* **2**:305–311.

Palmer, T., Bohnstedt, M., and Lewis, R. 1978. *The Evaluation of Juvenile Diversion Projects: Final Report.* Sacramento, Calif: Department of the Youth Authority.

Rossi, P., et al. 1979. *Participation of Target Populations and Monitoring of Delivery of Services.* Washington, D.C.: Law Enforcement Assistance Administration, Department of Justice.

Squire, L. and van der Tak, H. G. 1975. *Economic Analysis of Projects.* Baltimore: Johns Hopkins University Press.

Suchman, E. A. 1967. *Evaluative Research.* New York: Russell Sage.

Thompson, M. 1980. *Benefit-Cost Analysis for Program Evaluation.* Beverly Hills, Calif: Sage Publications.

U.S. Congress 1980. *Oversight on Scared Straight.* Hearings before the Subcommittee on Human Resources, Committee on Education and Labor. 96th Cong., 1st Sess. Washington, D.C.: U.S. Government Printing Office.

CHAPTER 8

DESCRIPTIVE STATISTICS: CENTRAL TENDENCY AND VARIABILITY

CHAPTER OUTLINE

MEASURES OF CENTRAL TENDENCY
  Mean
    Computing the mean
    Deviation from the mean
    Proportion
  Median
  Mode
INDICATORS OF VARIABILITY
  Variance
  Standard Deviation
  Mean Absolute Deviation from the Median
  Range
STANDARD SCORES

A major use of statistical work is to summarize sets of numbers so that their meaning can be conveyed in a simple and easy-to-understand manner. A series of numbers—7, 14, 8, 19, 27, and 6, for instance—can be represented by their *mean* as a single number, 13.5. The mean is derived by totaling the numbers and dividing by how many of them there are; that is, 81 (the total) is divided by 6 (the number of individual items). By use of the arithmetic mean, it becomes possible to determine things such as the average number of arrests in a jurisdiction in a given period, the "typical" age of members of a police force, and the average number of years of education of a group of prisoners.

This chapter will discuss the kind of summary information that can be gained from reducing a set of numbers to simpler dimensions.

Suppose you were asked to describe verbally a set of numbers such as the following: 6, 4, 19, 8, 9, and 5. You might try to do the job by calculating the mean (it is slightly more than 8). Or you might glance at the numbers and decide that their most interesting characteristic is that, generally, they are each less than 10. Or you could say, "Most of them fall between 5 and 10." Or if there were one number which shows up more than the others (there isn't in the set above), you might indicate which number this would be.

Numbers which are used as typical to indicate roughly where the members of a set are located are usually called *indicators of central tendency*. Sometimes they are also referred to as *indicators of location*. After you have indicated a typical measure to represent a series of numbers, you might next try to be more precise in regard to how typical the representative number is. You could say, for instance, in regard to the series we presented above: "Most of the numbers are between 5 and 10, but of the six numbers, one is below 5 and one is above 10." This is more precise, but the statement is beginning to become as cumbersome a method of representing the series as merely listing each number.

The attempt to determine the typicality of a number that represents a larger group of numbers is regarded as a measure of *variability*. If variability turns out to be small, then it becomes apparent that the numbers are pretty much alike, that is, that they do not differ one from the other very much. In such a case, the typical measure might be seen as describing them all quite well. On the other hand, a large variability indicates that the numbers differ considerably and the typical measure does not represent them very well. The point can readily be illustrated by trying to determine the mean weight of the five men on two police special weapons teams, one in the city of Toledo, say, and the other in Cincinnati. Table 6 gives the figures for the men in the two cities.

It takes only a quick glance to see that in Toledo the officers are very close together in weight and in Cincinnati they differ greatly, even though the totals and therefore the means for both cities would be exactly the same.

TABLE 6
WEIGHTS OF FIVE MALE PATROL OFFICERS IN TWO CITIES

Officer	Toledo	Cincinnati
A	165	120
B	175	212
C	168	140
D	172	187
E	166	187
Total	846	846

The aim of measures of variability is to try to represent such distinctions so that a person looking at the summary statement can understand something of the basic variation, such as that between the figures for the officers in Toledo and those for the officers in Cincinnati.

Indicators of variability are sometimes known as *indicators of dispersion* or *spread*. By the use of two numbers, the first giving an idea of the approximate location of the number set and the second providing an indication of the approximate dispersion of the same number set, you are able to convey to others considerable information about the sequence of numbers you are trying to abbreviate. The use of such summary numbers also makes the information conveyed easy to comprehend. This chapter will examine several measures of central tendency and of variability.

MEASURES OF CENTRAL TENDENCY

Mean

The most common measure of central tendency is the arithmetic mean. It is often referred to as the *average*, although technically any measure of central tendency is an average.

The mean, as you know, is used repeatedly in many contexts in American culture; it indicates, among other things, our interest in getting a lot of information in a quick and shorthand manner. We hear about the average IQ of law enforcement officers and of criminals. (Indeed, some years ago there was a flurry of newspaper publicity when a research worker compared the IQs of police officers in a rural southwestern town with those of the inmates of the local jail and discovered that the criminals' IQs were higher. The researcher made a feature story out of the material by wondering in print how it was possible for the criminals to be caught so often if they were "smarter" than those trying to apprehend them.) Television announcers constantly talk about the average weight of linemen on competing football teams and the average height of the forwards on different basketball teams.

Computing the Mean The symbol $\bar{x}$ is widely employed to denote the mean of a set of numbers. Its computational formula is:

$$\bar{x} = \frac{x_1 + x_2 + x_3 + \ldots + x_n}{n}$$

The formula may appear a bit forbidding at first glance, but its use becomes quite simple when you appreciate that x_1 is nothing but the first number in a full set of numbers, x_2 the second, and so forth. x_n then becomes the last number (or the nth) number of the set. If the numbers are 5, 4, and 6, then 5 is x_1 and 6 is x_n. The symbols $+ \ldots +$ mean no more than that you continue adding each number as you did the first ones until you get to the last, or the nth number. The preceding formula sometimes is shortened to the following form:

$$\frac{\sum_{i=1}^{n} x_i}{n}$$

It is important to react to the preceding as a *symbolic set of instructions,* not as an arcane and incomprehensible mathematical formula of complicated origin. With this in mind, it is very easy to follow through on the instructions themselves. It is essential not to confuse failure to remember what the symbols represent with difficulties in mathematical computation. The formula looks very different from what most people are accustomed to dealing with, but the arithmetic involved in working with it can be done by most junior high school pupils. People in our culture readily learn what a comma means, what a period stands for, and what a plus sign and multiplication symbol mean, and so on. Similarly, the formula just before this paragraph merely means that each number in a sequence is added to the others and divided by the total of the numbers in order to obtain the average.

Deviation From the Mean There is a specific feature of the mean that is of particular importance. This is the *deviation from the mean.* It is also called simply the *deviation* when the context in which the term is used makes it clear that the reference is to the mean.

The deviation of a number from the mean of a set of numbers in which the number is embedded is simply that number minus the mean. Take the following four numbers: 10, 8, 6, 4. Their mean is 7. For the number 10, the deviation is 3 (that is, 10 minus the mean of 7). In symbolic terms, the deviation from the mean is represented as $(x_1 - \bar{x})$, with the x_1 standing for the first number and $\bar{x}$, as we know, for the mean itself. The deviation of the second number, therefore, would be $(x_2 - \bar{x})$ (or, for the example: 8 minus 7, or 1). This can be continued for the set of numbers to the nth deviation which is represented as $(x_n - \bar{x})$.

We are now ready to point out an important characteristic associated with deviations: *The sum of the deviations from the mean is equal to zero.* Symbolically, the information can be indicated with the following two formulas:

$$(x_1 - \bar{x}) + (x_2 - \bar{x}) + (x_3 - \bar{x}) + \ldots + (x_n - \bar{x}) = 0$$

or

$$\sum_{i=1}^{n} (x_i - \bar{x}) = 0$$

(We shall prove that result formally later in this chapter.)

Test out the proposition with the set of four numbers noted above: 10, 8, 6, 4. We noted that their mean is 7; the deviation from the mean for 10 was seen to be 3; for 8 it is 1; for 6 it is minus 1 (or –1); and for 4, it is –3. When we take these numbers together we have a total of +4 and –4, or 0. The sum of the deviations from the mean must always equal 0 because of the nature of the operation by which it is derived. Our example illustrates how the numerical sum of deviations of numbers higher than the mean (the + deviations) is exactly equal to the numerical sum of deviations of numbers lower than the mean (the – deviations). In other words, deviations of numbers above the mean exactly balance deviations of numbers below the mean.

Proportion The term *proportion* is sometimes employed in statistical statements to provide a sense of the size of one part of a totality of things. Proportion actually represents a mean of a certain kind, one in which simple substitution of the number 1 is used for the objects whose proportion we are interested in determining and the number 0 for the other objects.

Suppose, for example, there have been 10 muggings within a particular jurisdiction. For each episode, the victim reported what he or she believed to be the sex of the offender. Seven of the muggings were said to have been carried out by men and three by women. The proportion of male muggers obviously is 7 of 10, which would more commonly be represented as .7 or 70 percent. Seventy percent indicates how many of the cases would appear if the total were 100 rather than 10. The word "percent" is a shorthand expression of "for each 100." Since the 10 cases are multiplied by a factor of 10 to reach 100, the number of men involved, 7, is also multiplied by 10 to make the percentage.

Now we assign the number 1 to each male mugger and 0 to each female mugger, and compute the mean of the ten numbers:

$$\frac{1 + 1 + 1 + 1 + 1 + 1 + 1 + 0 + 0 + 0}{10} = \frac{7}{10} = .70$$

We have seen how to convert this to a percentage:

$$\frac{7 \times 10}{10 \times 10} = \frac{70}{100} = 70 \text{ percent}$$

In summary: The proportion of objects in a group which contains two types of objects is exactly equal to the mean of the set of numbers resulting when 1 is assigned to the objects designated by the proportion and 0 is assigned to the other objects.

Median

The symbol *med* is used to denote the median of a set of numbers. The median is defined as the value falling at the midpoint of a set of numbers, that is, at the point where 50 percent of the numbers are above it and 50 percent fall below it. The word *median* derives from Latin, and means "in the middle." (The word *mediator* has the same derivation: a mediator who places himself or herself in the middle, between two disputants.)

To determine med, the set of numbers should be arranged in order from the smallest to the largest number. Take the following example of the crime rates per 100,000 persons for the five largest cities in a state:

$$20.6 \quad 21.2 \quad 23.7 \quad 25.8 \quad 26.4$$

The median crime rate for the largest metropolitan areas in the state is 23.7, the middle figure among the five numbers.

If the *n* (that is, the number of numbers there are) is uneven and the numbers are distinct, it is easy to pinpoint the unique middle figure. Otherwise, the matter becomes more complicated. Suppose, for instance, the *n* is even and the numbers numerically distinct, as in the following crime rates for the six largest areas in the same jurisdiction we considered a few sentences ago:

$$20.6 \quad 21.2 \quad 23.7 \quad 24.1 \quad 25.8 \quad 26.4$$

In cases such as this, the common practice is to take the median as lying halfway between the two midmost members when the set is arranged in numerical order. In the example we have given, these numbers are 23.7 and 24.1. Their average, 23.9, would be regarded as the median for the set.

If there are ties in the middle of the number set so that no single number can be designated as the middle one, the common practice is merely to take the numerical value of the tied scores as the median. Note the following example:

$$20.6 \quad 21.2 \quad 21.2 \quad 23.7 \quad 24.2$$

In this case, 21.2 would be regarded as the median, even though it appears both as the middle number and as the number immediately preceding it. If there are many ties in the middle of a range of numbers, the median probably is not a good indicator to employ as a designator. The problems that may arise concern generalizing from the data at hand to a much larger set of numbers; that is, when the five numbers noted above represent 50 or 500 numbers. But for purely descriptive purposes such difficulties usually are not very important and can be resolved by the simple rules we have indicated in the foregoing paragraphs.

The median should be understood as a balance point for the frequencies of numbers, much as the mean is a balance point for the deviations. The frequencies of measures above the median are balanced by the frequencies of measures below it.

Many times, reports which rely upon statistical materials indicate what they say is the "average" of a set of figures. Very frequently, they have reference to the median of the set of figures rather than the mean. "Average income" for the nation, for example, usually refers to the median income of the group. The reason for this is that very large incomes will produce a certain distortion in the mean, since most salaries are in the range of $10,000 to $25,000, and it is not possible to have a salary below zero.

To illustrate with an exaggerated set of figures, suppose that there are five incomes representing the salaries of the officers of a small rural police department, including the chief, as shown in Table 7. It could be said, with truth, that the "average" salary in the department is $17,580, but this figure would be highly misleading to a person who contemplated joining the force and wanted to know what salary he or she might reasonably look forward to. Nobody on the force except the chief earns more than the average; all the

TABLE 7
SALARIES OF POLICE OFFICERS

Officer	Salary/year
A	$12,400
B	12,400
C	13,800
D	14,200
E	35,100
	$87,900

officers are paid considerably less. The median figure of $13,800 provides a much more useful picture of what a recruit might reasonably anticipate earning—assuming, of course, that inflation did not affect the whole salary scale. It can be seen that a poor community or even one in which there are moderate income levels could be made to seem substantially affluent if there are a few multimillionaires and the mean income is calculated.

Mode

The *mode* of a series of numbers in a set is that number which occurs most frequently. Let us say that we are interested in the modal number of traffic citations issued by the patrol officers in a police department during a 10-day period. Table 8 gives the figures that we have on hand for the small northeastern community that we are studying. The mode for this array of numbers clearly is 5, the figure which appears most often in the set.

The concept of mode is frequently considered in terms of what is called a *relative mode*. A relative mode occurs when the frequency with which a given numerical value is found is larger than the frequencies of occurrence of the nearest neighboring numbers.

Take the following list:

$$1, \quad 2, \quad 2, \quad 3, \quad 5, \quad 5, \quad 5, \quad 6, \quad 7, \quad 7$$

The mode here, as with Table 8, is the number 5. The relative modes would be the numbers 2, 5, and 7. Sets of numbers often are classified according to the number of relative modes they contain. A set with a single mode is called *unimodal*. The figures in Table 8 represent a unimodal distribution. A set with two relative modes is called *bimodal*. One with three relative modes, such as the set in this paragraph, would be called *trimodal*.

TABLE 8
TRAFFIC CITATIONS ISSUED DURING 10-DAY PERIOD

Day	Number of citations
November 10	8
November 11	4
November 12	5
November 13	5
November 14	3
November 16	10
November 17	7
November 18	5
November 19	5
November 20	9

INDICATORS OF VARIABILITY

An indicator of variability is a number which provides information about how the numbers in a set are dispersed or spread out. If the numbers in the set all have approximately the same numerical value, their dispersion from one another is small. But if they are quite different in numerical value, their dispersion is large. An indicator of variability is a single number that reflects the extent to which the numbers are so dispersed or spread out.

When the numbers in a set are much alike in numerical values, they will all be close to their mean or median in numerical value. When they differ markedly in numerical value, there will be numbers in the collection which lie far below the mean or median and others which lie far above the mean or median. The indicator of variability may be regarded as a measure of the typicality of an indicator of central tendency. If the variability is small, the indicator of central tendency will not deviate much from the extreme members of the collection. If, on the other hand, the variability is large, there will be members of the set which have large positive deviations and others which have large negative deviations from the indicator of central tendency. The indicators of variability are based on some measure of the extent to which the individual members of the collection deviate from the mean or median of the collection.

Below, we describe three indicators of variability: the *variance,* the *standard deviation,* and the *mean absolute deviation from the median.* We also note a less basic measure, the *range.*

You might guess that you could use the average of all deviations from the mean or median as a measure of variability. This idea, though it seems reasonable on its face, is not correct. You may remember that when we discussed the mean, we pointed out that the positive deviations from the mean exactly balance the negative ones (that is, they will be something like $+32$ and -32 or any other two figures that together add up to 0). The mean deviation (that is, the sum of the deviations from the mean) will, therefore, always be zero and this result can provide no information about the variability of the collection of numbers.

Although the positive and negative deviations from the median would not exactly cancel out by adding up to zero, there would be sufficient cancellation to make the mean deviation from the median unacceptable as an indicator of variability.

For indicators of variability, the need is to eliminate the cancellation effect. This cancellation tendency (for the median) and cancellation effect (for the mean) can be overcome by squaring all the deviations before averaging. By squaring, we mean multiplying the number by itself: thus, if the deviation is $+2$, the square of the number is 4; if the deviation is -3, the square becomes 9, since two minus numbers when multiplied produce a plus result.

Another method is to take the mean of the absolute deviations, ignoring the minus signs. In this method, deviations from the mean of $+4$, $+2$, -4, and -2 would be totaled to 12 and the mean of the deviations would be 3.

In calculating *variance* and *standard deviation*, the cancellation is prevented by squaring the deviations. In calculating the *mean absolute deviation from the median*, the cancellation is prevented by taking absolute values.

Variance

The variance, designated as S^2, of a set of numbers is simply the sum of the squared deviations from the mean divided by the number of numbers in the set. The formula can be represented in the following symbolic manner:

$$S^2 = \frac{(x_1 - \bar{x})^2 + (x_2 - \bar{x})^2 + \ldots + (x_n - \bar{x})^2}{n}$$

or

$$S^2 = \frac{\sum_{i=1}^{n} (x_i - \bar{x})^2}{n}$$

The definition of the variance (S^2) of a set of numbers may be a new concept for you. If so, it probably has no meaning besides the instruction to add up the squared deviations from the mean and then to divide the sum by n. That is, you would not have any sense of the utility and information conveyed by the result of the process that you are undertaking. The variance does not enjoy the widespread popular use that averages do. Besides, as a means of describing numbers, the variance is completely dominated by a related concept, the standard deviation.

It is worth working through some numerical information in order to illustrate precisely how the variance is derived. Let us calculate the variance for the scores of a group of police recruits taking target shooting tests on the pistol range. The best score is 10 and the poorest score is 0. There are eight recruits in the group we wish to examine, and their reported scores, arranged in ascending order, are: 1, 3, 3, 4, 5, 6, 9, 9. The total for their scores is 40, and the mean therefore equals $40 \div 8$, or 5. We are now ready to substitute the numbers into the formula we presented above. It now reads:

$$S^2 = \frac{\begin{array}{c}(1 - 5)^2 + (3 - 5)^2 + (3 - 5)^2 + (4 - 5)^2 + (5 - 5)^2 + (6 - 5)^2 \\ + (9 - 5)^2 + (9 - 5)^2\end{array}}{8}$$

The calculation then proceeds as follows:

$$S^2 = \frac{(-4)^2 + (-2)^2 + (-2)^2 + (-1)^2 + (0)^2 + (1)^2 + (4)^2 + (4)^2}{8}$$

And thereafter:

$$S^2 = \frac{16 + 4 + 4 + 1 + 0 + 1 + 16 + 16}{8} = \frac{58}{8}$$

So that:

$$S^2 = 7.25$$

Standard Deviation

The standard deviation is the square root of the variance. Indeed, the reason the variance is symbolized by S^2 is to demonstrate its relationship to the standard deviation, which is symbolized by S. Thus, we have:

$$S = \sqrt{\frac{\sum_{i=1}^{n} (x_i - \bar{x})^2}{n}}$$

To provide a beginning intuitive feeling for the standard deviation, it can be noted that the standard deviation for IQ is either 15 or 16, depending upon the particular intelligence test being considered. Moreover, for most characteristics of human beings, about two-thirds of the measures or values fall between one standard deviation below the mean and one standard deviation above the mean. The standard deviation of intelligence as measured by the Stanford-Binet test is 16. Since the mean IQ is 100, one standard deviation below the mean is 84 (100 minus 16) and one standard deviation above the mean is 116 (100 plus 16). Thus, about two-thirds of the IQs of children given the Stanford-Binet test will be between 84 and 116.

Do not be concerned if you do not believe that you have a solid grasp of the meaning of standard deviation as yet. If we assume that you have had no previous encounters with the concept, all you have so far is a formal definition and an example of the application. The definition tells only how to compute the standard deviation from a given set of numbers, and nothing more. Satisfactory understanding or intuitive grasp will come only with exposure to the concept in many contexts, both in this book and subsequently.

You will remember that in the illustration we provided of the variance, S^2 = 7.25. The square root of 7.25 (it can be located in tables which provide square roots, or it can be calculated if you know the method) is 2.69, or, rounded off, 2.7. This means that the pistol range scores showed a mean of 5 with a standard deviation of 2.7. Scores of 2.3 or above (5.0 – 2.7) were within one standard deviation below the mean, and those of 7.7 or below (5.0 + 2.7) were within one standard deviation above the mean. It will be seen that of the eight range scores, five, or about 63 percent, fell within one standard deviation above and below the mean (the scores of 3, 3, 4, 5, and 6). Three (1, 9, 9) fell outside this range.

Mean Absolute Deviation From the Median

The absolute value is defined as the positive value (the + value) of a number, irrespective of whether its sign is plus or minus. Perpendicular lines are put to the left and to the right of a number to specify its absolute value. Thus:

$$| +5 | = | -5 | = 5$$

Therefore, $| x_1 - \text{med} |$ is a positive number regardless of whether x_1 is smaller than the median or larger. $| x_1 - \text{med} |$ represents an absolute deviation from the median, and the same process can be used to calculate the absolute deviation from the mean for each number in the set. Since the results all are positive, we do not have any difficulty that would otherwise occur when the minus values cancel the positive values if the figures are added up.

The mean of the absolute deviations from the median, or the indicator of variability of concern to us now, is indicated as:

$$AD = \frac{| x_1 - \text{med} | + | x_2 - \text{med} | + \cdots + | x_n - \text{med} |}{n}$$

or

$$AD = \frac{\sum_{i=1}^{n} | x_i - \text{med} |}{n}$$

We can return to the illustration earlier in which we took the pistol-range scores of eight police recruits and use the same material to demonstrate how to calculate the mean absolute deviation from the median. The scores were 1, 3, 3, 4, 5, 6, 9, 9. The median for the set is the middle figure. It will be remembered that when there are two figures in the middle (4 and 5 in this instance), the common practice is to take the average of the two, or, for this set, 4.5. Substituting in the formula presented above we now have:

$$AD = \frac{\begin{array}{c} | 1{-}4.5 | + | 3{-}4.5 | + | 3{-}4.5 | + | 4{-}4.5 | + | 5{-}4.5 | \\ + | 6{-}4.5 | + | 9{-}4.5 | + | 9{-}4.5 | \end{array}}{8}$$

This (eliminating the minus sign because of the | | in the formula) reduces to:

$$AD = \frac{|-3.5| + |-1.5| + |-1.5| + |-.5| + |.5| + |1.5| + |4.5| + |4.5|}{8}$$

or

$$AD = \frac{18}{8} = 2.25$$

The mean absolute deviation from the median (AD) is the appropriate indicator of dispersion when it is necessary to use the median rather than the mean as a measure of central tendency. This would be true, for example, in the cases of incomes where there is a distortion in the mean as a representative figure because of a very few extremely high incomes in the distribution. In practice, however, in most contexts in which the median of a set of numbers is given, no indicator of variability accompanies it. Given that state of affairs, together with the fact that S and S^2, but not AD, have great importance in inferential statistics, you may never see the AD mentioned outside of an introductory book such as this one. And if you did run across it in specific applications, it is not likely that a background of meaning will be acquired as with standard deviation, so that a feeling for the importance and sense of the *AD* figure will not become intuitive.

Range

The *range* represents the simplest way of describing the dispersion of a set of numbers. It is simply the highest number in the set minus the lowest number. Clearly it is not a very discriminating indicator, since it depends solely on the values of the highest and lowest numbers. The following two sets of numbers, it can be seen, will have the same range. But we would probably not be comfortable in saying that they have the same dispersion:

Set 1:	4,	5,	5,	5,	5,	6,	6,	47		
Set 2:	4,	8,	12,	16,	18,	24,	27,	31,	39,	47

The usefulness of the range is, consequently, extremely limited.

STANDARD SCORES

Suppose that we have a situation where two numbers are associated with each individual in a certain grouping. For example, the grouping might consist of all police cadets in a certain department. Of the two numbers associated with each cadet, one could be a score of physical agility and the other could be a measure of intelligence. We have, in essence, two sets of numbers, one set consisting of all physical-agility scores (one score associated with each cadet) and one set consisting of all intelligence measures (one measure associated with each cadet). If we learn that cadet A has scores of 281 in physical agility and 57 in intelligence, we might conclude that cadet A is strong and agile but not very bright. But how reasonable is that type of conclusion?

If we are told that the mean of physical agility scores is 331 and the mean of intelligence measures is 42, we have to revise our conclusions about cadet A very drastically. In this case, obviously, cadet A is below average in physical agility and above average in intelligence. The previous conclusion obviously was totally false.

The illustration makes it clear that numbers from two sets can be compared in terms of relative levels only if the sets have identical means. If they have different means, however, it is possible to convert the number sets that we have to other sets in such a manner that equal means can be obtained. Then we can make comparisons that will be informative rather than misleading.

To illustrate: We want to determine the mean of the figures that represent the numbers of traffic tickets written by five traffic control officers in a city during the day that we are examining. We will use the symbol $\bar{x}$ to represent the mean of this set of numbers and $\bar{x}_m$ for the mean of the transformed set. Suppose the traffic figures are as follows: 5, 10, 15, 20, and 25. The mean is 15; that is, $\bar{x} = 15$. If we want to convert this set to a new set that has a mean $\bar{x}_m$ equal to 0 we would only have to subtract 15 from each number in the original set. The new set then becomes –10, –5, 0, 5, 10; and the mean of the new set is 0 ($\bar{x}_m = 0$).

In general, if we have

$$x_1, x_2, x_3, \cdots, x_n \tag{1}$$

as our original number set, with mean equal to $\bar{x}$, then a new set obtained by subtracting $\bar{x}$ from each of these numbers, produces

$$x_1 - \bar{x}, x_2 - \bar{x}, x_3 - \bar{x}, \cdots, x_n - \bar{x} \tag{2}$$

which has mean $\bar{x}_m = 0$.

To prove that $x_m = 0$, remember that, by definition,

$$\bar{x}_m = \frac{(x_1 - \bar{x}) + (x_2 - \bar{x}) + \cdots + (x_n - \bar{x})}{n} \tag{3}$$

or

$$x_m = \frac{\sum_{i=1}^{n} (x_i - \bar{x})}{n} \tag{4}$$

Rearranging terms in the first of these produces

$$\bar{x}_m = \frac{(x_1 + x_2 + \cdots + x_n) - (\bar{x} + \bar{x} + \cdots + \bar{x})}{n} \tag{5}$$

And this can be written as

$$\bar{x}_m = \frac{x_1 + x_2 + \cdots + x_n}{n} - \frac{n\bar{x}}{n} \tag{6}$$

since there are n values of $\bar{x}$ in the second parentheses (one for each number in the set of n numbers).

And, we have

$$\bar{x}_m = \bar{x} - \bar{x} = 0 \tag{7}$$

Let us substitute numbers in formula (5) above, using the traffic ticket totals that we discussed a moment ago. The formula with the numbers inserted looks like this:

$$\bar{x}_m = \frac{(5 + 10 + 15 + 20 + 25) - (15 + 15 + 15 + 15 + 15)}{5}$$

$$= \frac{75 - 75}{5} = \frac{0}{5} = 0$$

Thus, if we have one set of scores with mean $\bar{x}_1$ and another with mean $\bar{x}_2$, we can convert them to two different sets, each with mean 0, by subtracting $\bar{x}_1$ from each number in set 1 and $\bar{x}_2$ from each number in set 2.

This process represents a move in the right direction in order to make comparisons like the one between scores on physical agility and on intelligence that we noted at the outset of this discussion. But it is not enough. The reason why this is so is that the two sets of numbers may differ markedly in terms of their standard deviations. Even though each original set of numbers may be converted to a set with a mean of zero, a given number may be far above the mean for one set and just barely above the mean for the other set. It would, as we know, be far above the mean if all numbers were tightly compacted around the mean (that is, if there were a small standard deviation) and just barely above the mean if the numbers were widely spread out, as, for example, if they were between −1000 and +1000 (in which case they would have a large standard deviation).

It would seem desirable, therefore, to equate standard deviations between the two number sets. A widely used convention is to employ a standard deviation of 1 (that is, $S = 1$) as the basis.

Conversion to a standard deviation of 1 is accomplished by using the set that has a mean equal to zero. In our example, this was the set that we converted from 5, 10, 15, 20, 25, to −10, −5, 0, 5, 10, and whose mean then became 0 ($\bar{x}_m = 0$). The set with −10 as its first number is the one that is employed for conversion to a standard deviation of 1. Each number of the set is divided by the original standard deviation. It should be noted that the standard deviation of the original set of numbers is not changed by the process of subtracting a constant (in this case $\bar{x}$) from each number. That is, the standard deviation of the set with mean zero is equal to the standard deviation of the original set.

In symbolic form, the full conversion takes the form:

$$\frac{x_1 - \bar{x}}{s}, \quad \frac{x_2 - \bar{x}}{s}, \quad \ldots, \quad \frac{\bar{x}_n - \bar{x}}{s}$$

That is, the original mean is subtracted from each number, and this difference is then divided by the original standard deviation.

The first step is to calculate the denominator of the formula for conversion. It might be useful to review this process here. First, we know that the mean of the five numbers (5, 10, 15, 20, and 25) is 15; that is, the total 75 divided by the number 5. Then we substitute in the formula as follows:

$$S^2 = \frac{(5 - 15)^2 + (10 - 15)^2 + (15 - 15)^2 + (20 - 15)^2 + (25 - 15)^2}{5}$$

$$= \frac{(-10)^2 + (-5)^2 + (0)^2 + (5)^2 + (10)^2}{5}$$

$$= \frac{100 + 25 + 0 + 25 + 100}{5}$$

$$= \frac{250}{5}$$

$$= 50$$

S^2 therefore equals 50. And to obtain the standard deviation we take the square root of 50, which is 7.07. We have now located the denominator. Next, we are required to divide each number in the new set by the original standard deviation. Therefore, we have:

$$\frac{-10}{7.07}, \quad \frac{-5}{7.07}, \quad \frac{0}{7.07}, \quad \frac{5}{7.07}, \quad \frac{10}{7.07}$$

This produces a new set of numbers, which are in turn: -1.41, -.707, 0, .707, and 1.41. The numbers in the new set are called *standard scores* because they provide a standard for comparing different sets. Standard scores take on even more meaning when the numbers follow a normal distribution, but much more of that comes later in the book. The reason the word *scores* is used (rather than merely *numbers*) in the expression *standard scores* is that the method of conversion has the widest use in the realm of educational and psychological testing, where test results are called scores.

The calculation of the new standard deviation for this series would adhere to the following process. Note that the mean of the set is 0, so that the S^2 formula looks as follows with the numbers inserted.

$$
\begin{aligned}
S^2 &= \frac{(-1.41 - 0)^2 + (-.707 - 0)^2 + (0 - 0)^2 + (.707 - 0)^2 + (1.41 - 0)^2}{5} \\
&= \frac{1.99 + .50 + 0 + .50 + 1.99}{5} \\
&= \frac{4.98}{5} \\
&= 1.0 \text{ approximately}
\end{aligned}
$$

The square root of 1.0 is, of course, 1.0 (that is, 1 and 1 are the numbers that multiplied together give 1). The new set of numbers therefore has a standard deviation of one ($S_n = 1$).

A standard score, often designated by the letter z, is expressed in general form as:

$$
z = \frac{x - \bar{x}}{s}
$$

where no ambiguity results from omission of subscripts.

CHAPTER 9

DESCRIPTIVE STATISTICS: CORRELATION

CHAPTER OUTLINE

THE PRODUCT-MOMENT CORRELATION COEFFICIENT

THE MEANING OF CORRELATION

Scatter Diagrams

Correlation in Everyday Phenomena

Examples of Use of Correlation Coefficients

Poverty and crime

Peer group approval and female delinquency

OTHER MEASURES OF CORRELATION

Curvilinear Relationships

Dichotomous Data

Point-biserial correlation coefficient

Phi coefficients

Ranked Data

Spearman's rank-order correlation coefficient

Kendall's tau

CORRELATION AND CAUSATION

REFERENCES

The terms *relation* and *relationship* indicate a connectedness between two or more objects, events, or people. There is, for example, a relationship between the amount of forcible rape and the time of the year, with virtually all studies indicating that the rate of the offense increases during the summer. Most crimes of violence, in fact, go up when the weather turns hot. There is also a relationship of sorts between a prison guard and an inmate; indeed, an excellent study of this relationship by Gresham Sykes shows how members of each group adjust their behavior considerably in order to appease and get along with each other. It seems on first glance that all the power resides with the prison guards, but closer scrutiny shows that subtle kinds of retaliation by prisoners, including sarcasm, slow response, and constant hassling can make the guards' lives miserable; so an accommodation is reached. Thus, we have another illustration of a kind of relationship or connectedness between groups.

In the same fashion, there can exist relationships of diverse kinds between sets of numbers. For example, we can have two sets of numbers that represent the scores of persons who are studying for promotion within the probation department. In the realm of statistics, the word *correlation* is employed to refer to a particular kind of relationship between sets of numbers. Let's look for the moment at the two sets of numbers shown in Table 9, all of which represent different scores on tests earned by the persons in the training class.

Let us assume that set A_1 represents the scores of members of the class for a test on leadership given in November; and set A_2 their scores on a December examination. The small letters, such as "a" and "b," represent the individual members of the class. Let sets B_1 and B_2 represent the scores of the same group of students at the same time periods for a test on criminal law.

It seems obvious on inspection that the sets B_1 and B_2 go together more than sets A_1 and A_2 do. That is, where B_1 is high, B_2 tends to be high; where B_1 is low, B_2 tends to be low; and so forth over the range of paired values. This is not the case for the A_1-A_2 pairs. Just look at the numbers under *a* for all four sets. In the B pair, the figures are 23 and 20, numbers much closer

TABLE 9
TEST SCORES (ARRANGED BY SETS) IN A TRAINING CLASS

Pair	Class members							
	a	b	c	d	e	f	g	h
Set A_1	21	17	14	14	11	9	8	4
Set A_2	11	6	9	22	3	18	7	14
Set B_1	23	19	15	14	9	9	6	5
Set B_2	20	17	18	12	12	10	7	3

together than the 21 and 11 that we find under the A pairs; and the same situation pretty well holds for the rest of the figures in the four sets, those in the B group coming closer together than those in the A group. If necessary we could predict the other member of a pair when the value of only one is known more easily in the case of the B_1-B_2 group than in the case of the A_1-A_2 group. Later we will see that the principles of correlation and prediction are related.

THE PRODUCT-MOMENT CORRELATION COEFFICIENT

We would like to have a single number to express the degree of relationship between two sets of numbers in the sense that high numbers in one set go with high numbers in the other set, low numbers with low numbers, and so forth. The aim again is to reduce complexity so that we have a simpler representation and, at the same time, an informative shortened manner of conveying important information about numbers. How can we proceed with the present question?

Suppose, as a first attempt to arrive at a descriptive number of the sort we desire, we multiply the paired numbers and add up the results of the multiplication process. The results for two number pairs for a different set of scores would look like Table 10. Examination and comparison of the sets represented by C_1 and C_2 indicate that the C numbers go together more closely than the D numbers. Assuredly, two of the figures in the D sets (the pair of 6's and the 8 and 9) are very close together, but note that the highest number in D_1 is paired with the second lowest number in D_2. In the C sets, highest goes with highest, lowest with lowest, and so on. This observational conclusion is reflected in the products, which show C at 185, which is larger than the sum for D (172). So far so good.

Let us try the same process on another two sets, as shown in Table 11. The sum of cross-products again produces the desired result: the higher total appears with the number pairs that seem more closely related; that is,

TABLE 10
SCORES ARRANGED BY SETS WITH THE PRODUCTS CALCULATED

Sets C			Sets D		
C_1	C_2	Product	D_1	D_2	Product
10	9	90	10	5	50
8	6	48	8	9	72
7	5	35	7	2	14
6	2	12	6	6	36
		Sum 185			Sum 172

TABLE 11
SERIES ARRANGED BY SETS WITH PRODUCTS CALCULATED

Sets E			Sets F		
E_1	E_2	Product	F_1	F_2	Product
23	25	575	23	3	69
17	19	323	17	12	204
14	12	168	14	25	350
9	8	72	9	8	72
7	8	56	7	19	133
2	3	6	2	8	16
		Sum 1200			Sum 844

the total 1200 appears with the E sets, and the total 844 appears with the F sets.

There are, however, problems associated with using the sum of the cross-products. We camouflaged one problem by the way that we arranged the various sets of numbers. If you want to check it out, you will be able to see that the numbers in C and D and those in E and F are, when examined individually, exactly the same. Take the E and F sets for example: arranged in ascending order, E_1 has: 2, 7, 9, 14, 17, and 23. F_1 has precisely the same numbers. Similarly for E_2 and F_2, the only difference being the manner in which the numbers were put together, that is, how they were ordered. The four sets were rigged in that manner to avoid the problem of higher cross-products resulting primarily from higher number values. That is, even when a given pair of number sets seem more closely correlated than another pair, the sum of cross-products of the latter may be higher than the sum of cross-products of the former if the numbers themselves are larger.

Table 12 illustrates the process.

TABLE 12
SERIES ARRANGED BY SETS WITH PRODUCTS CALCULATED

Sets G			Sets H		
G_1	G_2	Product	H_1	H_2	Product
15	17	255	36	17	612
9	14	126	29	15	435
8	11	88	19	32	608
4	7	28	12	8	96
		Sum 497			Sum 1751

TABLE 13
MEANS AND STANDARD DEVIATIONS FOR FOUR SETS OF NUMBERS

	G_1	G_2	H_1	H_2
Mean	9.00	12.25	24.00	18.00
Standard deviation	3.94	3.70	9.19	8.75

The sum of cross-products is considerably higher for the pairs in sets H than in sets G—1751 versus 497. But it seems clear that the correlation is higher between the pairs in G than it is between the pairs in H.

Let us see what happens when we convert all numbers to standard scores (Z scores) and then again compute the sum of the cross-products. For that conversion, we first calculate the information shown in Table 13.

Let's do the mathematics on sets G, to make certain we know the process by which the numbers in Table 13 were derived.

The mean of G_1 is reached by adding $15 + 9 + 8 + 4$ and dividing the number of numbers in the column by 4, so that $36 \div 4 = 9$. Then we move to the following calculation to obtain the standard deviation:

$$S^2 = \frac{(15 - 9)^2 + (9 - 9)^2 + (8 - 9)^2 + (4 - 9)^2}{4}$$
$$= \frac{6^2 + 0^2 + (-1)^2 + (-5)^2}{4}$$
$$= \frac{36 + 0 + 1 + 25}{4} = \frac{62}{4} = 15.5$$

The variance, then, is 15.5, and the square root of 15.5 is 3.94.

To obtain standard scores we proceed as follows:

$$\frac{15 - 9}{3.94}, \quad \frac{9 - 9}{3.94}, \quad \frac{8 - 9}{3.94}, \quad \frac{4 - 9}{3.94}$$

which gives us the figures listed in Table 14 for column G_1. Similar procedures provide the figures for sets G_2, H_1 and H_2 shown in Table 14.

The sum of cross-products for G (3.83) is now considerably higher than for H (0.29), as one would expect on the basis of overall observation of the original number sets G and H. In terms of the notation used in the book, the symbolic expression for the sum of cross-products of standard scores is:

$$\sum_{i=1}^{n} z_{x_i} z_{y_i}$$

TABLE 14
SUMS OF PRODUCTS OF STANDARD SCORES FOR FOUR SETS OF NUMBERS

Set G (z scores)			Set H (z scores)		
G₁	**G₂**	**Product**	**H₁**	**H₂**	**Product**
+ 1.52	+ 1.28	+ 1.95	+ 1.31	− .12	− .16
0	+ .47	0	+ .54	− .34	− .18
− .25	− .33	+ .08	− .54	+ 1.60	− .86
− 1.27	− 1.42	+ 1.80	− 1.31	− 1.14	+ 1.49
		Sum 3.83			Sum .29

where n is the number of pairs, z_{x_i} is the z score corresponding to the number x_i, and z_{y_i} is the z score corresponding to the number y_i. In terms of the z scores for sets G this quantity is:

$$(1.52)(1.28) \ + \ (0)(.47) \ + \ (-.25)(-.33) \ + \ (-1.27)(-1.42) \ = \ 3.83$$

The sum in the foregoing equation is a function of the number of z scores being added. In our examples we avoided this difficulty by arranging to have all comparison sets of equal size. Thus, sets C and D have four numbers each, sets E and F six numbers each, and sets G and H four numbers each. But, clearly, if one set has very few number pairs and another set has many number pairs, the sum of z-score cross-products for the set with many numbers may be larger even when the pairs have a lower relationship.

That difficulty is overcome by dividing the sum of cross-products by the number of pairs. That compensates for different sizes by providing an average cross-product of z scores. The resulting form is:

$$\frac{\sum\limits_{i=1}^{n} z_{x_i} z_{y_i}}{n}$$

Indeed, that is the definition of *product-moment correlation coefficient*. It was originally proposed by Karl Pearson and is designated by the letter r. Another form in which r is frequently expressed is obtained by substitution of the x and y equivalents for z_{x_i} and z_{y_i} respectively. Thus, we use

$$z_{x_i} \ = \ \frac{x_i - \bar{x}}{S_x}$$

and

$$z_{y_i} \ = \ \frac{y_i - \bar{y}}{S_y}$$

And we have

$$r = \frac{\sum\limits_{i=1}^{n} z_{x_i} z_{y_i}}{n} = \frac{\sum\limits_{i=1}^{n} \left(\frac{x_i - \bar{x}}{S_x}\right)\left(\frac{y_i - \bar{y}}{S_y}\right)}{n}$$

$$= \frac{\sum\limits_{i=1}^{n} (x_i - \bar{x})(y_i - \bar{y})}{nS_x S_y}$$

In actual practice, the formula is rarely used, since there are simpler forms (for calculational purposes) that can be readily derived algebraically. Moreover, one of the available computer programs should be used where there are more than a few calculations necessary.

A simpler calculational form is the following:

$$r = \frac{\sum\limits_{i=1}^{n} x_i y_i - n\bar{x}\,\bar{y}}{nS_x S_y}$$

This form has the advantage of avoiding the necessity of calculating standard scores.

Using the definition of the correlation coefficient, we obtain the following coefficients for sets G and H, using both the original form and the direct computational form:

For sets G, we have

$$r = \frac{\sum\limits_{i=1}^{n} z_{x_i} z_{y_i}}{n}$$

$$= \frac{(1.52)(1.28) + (0)(.47) + (-.25)(-.33) + (-1.27)(-1.42)}{4}$$

$$= \frac{1.95 + 0 + .08 + 1.80}{4} = \frac{3.83}{4} = .96$$

or $\quad r = \dfrac{\sum\limits_{i=1}^{n} x_i y_i - n\bar{x}\,\bar{y}}{nS_x S_y}$

$$= \frac{(15)(17) + (9)(14) + (8)(11) + (4)(7) - 4(9.00)(12.25)}{4(3.94)(3.70)}$$

$$= \frac{497 - 441}{58.31} = \frac{56}{58.31} = .96$$

Now, for sets H:

$$r = \frac{\sum_{i=1}^{n} z_{x_i} z_{y_i}}{n} = \frac{.29}{4} = .07 = \frac{\sum_{i=1}^{n} x_i y_i - n\,\bar{x}\bar{y}}{n S_x S_y}$$

$$= \frac{1751 - 4(24.00)(18.00)}{4(9.19)(8.75)} = \frac{1751 - 1728}{321.65} = \frac{23}{321.65} = .07$$

There is a complication which we have been avoiding thus far. The correlation is higher, in a numerical sense, if high numbers in the first set go with low numbers in the second set, middle numbers in the first set go with middle numbers in the second set, and low numbers in the first set go with high numbers in the second set. The relationship where high goes with low and low with high is referred to as a *negative relationship*—as opposed to a *positive relationship*, where high goes with high and low with low. Indeed, when high goes with low and low with high, the correlation coefficient is a negative number, as we shall show you with various illustrations.

The numerical value of a correlation coefficient, then, indicates the degree of relationship, and its sign (positive or negative) indicates the direction of the relationship. The highest possible correlation is 1.00, which is +1.00 in the case of a positive relationship and −1.00 in the case of a negative relationship. The lowest possible correlation is 0, indicating no relationship (or predictability) between number sets.

We found the following correlations: for sets G, $r = .96$ and for sets H, $r = .07$. Now, suppose the numbers in columns G_2 and H_2 were reversed to produce the sets shown in Table 15. Notice that G_1' and G_2' are just as predictable from each other as are G_1 and G_2. Only now one predicts a low number corresponding to a high number and a high number corresponding to a low number. And H_1' and H_2' remain unpredictable from each other in the sense that one does not know whether to predict high or low in H_2' when given a high number (or a low number) in H_1' (and vice versa).

TABLE 15
REARRANGEMENT OF NUMBER SETS G_1 AND G_2, AND H_1 AND H_2

Sets G'		Sets H'	
G_1'	G_2'	H_1'	H_2'
15	7	36	8
9	11	29	32
8	14	19	15
4	17	12	17

TABLE 16
PRODUCT SUMS OF G′ AND H′

Sets G′			Sets H′		
G_1'	G_2'	Product	H_1'	H_1'	Product
15	7	105	36	8	288
9	11	99	29	32	928
8	14	112	19	15	285
4	17	68	12	17	204
		Sum 384			Sum 1705

We now compute the correlations as in Table 16. For G′:

$$r = \frac{\sum_{i=1}^{n} x_i y_i - n\,\bar{x}\bar{y}}{nS_x S_y} = \frac{384 - 441}{58.31} = \frac{-57.00}{58.31} = -.98$$

And for H_1':

$$r = \frac{1705 - 1728}{321.65} = \frac{-23}{321.65} = -.07$$

THE MEANING OF CORRELATION

The definition of the correlation coefficient is not very helpful in providing an intuitive grasp for those who have not been exposed to the concept before. So far, the result of the calculations seems to be no more than merely a number that appears to reflect the degree to which numbers in one set go with numbers in another set—high with high, and low with low. Our next task is to provide illustrative information, starting a process that will lead to a general understanding of the meaning and implications of a correlation coefficient, so that if you are told that $r = .56$, you will have some feeling for the term in regard to the information it conveys about the world of relationships.

Scatter Diagrams

A start toward fleshing out the bare bones of the idea of the correlation coefficient can be made by a visual depiction. A pictorial representation that has a point for every pair of numbers being correlated is called a *scatter diagram*.

TABLE 17
SENTENCES OF JUDGES IN SIMULATED TRIALS,
BY MONTHS

Defendant	Judge A (x axis)	Judge B (y axis)
a	10	8
b	7	9
c	5	2
d	8	6
e	6	4
f	1	2
g	7	6

Consider the sets of numbers in Table 17, for example. We will proceed with producing a scatter diagram for the number pairs. The numbers on the x axis may be taken to represent the sentences assigned to each of seven convicted defendants by one judge in a simulated trial; the numbers on the y axis represent sentences by another judge in the simulated trials.

To plot the scatter diagram for these figures, we merely set up a graph with a y axis (running from bottom to top on the figure) and an x axis (running from left to right on the figure). Then we plot the numbers for Judge A on the x axis and those for Judge B on the y axis for each defendant, with the scatter diagram shown in Figure 3 emerging.

Let us now consider the scatter diagrams for three special cases, where r = +1.00, r = −1.00, and r = 0; see Figures 4, 5, and 6.

As may readily be seen, when there is a perfect positive correlation (that is, r = +1.00) or a perfect negative correlation (that is, r = −1.00), all the points on the scatter diagram fall in a straight line. That state of affairs reflects the fact that the product-moment correlation measures linear relationships between number sets. The line moves from lower left to upper right when r = +1.00 (since low goes with low and high with high) and from upper left to lower right when r = −1.00 (since high goes with low and low with high). When the correlation is zero, the points are scattered throughout the scatter diagram without any indication of relationship between the numbers.

It is easy to comprehend in the three scatter diagrams the relationship of correlation to predictability. When the correlation is perfect, knowing any number on one axis allows immediate determination of what its pair-mate is on the other axis. Suppose, for example, we correlated two sets of target-shooting scores, x (for a rifle) and y (for a handgun), and found a correlation of +1.00. If an individual comes along with a score on test x but none on test y, we can predict his or her score on y immediately by going up vertically from the score on the x axis of the scatter diagram (for +1.00) to the intersection of that vertical line with the line connecting the points in the

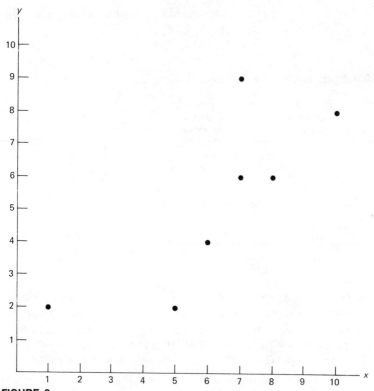

FIGURE 3
Scatter-diagram representation of numbers in Table 17.

FIGURE 4
Scatter diagram for $r = +1.00$.

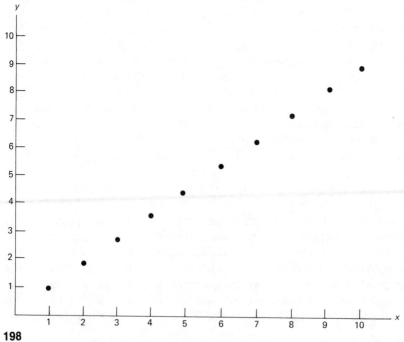

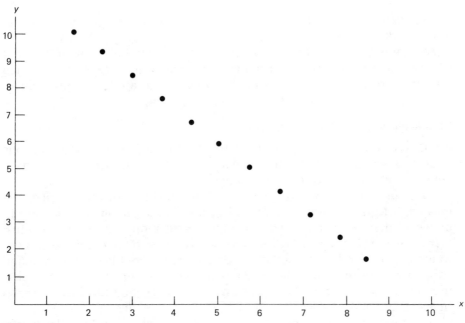

FIGURE 5
Scatter diagram for $r = -1.00$.

FIGURE 6
Scatter diagram for $r = 0$.

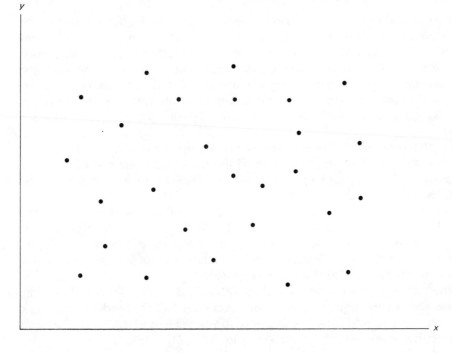

scatter diagram, then reading the corresponding y score on a horizontal move to the y axis.

The same predictability is apparent when $r = -1.00$. But notice that when $r = 0$, there is no way of predicting a y value when an x is known, since the same array of y values is associated with each and every possible x.

Correlation in Everyday Phenomena

Another way of assigning meaning to correlation coefficients of various sizes is to anchor them to phenomena and relationships for which we have general cultural or intuitive knowledge.

Thus, people are generally aware of the meaning of intelligence, the meaning of grade point average (GPA), and the approximate relationship between them. Knowing the approximate correlation between intelligence test score and GPA, therefore, allows one to attach a bit of empirical content to the actual correlation coefficient. At the high school level, the obtained correlations between total score on a group intelligence test (in particular, the School and College Ability Tests, Series II, Level 2) and GPA ranged between .59 and .68 over the four high school grades.

And tests of general intellectual ability used at the college level (the Scholastic Aptitude Test and the American College Testing Program Battery) show correlations of about .50 with college GPAs.

Examples of Use of Correlation Coefficients

Poverty and Crime The manner in which correlation coefficients may be employed to provide understanding of relationships among diverse forms of information can be gleaned from Table 18. The table is taken from a book that seeks to demonstrate the association between economic indices and the amount of crime that emerges in a social system. The paired numbers for each correlation determination are index crime rates and measures of relative poverty; for each such correlation there are 193 pairs (one for each city).

The table offers 14 different correlation coefficients. The author reaches the conclusion set out below. Examine the table and make certain that you understand the relationships indicated. It should be understood that he uses the term *significantly related* to refer to a certain level of correlation, a matter which we have not yet come to. But the fundamental reach of the conclusion is easily determined from the table. So too can the student obtain some idea of the range and direction of different correlation coefficients that can be derived from an examination of sets of numbers (in this case crime rates and indices of poverty).

The author's conclusion, based on Table 18, is: "Percentage of families below the poverty line and percentage receiving half the median income or less are both significantly related only to homicide and aggravated assault out of the seven offenses" (Braithwaite, 1979:213–214).

TABLE 18
CORRELATIONS BETWEEN UCR INDEX CRIME RATES AND TWO ECONOMIC INDICES OF INCOME INEQUALITY
FOR 193 UNITED STATES CITIES

		Homicide	Rape	Robbery	Aggravated assault	Burglary	Grand larceny	Automobile theft
% below poverty line	r	.351	.087	-.121	.310	.049	-.081	-.158
% receiving half the median income or less	r	.255	.087	-.048	.251	.070	.004	-.043

TABLE 19
REFERENCE GROUP SUPPORT FOR DELINQUENCY
IN RELATIONSHIP TO SELF-REPORTED INVOLVEMENT (n = 191)

	Whites		Blacks	
	Mean approval	Association with delinquent activity *r*	Mean approval	Association with delinquent activity *r*
Girls I hang around with	29.38	.33	27.00	.29
Guys I hang around with	26.97	.01	24.74	.24
Boyfriend	22.74	.02	26.15	.18

Peer Group Approval and Female Delinquency   Another illustration of the use of a correlation coefficient to highlight research findings appears in the work of Giordano (1978) on female delinquency. As part of her work, Giordano obtained information on the relationship between the amount of support black and white delinquent girls believed they had from persons in their peer groups and the amount of delinquent behavior in which they participated.

The resultant table (Table 19) shows the scores of approval, using a mean indicator with whose calculation you are familiar, and then supplying the correlation coefficient.

The n = 191 in the title of Table 19 indicates the number of persons who were included in the study; that is, the number of pairs in each correlation determination.

The author's conclusion is one that, at this point, you could supply yourself after you had properly calculated the tables. Giordano notes:

> The correlation between the perception of approval from other reference groups and actual delinquency involvement is also presented in [the table]. There are significant correlations, for both black and white subsamples, between the extent of approval from other *girlfriends* and actual participation in delinquency (p. 131).

Again, as noted earlier, the idea of significance involves a calculation a bit beyond those we have explored so far, but the general idea of relationship as expressed by correlation coefficient can be comprehended from the figures in the table.

OTHER MEASURES OF CORRELATION

Curvilinear Relationships

The product-moment correlation coefficient describes the linear relationship between two sets of numbers. It is insensitive to many relationships that may be curvilinear in form.

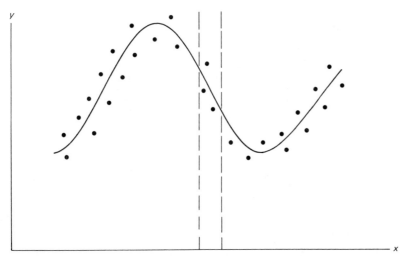

FIGURE 7
Scatter diagram showing a curvilinear relationship between two sets of numbers.

Consider, for example, the points in Figure 7, a scatter diagram showing a curvilinear relationship between two sets of numbers. The product-moment coefficient is very nearly zero, but there is clearly some relationship, as may be seen by a wavy line that has been added to the diagram to follow the general trend of the points. That is, while the number sets have no linear relationship (high with high, low with low, etc., or high with low, low with high, etc.), they are related in some more complicated manner, as shown by the curve. It is occasionally desirable to describe the degree of curvilinear relationship between the two number sets, and various measures have been developed for this purpose.

One such measure is the *correlation ratio* or *eta coefficient*. The eta coefficient is defined in terms of the increase in predictive precision created by the curvilinear relationship. Suppose we are predicting from x to y and that there is a large enough set of number pairs such that each value of x has several different values of y associated with it. By that we mean that there may be pairings like those in Table 20.

The x value 12, it can be seen readily, has the y values 21, 14, 24, and 8 associated with it, and the x value 14 has 7 and 16 associated with it, and so on. Take a given x: the y's associated with it fall in a column like that shown in the dotted lines in Figure 7. To predict the y value corresponding to that x value, a reasonable choice would be to pick the mean y for the points that fall in the column, or, in other words, the mean of the y value associated with that x. And that would entail a different prediction depending upon the location of the column, or, in other words, the particular x value used in the prediction.

TABLE 20
NUMBER SETS AS BASIS FOR
CORRELATION RATIO MEASURE

x	y
12	21
12	14
12	24
12	24
12	8
13	16
14	7
14	16
15	8
15	24
15	18

If you did not know the curvilinear relationship between x and y, you could make only a grosser prediction on the basis of the entire set of y values. Thus, the curvilinear relationship clearly enhances predictability.

You can define the mean of the y's associated with the value x_i as $\bar{y}_i'$. In the above table, for example, the $\bar{y}_i$ corresponding to the x value 12 is

$$\frac{21 + 14 + 24 + 24 + 8}{5} = 18.2$$

The $\bar{y}_i'$ values are the ones we used in predicting y from x. The eta coefficient is defined as

$$\eta = \frac{\text{standard deviation of the } \bar{y}_i' \text{ values}}{\text{standard deviation of all } y\text{'s}}$$

There are, of course, as many values of $\bar{y}_i'$ as there are of x.

Unlike the situation with the product-moment correlation coefficient, there are two correlation ratios in each relevant case. In addition to the one illustrated above, there is one for the prediction from y to x. The two ratios very rarely will be equal. To determine the correlation ratio for the prediction y to x, one uses the mean value of the x's associated with y_j ($\bar{x}_j'$) and proceeds in the manner just described.

The correlation ratio is not a widely used descriptive measure, but appreciating its status gives insight into limitations of the product-moment correlation coefficient. A more extended discussion of the correlation ratio, including its ties with more advanced statistical analyses and arguments for its relevance, may be found in Guilford and Fruchter (1973).

Dichotomous Data

In all examples presented thus far, there were n pairs of numbers where the numbers in each pair came from a certain range of values. For example, intelligence quotients are values in the range of (roughly) 90 to 160 for high school and college students, and GPAs are in the range .5 to 4.0. One person might have an IQ of 129 and a GPA of 3.6; a second person, an IQ of 107 and a GPA of 2.3; a third person, an IQ of 158 and a GPA of 2.7, and so forth over the ranges.

Sometimes, however, we do not have paired numbers of that sort but only dichotomous categorical information, that is, information that people fall into one of two categories. The dichotomous categorization may be the case for either or both variables. Dichotomous variables that might appear are: male or female, black or white, married or single, "police officer used deadly force" or "police officer did not use deadly force," "bachelor's degree obtained in criminal justice" or "bachelor's degree obtained in some other field."

Point-Biserial Correlation Coefficient An approach to obtaining a correlation with a dichotomous variable is to assign the value 0 to one of the categories and the value 1 to the other.

In the dichotomy "male or female" we might, thus, assign 0 to male and 1 to female (or vice versa). We would then compute a product-moment correlation coefficient in the usual way. Suppose we wish to determine if there is any relationship between sex and fear of crime. We can develop a questionnaire that produces a measure of fear of crime in the range 0 (no fear) to 25 (maximum fear). The results from a sample of both sexes are shown in Table 21.

TABLE 21
RESULTS OF SURVEY OF FEAR OF CRIME,
BY SEX

Fear of crime	Sex
14	M
15	F
2	M
22	F
11	F
7	M
9	M
14	M
24	F
11	M
19	F

TABLE 22
RESULTS OF SURVEY OF FEAR OF CRIME
WITH SEX INDICATED AS M = 0; F = 1

Case	Fear of crime	Sex
A	14	0
B	15	1
C	2	0
D	22	1
E	11	1
F	7	0
G	9	0
H	14	0
I	24	1
J	11	0
K	19	1

Assigning a 0 to each M and a 1 to each F, we use the number pairs shown in Table 22 to compute a product-moment correlation coefficient.

The correlation coefficient has a special name and a special computational formula when the data are dichotomous for one variable, despite the fact that it is a product-moment coefficient. It is called the *point-biserial correlation coefficient,* symbolized as r_{pbi}. One can obtain r_{pbi} by use of one of the defining formulas for the product-moment coefficient. However, because of the special assignment of the values 0 and 1 to one variable, a simplified form is available. Let the *x* variable be the one with a full range of numbers (like "fear of crime" above) and the *y* variable be the dichotomous one with values 0 and 1; the formula may then be written:

$$r_{pbi} = \frac{\bar{x}_p - \bar{x}_q}{S_x} pq$$

where $\bar{x}_p$ = mean of those *x*'s corresponding to *y*'s equal to 1
  $\bar{x}_q$ = mean of those *x*'s corresponding to *y*'s equal to 0
  S_x = standard deviation of all *x*'s
  p = proportion of *y*'s with values equal to 1
  q = proportion of *y*'s with values equal to 0

In the data shown in Table 22,

$$\bar{x}_p = \frac{15 + 22 + 11 + 24 + 19}{5} = \frac{91}{5} = 18.20$$

$$\bar{x}_q = \frac{14 + 2 + 7 + 9 + 14 + 11}{6} = \frac{57}{6} = 9.50$$

$$S_x = 6.21$$

$$p = \frac{5}{11} = .45$$

$$q = \frac{6}{11} = .55$$

so that

$$r_{pbi} = \frac{18.20 - 9.50}{6.21} \, (.45) \, (.55) = .35$$

Phi Coefficients   When the data of both variables are dichotomous, you can assign a $+1$ to one of the two categories in each case and a 0 to the other. We have done this in Table 23, with "fear of crime" represented as 1 when it is high and 0 when it is low. In particular, if the "fear of crime" measure is 14 or above, it is considered high and assigned 1; if the measure is 11 or below, it is considered low and assigned a 0. The sex designations are similar to those we employed earlier, with the 0s representing the males and the 1s the females.

When $+1$ and 0 are assigned to each of the dichotomous variables in this way, one can proceed to calculate a product-moment coefficient in the usual way. However, owing to the simplicity of the form of the data, there is again a simplified formula for calculational purposes. The resulting correlation value is called the *phi coefficient*. Consider Table 24, which would result from a situation like that described.

Table 24 represents the case where *a* cases received a 1 on the vertical variable and a 0 on the horizontal variable, *b* received 1 on both variables, *c*

TABLE 23
FEAR OF CRIME DICHOTOMIZED BY SEX

Case	Fear of crime	Sex
A	1	0
B	1	1
C	0	0
D	1	1
E	0	1
F	0	0
G	0	0
H	1	0
I	1	1
J	0	0
K	1	1

TABLE 24
SUMMARIZING DATA FOR PHI COEFFICIENT

	0	+1	
+1	a	b	a + b
0	c	d	c + d
	a + c	b + d	n

received 0 on both variables, and d received 0 on the vertical variable and 1 on the horizontal variable. The phi coefficient, which is written as ϕ, is then

$$\phi = \frac{bc - ad}{\sqrt{(a + b)\,(a + c)\,(b + d)\,(c + d)}}$$

The number value for a is 2, the total of instances with a 1 on the first axis and a 0 on the second (cases A and H). For b, we have 4 (cases B, D, I, and K); for c, 4 (cases C, F, G, and J); and for d, 1 (case E).
Thus,

$$\phi = \frac{(4)\,(4) - (2)\,(1)}{\sqrt{(2 + 4)(2 + 4)(4 + 1)(4 + 1)}} = \frac{16-2}{\sqrt{6\cdot6\cdot5\cdot5}} = \frac{14}{30} = .47$$

Notice that the obtained ϕ of .47 differs from the previously obtained r_{pbi} of .35 for the data when the actual measures, rather than 1 and 0, were used for "fear of crime." The difference between the magnitudes of these correlations reflects the loss of information in substituting 1s and 0s for more discriminating numbers.

Because phi is a product-moment correlation coefficient, it can have any value between +1.00 and −1.00. But in specific practice, the values

$$p = \frac{a + b}{n}$$

$$q = \frac{c + d}{n}$$

$$p' = \frac{b + d}{n}$$

$$q' = \frac{a + c}{n}$$

put lids on the maximum possible value of phi. Thus, phi can reach a value of +1.00 only when $p = p'$ (and $q = q'$). As another example, when $p = .50$

and $p' = .75$, the maximum possible value of phi is .58. That situation is not absurd, as it may seem on casual glance, because the values of the proportions p and p' do affect predictability from one variable to the other, and decreased predictability is reflected in a decreased value of phi.

Ranked Data

Several correlation coefficients have been developed for variables that are expressed in the form of ranks.

Ranked data result when, for example, one is asked to order a group of police officers from worst to best in performance on written tests. If there are 10 police officers, the worst would be placed at rank 1, the second worst at rank 2, the third worst at rank 3, and so on to the best at rank 10. The same officers might also be ranked in terms of previous education to produce the results shown in Table 25. Where there are ties at a given rank—as when two or more individuals have precisely the same previous education—an average rank is assigned, the average of the ranks that would have been assigned if the tie didn't exist. In the case of a tie of two when rank 4 is reached, for example, each of the two tied individuals is assigned a rank of 4.5, so that the ranking appears as 1, 2, 3, 4.5, 4.5, 6, 7, 8...The tied individuals take up positions 4 and 5, although they are each assigned the rank of 4.5. If there were three people tied for the same position, the rank of 5 would be assigned.

Spearman's Rank-Order Correlation Coefficient Spearman's rank-order correlation coefficient, r_s, was developed for the purpose of correlating ranked data. The simple calculational approach consists in taking the difference in rank for each pair, squaring the difference, adding up all

TABLE 25
PERFORMANCE AND EDUCATION OF POLICE OFFICERS

Officer	Performance rank	Education rank
A	1	3
B	2	1
C	3	4
D	4	2
E	5	7
F	6	5
G	7	6
H	8	10
I	9	8
J	10	9

squared differences, and then applying constants that adjust the resulting value to +1.00 or –1.00 when the correlation is perfect. The actual formula is

$$r_s = 1 - \frac{6 \sum_{i=1}^{n} D_i^2}{n(n^2 - 1)}$$

where D_i is the difference for the ith pair and n is the number of pairs.

To illustrate, using the data on police officers given in Table 25, we proceed as shown in Table 26. The rank-order correlation coefficient is, then,

$$r_s = 1 - \frac{6(22)}{10(100 - 1)} = 1 - \frac{132}{990} = 1 - .13 = .87$$

In earlier years, the Spearman correlation was used as a quick approximation for the Pearson r (by converting available measures to ranks) because of its ease of calculation relative to the Pearson r. Since Spearman's coefficient is actually the Pearson coefficient that would be obtained by correlating ranks, considered as ordinary variates, with the usual product-moment correlation formula, the resulting approximation makes sense. However, the Pearson r differs from the Spearman r_s that would have been obtained from the original data, because of the loss of information in converting to ranks from the original measures. At the present time, the ready availability of computer programs has markedly reduced the need for the approximation, since the Pearson r can now be produced so readily.

TABLE 26
PERFORMANCE AND EDUCATION OF POLICE OFFICERS
WITH CALCULATIONS OF DIFFERENCES (D) AND SQUARED DIFFERENCES (D^2)

Officer	Performance rank	Education rank	Difference (D)	Difference squared (D^2)
A	1	3	-2	4
B	2	1	1	1
C	3	4	-1	1
D	4	2	2	4
E	5	7	-2	4
F	6	5	1	1
G	7	6	1	1
H	8	10	-2	4
I	9	8	1	1
J	10	9	1	1
				Sum 22

Kendall's Tau Kendall's tau (τ) is another measure of correlation based upon ranks. Unlike Spearman's correlation (and the point-biserial and phi coefficients), τ is not a special case of the product-moment correlation coefficient. Kendall's tau is computed on the basis of "concordances" and "discordances" between the two sets of ranking. A concordance occurs whenever a comparison among ranks on one variable shows the same ordering as the comparable comparison on the other variable; a discordance occurs when the rank orderings differ. Let us return to the ranked data on police officers in Table 25 to illustrate the calculation of tau.

Let's first look at the case of officer A (and let's assume that officer A is a man). His performance rank of 1 places him at a lower numerical level than any of the other officers. If there were perfect concordances for officer A, his education rank also would be at a lower numerical level than that of any other officer. This could be the case only if his education rank were 1. The actual rank of 3 produces a discordance in comparison with the education rank of officer B, which is 1. In other words, officer A ranks lower than officer B on performance but higher on education, thus creating the discordance. On the other hand, a comparison between officers A and C produces a concordance, because the rankings are in the same order, 1 and 3 in performance and 3 and 4 in education.

Kendall's tau depends on counting all these concordances and discordances over pairs of officers and then using the results in the formula

$$\tau = \frac{c - d}{\frac{1}{2}n(n - 1)}$$

where c is the total number of concordances and d is the total number of discordances.

Let us proceed with the calculations. In the case of officer A, there are seven concordances and two discordances calculated as follows. There are nine comparisons involving officer A with officer B, with C, with D, and so forth. In the case of the A-B comparison, there is a discordance, since the performance ranks are 1–2 while the education ranks are 3–1—that is, there is a different direction of ordering. The A-C comparison produces a concordance, since the performance and education ranks are in the same direction; they are, respectively, 1–3 and 3–4. The A-D comparison produces a discordance, since the performance ranks (1–4) are in reverse order to the education ranks (3–2). Proceeding through comparisons A-E, A-F, A-G, A-H, A-I, and A-J, one gets the seven concordances and two discordances.

Turning to officer B, we start with comparison B-C, since the comparison with A was completed above. B-C produces a concordance, since the ordering of the performance ranks (2–3) is in the same direction as the ordering of the education ranks (1–4). B-D also produces a concordance, since the ordering of the performance ranks (2–4) is in the same direction

TABLE 27
CONCORDANCE AND DISCORDANCE OF OFFICER RANKS
ON PERFORMANCE AND EDUCATION

Officer	Concordances	Discordances
A	7	2
B	8	0
C	6	1
D	6	0
E	3	2
F	4	0
G	3	0
H	0	2
I	1	0
J	0	0
	Sum 38	Sum 7

as the ordering of the education ranks (1–2). And so the comparisons proceed, bringing eight concordances and no discordances.

Proceeding in that fashion, one calculates the entire set of concordances and discordances shown in Table 27.

Kendall's tau is

$$\tau = \frac{38 - 7}{\frac{1}{2}(10)(9)} = \frac{31}{45} = .69$$

The obtained value, .69, does differ, of course, from the .87 that was obtained by Spearman's rank-order formula using the same rankings. But that degree of difference can be expected, given the differing assumptions behind the calculational formulas. An analysis of these differences, together with an interesting general theory of rank correlation that encompasses both Kendall's tau and Spearman's rho may be found in Kendall (1955). In that book, Kendall (p. 7) describes tau as providing "a kind of average measure of the agreement between pairs of members ('agreement,' that is to say, in respect to order) and thus has evident recommendations as a measure of the concordance between two rankings."

To show that tau has the right properties for a measure of correlation, let us compute τ for the cases when the two rankings are in perfect agreement and when they are in perfect disagreement. First, we illustrate perfect agreement; see Table 28.

Clearly, there are no discordances, and so we need tally only concordances. They are, as follows for the various officers: A, 9; B, 8; C, 7; D, 6; E, 5; F, 4; G, 3; H, 2; I, 1, for a total of 45 concordances. Therefore,

$$\tau = \frac{45 - 0}{\frac{1}{2}(10)(9)} = \frac{45}{45} = 1.00$$

TABLE 28
PERFORMANCE AND EDUCATION RANKS OF OFFICERS

Officer	Performance rank	Education rank
A	1	1
B	2	2
C	3	3
D	4	4
E	5	5
F	6	6
G	7	7
H	8	8
I	9	9
J	10	10

Next, we illustrate perfect disagreement; see Table 29. Clearly, in this case, there are no concordances. In the instance of officer A, for example, all other officers have a higher ranking on performance and a lower ranking on education. Tallying discordances produces: A, 9; B, 8; C, 7; D, 6; E, 5; F, 4; G, 3; H, 2; I, 1; for a total of 45. Therefore

$$\tau = \frac{0 - 45}{45} = -1.00$$

Thus, Kendall's tau has the values we expect at the extremities.

The calculation of tau when there are ties is a good deal more complicated. See Blalock (1972) for an explanation and illustrative example.

TABLE 29
PERFORMANCE AND EDUCATION RANKS OF OFFICERS

Officer	Performance rank	Education rank
A	1	10
B	2	9
C	3	8
D	4	7
E	5	6
F	6	5
G	7	4
H	8	3
I	9	2
J	10	1

CORRELATION AND CAUSATION

Suppose, during a particularly intense summer storm, lightning strikes a barn and the barn catches fire. One would ordinarily say under these circumstances that the fire was "caused" by the lightning, and the police would proceed no further with a possible arson investigation. Similarly, if a police officer shoots and kills a suspect who was brandishing a rifle, we say that the suspect's death was "caused" by the officer's bullet.

Those examples convey our general understandings that A caused B if the occurrence of A led to the occurrence of B and that if A had not occurred, B would not have happened. In addition to the sequencing of A and B in time, we use the term *cause* only when we have some understanding or explanation of why the occurrence of A leads to the occurrence of B. A dictionary definition of cause reflecting that understanding is as follows (Webster's Seventh New Collegiate, 1963): "Something that occasions or effects a result; a person or thing that is the occasion of an action or state, esp: an agent that brings something about."

Unfortunately, however, a philosophical analysis of the meaning of *cause* raises a good deal of difficulty. Philosophers of the stature of David Hume, Bertrand Russell, John Stuart Mill, W. V. Quine, and K. B. Popper have been writing on the subject of causality for hundreds of years. Yet, in a broad survey of "The Concept of Cause" in a book published in 1979, we find the following statement (Cook and Campbell, p. 10):

> The epistemology of causation. . .is at present in a productive state of near chaos. In our treatment of causality we shall touch upon only a small part of the current ferment. We are far from satisfied with our treatment here and find in it no completely satisfying resolution to the major problems of causality.

And, indeed, when one reads the overview of causality presented in the book, one must readily agree with the negative evaluation of the authors. The fault (cause?) lies in the difficulty of the concept, not in the capabilities of the writers.

Because of that difficulty we will claim no more specific meaning for causality than that contained in the dictionary definition above. We believe that this definition adequately reflects the general cultural understanding of its meaning.

We are now ready to consider the relation of correlation to causation in that broad sense. The correlation coefficient, it should be recalled, is purely descriptive of the extent to which paired numbers go together—high with high, low with low, and so forth, or high with low, low with high, and so forth. The coefficient is completely insensitive to the sources of the two number sets, regardless of its size, and so can carry no implications for any causal relationship between the variables represented. Thus, if one correlated the weekly church attendance and the amount of reported crime over cities in the United States, one would obtain a high positive correlation. It would, of course, be foolish to infer from that correlation that church attendance encourages (causes) crime—or that crime encourages (causes) church attendance. Clearly, both church attendance and crime rates vary with the size of cities—highly populated cities have both high church attendance and high crime rates, less-populated cities have lower church attendance and lower crime rates.

One can explain the high correlation between church attendance and crime on the basis of the third variable, city size. But it is possible to obtain a high correlation between two sets of paired numbers even when there is no apparent explanation at all. For example, a researcher reports the finding of a significant correlation over several years between the number of divorces in Great Britain and the number of apples imported into the country. It is quite unlikely that the flow of apples into a country causes divorces or that increases in divorces cause greater amounts of apples to be imported. The correlation simply provides an index of agreement between two sets of numbers and no information about the reasons why they agree (or disagree). The causal analysis must come from a thinking person using prior knowledge of the characteristics of the variables of concern.

REFERENCES

Blalock, H. M., Jr. 1972. *Social Statistics* (2d ed.). New York: McGraw-Hill.

Braithwaite, J. 1979. *Inequality, Crime and Public Policy*. London: Routledge and Kegan Paul.

Cook, T. D., and Campbell, D. T. 1979. *Quasi-Experimentation: Design and Analysis Issues for Field Settings*. Chicago: Rand McNally.

Giordano, P. C. 1978. "Girls, Guys and Gangs: The Changing Context of Female Delinquency." *Journal of Criminal Law and Criminology*, **69**:126–132.

Guilford, J. P., and Fruchter, B. 1973. *Fundamental Statistics in Psychology and Education* (5th ed.). New York: McGraw-Hill.

Kendall, M. G. 1955. *Rank Correlation Methods* (2d ed.). London: Griffin.

CHAPTER 10

PROBABILITY AND PROBABILITY DISTRIBUTIONS

CHAPTER OUTLINE

PROBABILITY
  Sample Space
  Equal Likelihood
  Mutually Exclusive Events
  Properties of Probability
  Probabilities in the General Case
PROBABILITY DISTRIBUTIONS
  Binomial Distribution
  Normal Distribution

PROBABILITY

The idea of *probability* is widespread in American culture. Such concepts as likelihood, chance, uncertainty, and odds for or against are aspects of probability. Detectives in a police department will say that they think there is about a 40 percent chance that this or that suspect truly is guilty of the defense. Students in a criminal justice research class were asked what it was they thought of when they dealt with matters of probability. The following responses were forthcoming: "The probability that a number will occur is the chance it will come out as compared with another number." "With probability there is always an element of doubt involved." "Probability means that the results are beyond your control." "Probability is the likelihood of an act occurring or the chance of something happening." "Probability is full of surprises." And, last: "Probability must be based on knowledge of previous events."

These ideas indicate a general grasp of the concept of probability. The concept can be narrowed down to arithmetic terms. If someone asks you what the probability is that a head or a tail will come up on the toss of a perfectly balanced coin, you would not hesitate to supply the correct answer: "One-half," or "One out of two." If the question was the probability of any one of six possible numbers coming up in the throw of a die (the singular of dice), the response would be "One-sixth," or "One out of six." With the coin, you might also say: "There is a fifty-fifty chance." The fifty-fifty chance can be represented as .50 - .50, meaning a probability of .50 (1/2) that a particular result will take place and .50 (1/2) that it will not take place.

It can be seen that we all have a general understanding of probability, even though we have made no formal study or investigation of the subject. Life is full of uncertainty: we need only note predictions of what the weather is going to be. We try to deal with such uncertainty by expressing it in terms of probability. Somebody will say to you that "maybe" or "perhaps" this or that will take place. If you want a better or more precise estimate of what is meant by such words, you could ask to have the matter expressed in probabilistic terms: "Do you think there is a 40 percent chance that it will happen, or do you think the likelihood is nearer to 80 or 90 percent?" The answer will provide a better understanding of the estimate of probability. The following discussion of probability builds upon our intuitive and commonsense understanding of the idea.

Sample Space

Where there is probability (or likelihood or chance), there must be a result or outcome to which the probability refers. That outcome might be a head or a tail in the case of tossing a coin; or a 1, 2, 3, 4, 5, or 6 in throwing a die. We can represent each of these two sets of outcomes as shown in Figure 8. Each of these representations is what we call a *sample space*. There must be an element, or a sample point, in each sample space for each possible outcome.

The activity of interest, such as the toss of the coin, is often referred to as an experiment or a trial. The sample space reflects the increased number of

FIGURE 8
Sets of outcomes for (*left*) the toss of a coin and (*right*) the throw of a die.

outcomes as the activity of interest becomes more complex. The trial of tossing a coin twice, for example, has the following possible outcomes: head-head, head-tail, tail-head, tail-tail, with the first designation indicating the outcome of the initial toss and the second the result of the following toss. Similarly, throwing a die twice has the following possible outcomes: 1–1, 1–2, 1–3, 1–4, 1–5, 1–6, 2–1, 2–2, 2–3, 2–4, 2–5, 2–6, 3–1, 3–2, 3–3, 3–4, 3–5, 3–6, 4–1, 4–2, 4–3, 4–4, 4–5, 4–6, 5–1, 5–2, 5–3, 5–4, 5–5, 5–6, 6–1, 6–2, 6–3, 6–4, 6–5, 6–6.

Equal Likelihood

We have confined our illustrations to die and coin tosses because in the realm of criminal justice work, the probabilities of one thing or another are not so straightforward. There may be five suspects under consideration by the police after a store burglary, but the chances are that not each of them is considered equally likely to have committed the offense. Suspect A may have an alibi for the time of the burglary, and though it is far from foolproof, it reduces the chances that suspect A committed the act. Similarly, each of the others, to a greater or lesser extent, seems likely to be culpable, or guilty of the violation of the law.

For the moment, however, we are concerned with outcomes that have equal likelihoods of coming about. In the toss of a coin or the throw of a die, the intuitive expectation is that each outcome is equally likely. We have a feeling that for the coin, the probability of either of the two outcomes is 1/2 and for the die, the probability of each of the six outcomes is 1/6. That each possible outcome has the same probability of occurring is what we mean by the term *equal likelihood*. If there are two possible outcomes, each has a probability of ½; if there are three outcomes, each has a probability of 1/3; and with four possible outcomes, the probability becomes ¼. In the general case, if there are k possible outcomes, each has a probability of $1/k$.

But how do you know that the outcomes are equally likely in a given case? Police officers chasing a fleeing felon know that there is a fork in the road up ahead, and they can radio to the standby patrol car some distance away to move into position along the left fork or the right fork. Which fork will the car they are chasing take? In theory, the chances seem equal, but we know from experience that they are not so, that people have preferences for right or left, that their past experiences or their expectations or the cues they use make them more likely to go one way than the other. It is the shrewd person who can calculate all these likelihoods and reach a reasonable estimate of probability.

It is important to distinguish between knowing likelihoods and knowing what is going to happen. If we take a coin out of a pocket and toss it, we can only anticipate the probability of the outcome. We have had extensive past experience with coins: dropping them, tossing them, spinning them, and making decisions or losing bets on the basis of the outcome. We have a deep-down feeling that a head is as likely to eventuate as a tail. Therefore, when we deal with a coin that we have not used before, we expect it to behave just like all the other coins we have used.

Of course, it may not! The coin that we take at random from our pocket may be so weighted that it comes up heads almost always in a free toss. The probability that a head will come up may be 9/10, 99/100, or 999/1000. When a coin is so weighted that the probability of a head or a tail is not ½, we say that the coin is *biased*.

The conjecture or belief that a coin selected from your pocket is unbaised (that is, that the probability of a head = the probability of a tail = ½) is equivalent to a hypothesis, in the sense that we have discussed hypotheses earlier in this book. The hypothesis may be tested by tossing the coin freely a number of times. If the selected number of tosses is 50, we would expect an unbiased coin to show about 25 heads and 25 tails. If the actual numbers of heads and tails obtained in 50 tosses differs markedly from 25, the experimenter may have reason to doubt the hypothesis.

The trial and its outcome refer more specifically to a relationship between probability and frequency of occurrence. In the preceding example, it is clear that there are two possible outcomes and that each has a probability of ½. We then expect that in n trials (such as tosses), we will see ½n of one outcome and ½n of the other outcome. In the example we have just given of the 50 tosses, n equals 50, and ½n then becomes 25. Probability and frequency of occurrence are closely associated in popular thinking. Where the probabilities are 1/6, as in the case of the throw of the die, we expect in 600 throws to get about 100 (1/6 of 600) of each possible outcome. The same probability-frequency of outcome relationships prevails whether the probabilities are 1/3, 1/4, 1/9, or, as we put it for the general case, 1/k.

Suppose, for example, that there are k possible outcomes, all with equal probability of occurrence. For convenience, we designate the set of possible outcomes by the numbers 1, 2, 3, 4...k. The probability of each is 1/k. The symbol $P[]$ is very generally used to designate the probability of whatever outcome is placed within the brackets. In the example of k

outcomes, $P[1] = 1/k$, $P[2] = 1/k$, $P[3] = 1/k$, and so forth. Or if we use x_i to represent any of the numbers, $P[x_i] = 1/k$.

To put the above in concrete form, let us return to the throw of the die. The full set is 1, 2, 3, 4, 5, 6, where $k = 6$. In this case $P[1] = P[2] = P[3] = P[4] = P[5] = P[6] = 1/6$.

In the general case of k outcomes, if a person were asked to specify the probability that the outcome will be either a 1 or a 2, the intuitive response would very likely be $2/k$ (that is, $1/k + 1/k$). Similarly, if the probability of either a 1 or a 2 or a 3 were the matter in question, the response would very likely be $3/k$ (or $1/k + 1/k + 1/k$). In the case of the die, the probability that a 1 or a 2 will show would be 2/6 (or 1/6 + 1/6). And the probability of either a 1, a 2, or a 3 would be 3/6 (or 1/6 + 1/6 + 1/6). The last, of course, indicates that the chances are 1/2 (that is, 3/6 reduced) that a single toss of the die will produce either a 1, a 2, or a 3. This makes perfect sense when we note that the chance of either a 4, a 5, or a 6 comes to exactly the same likelihood (3/6, or 1/2).

The formal definition of the probability of any one of a grouping of possible outcomes reflects the foregoing intuitions, making the examples special cases of a more general definition.

Symbolically, the probability of any one of two or three possible outcomes is expressed as $P\,[1\text{ or }2]$ in the case of two outcomes, and $P\,[1\text{ or }2\text{ or }3]$ in the case of three outcomes. We then have, for equally likely outcomes,

$$P[1 \text{ or } 2] = \frac{2}{k}$$

and

$$P[1 \text{ or } 2 \text{ or } 3] = \frac{3}{k}$$

The foregoing formula would apply no matter which of the two or three outcomes were selected. If we were interested in outcomes which were more general, we might, if there were two of them, designate them as a and b. In that case the formula would read

$$P[a \text{ or } b] = \frac{2}{k}$$

Or, if there were three different outcomes that we were concerned with, we would represent the situation as follows:

$$P[a \text{ or } b \text{ or } c] = \frac{3}{k}$$

Outcomes grouped together in the fashion that we have them above are called *events.* In technical terms, an event is any subset of the sample space for which we wish to specify the probability. An event could be the outcomes (1, 2) or (1, 2, 3), as discussed previously, or (1, 3) or (2, 6) or (1, 2, 6) or (2, 4, 6) or (1, 2, 5, 6). It is on occasion possible to express an event conceptually. In the case of the die toss, for example, the event consisting of 1, 3, 5 could be expressed as an *odd number,* and the event consisting of 2, 4, 6 could be expressed as an *even number.* The probability that an odd number will show up on a toss of a die can be represented in symbolic form in the following manner:

$$P[1 \text{ or } 3 \text{ or } 5] = \frac{3}{6} = \frac{1}{2}$$

And the probability of an even number is

$$P[2 \text{ or } 4 \text{ or } 6] = \frac{1}{2}$$

We are ready to move along to somewhat more complex situations in order to understand probability as it applies to a variety of circumstances. Take a deck of playing cards. It has four suits—spades, hearts, diamonds, and clubs. There are 13 numbers and pictures within each of the four suits: 1, 2, 3, 4, 5, 6, 7, 8, 9, 10, jack, queen, and king. Since there are 52 playing cards ($k = 52$), the probability that any one card (such as the ace of spades or the ace of hearts) will turn up in an experiment in which you select one card from a well-shuffled deck is 1 out of 52 or 1/52. The probability that you will turn up either the ace of spades or the ace of hearts is 2/52.

Suppose we want to determine the probability of turning up *any* ace: the ace of spades, the ace of hearts, the ace of diamonds, or the ace of clubs. The probability of an ace of any suit is

$$P[\text{ace}] = \frac{4}{52}$$

Or suppose that our interest is in turning up a heart of any kind. Since there are 13 hearts in the deck, the probability can be expressed in the following way:

$$P[\text{heart}] = \frac{13}{52}$$

Considerations of events such as "ace" and "hearts," as we have indicated above, and their associated probabilities make apparent the basis of one of the most common formal definitions of probability. In this definition, the outcomes that are grouped together to form the event of interest are referred to as *favorable outcomes*. Occurrence of any ace, for example, consists of the favorable outcomes of drawing an ace of spades, ace of hearts, ace of diamonds, or ace of clubs. The probability of an event then may be specified in this form:

$$P[\text{favorable outcome}] = \frac{\text{number of favorable outcomes}}{\text{number of possible outcomes}}$$

assuming, of course, that the outcomes are equally likely to occur. In the example of occurrence of an ace, there are four favorable outcomes; for the occurrence of hearts (or any other individual suit), there are 13 favorable outcomes.

Remember that a die has six sides. Now, let us suppose that we paint two sides of the die red, three sides white, and one side blue. We are interested in the probability that a red side will turn up in a throw of the die. That probability will be

$$P[\text{red}] = \frac{\text{number of favorable outcomes}}{\text{number of possible outcomes}} = \frac{2}{6} = \frac{1}{3}$$

And the probability for white (which has been painted on three sides) would then be

$$P[\text{white}] = \frac{\text{number of favorable outcomes}}{\text{number of possible outcomes}} = \frac{3}{6} = \frac{1}{2}$$

And, then, for the one side painted blue,

$$P[\text{blue}] = \frac{\text{number of favorable outcomes}}{\text{number of possible outcomes}} = \frac{1}{6}$$

For illustrative purposes, we can convert these to frequencies. In 300 throws of the die we would expect about 100 red faces to come out on top ($1/3 \times 300$), about 150 white ones ($1/2 \times 300$), and about 50 blue ones ($1/6 \times 300$).

To obtain a working formula for probability, we designate the event of interest as A. This could represent the occurrence of an ace, a heart, a red side on top, or whatever. If there are k possible outcomes and the event A

contains m outcomes (or, in other words, there are m favorable outcomes), the probability of A is

$$P[A] = \frac{m}{k}$$

Mutually Exclusive Events

The events A and B are said to be *mutually exclusive* if they have no outcomes in common; that is, if *only* one event can occur. In a trial of throwing a die, for example, the event "odd number appearing" and the event "even number appearing" are mutually exclusive; no toss of one die can give *both* an odd number and an even number at the same time. The first event consists of the outcomes 1, 3, 5 and the second of 2, 4, 6. On the other hand, the event "odd number appearing" and "1 or 2 appearing" are not mutually exclusive. If the number 1 comes out on top, it falls into both categories: it is an odd number, and as a 1, it meets the requirement in the second category.

In a deck of cards, similarly, the events "ace occurring" and "queen occurring" are mutually exclusive, since they have no cards in common. But the events "ace occurring" and "heart occurring" are not mutually exclusive. These latter two events have the ace of hearts in common.

Figure 9 illustrates the concept of mutual exclusiveness; the letters A, B, and C represent events. There are k points in the sample space which

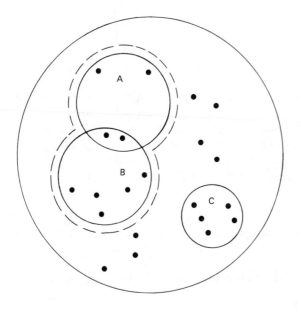

FIGURE 9
Mutual exclusiveness;
A, B, and C are events.

represent k possible outcomes in regard to a given experiment. Looking at the diagram, we see that there are four points or outcomes in event A, seven points in event B, and five points in event C. Since events A and B have two points in common, they are not mutually exclusive. Events A and C, however, are mutually exclusive, as are events B and C.

Properties of Probability

The probabilities assigned to the outcomes and events above were all positive numbers. Probabilities are never negative. If an event is impossible—that is, if it cannot occur—we say that its probability is zero. Take, for instance, the question whether the number 7 will turn up in the throw of a die. Since the die contains only numbers as high as 6, there is no likelihood that a 7 or anything higher will appear.

Therefore, we can regard an initial property of probability as the fact that it is always a positive number or zero.

We noted in the earlier discussion that the probability of any one of two, three, or more outcomes is the sum of their separate probabilities. The matter may be represented as follows for a, b, c, or d as outcomes in a space that has k total outcomes:

$$P[a \text{ or } b] = \frac{1}{k} + \frac{1}{k} = \frac{2}{k}$$

$$P[a \text{ or } b \text{ or } c] = \frac{1}{k} + \frac{1}{k} + \frac{1}{k} = \frac{3}{k}$$

$$P[a \text{ or } b \text{ or } c \text{ or } d] = \frac{1}{k} + \frac{1}{k} + \frac{1}{k} + \frac{1}{k} = \frac{4}{k}$$

We now have a second important property of probability—its additive nature.

It is clear, also, that the probability of any outcome within a space is equal to 1. That is, the probability of a head or a tail in the toss of a coin is 1: there is certainty that a coin will come up *either* head or tail; any reasonable person would be quite willing to bet on that. Similarly, the probability of a 1, 2, 3, 4, 5, or 6 in the toss of a die is 1. Using the additive property of probability that we noted above, the probability of one of k possible outcomes can be represented in the following form:

$$P[\text{any one of the } k \text{ outcomes}] = \frac{1}{k} + \frac{1}{k} + \frac{1}{k} + \frac{1}{k} \cdots + \frac{1}{k}$$

Since there are k of these $1/k$'s in the sum, we can rewrite the formula as follows:

$$P[\text{any one of the } k \text{ outcomes}] = k\,\frac{1}{k} = 1$$

It is always the case that the probabilities assigned to either the outcomes in a space or a set of mutually exclusive events satisfy these three properties that we have indicated. First, the probabilities are positive numbers or zero. Second, for any grouping of more than one outcome or more than one event (where they are mutually exclusive, of course), the probability of an outcome in the new grouping is equal to the sum of the separate probabilities of the outcomes or events in the grouping. And third, the probability of any outcome in the space, where the probabilities are defined on outcomes or on events, is equal to 1.

Probabilities in the General Case

Probabilities may be calculated even when we do not have equally likely outcomes that may be grouped into sets as in the instances that we have used so far in this chapter. We might be interested, for example, in the likelihood that any given officer, of a total of 20, will win a target-shooting contest in a particular law enforcement department. If all the men and women in the contest were equally skilled and prepared and lucky (and otherwise equal in all the relevant requirements), then we could say that the probability that any one of the 20 will win would be equal. But this obviously is far from the actual situation in virtually any kind of complex competition. Officer A may be highly skilled and may have won a number of competitions in the past. His probability of winning may seem to be about 1/4. Officer B may be almost as good as A, and we perhaps would rate her chances at 1/5. On the other end, officer T may be so unskilled that his chance of coming out first seems to lie in the vicinity of 1/1000.

Take another example. We might ask people in a shopping center about their attitudes toward the criminal justice system. We have a series of items on a questionnaire that we are going to employ to determine public opinion, at least as it is expressed by those persons who frequent this particular shopping center at this time on this day. One question might be framed as follows:

Please indicate your feelings about the present chief of police in this township by choosing one of the five following responses: (1) He is a militarist who cares more about style than about delicate aspects of human relationships. (2) He tends toward the military outlook but shows a spark of human concern here and there. (3) He is an average type of police officer in the balance between military style and community concern. (4) He tends to be more community-oriented than concerned with military organization. (5) He is oriented toward the needs of the people in the community and tolerates military style only to the minimum degree necessary for the maintenance of the police organization.

The probabilities associated with the five items for a militaristic chief might be:

$$P[1] \quad = \quad .50$$
$$P[2] \quad = \quad .25$$
$$P[3] \quad = \quad .12$$
$$P[4] \quad = \quad .10$$
$$P[5] \quad = \quad .03$$

On the other hand, the probabilities associated with the five items for a community-oriented chief might be:

$$P]1] \quad = \quad .01$$
$$P[2] \quad = \quad .02$$
$$P[3] \quad = \quad .14$$
$$P[4] \quad = \quad .18$$
$$P[5] \quad = \quad .65$$

The preceding are entirely fictitious probabilities, chosen so as to reflect choices when the chief is quite military in operation and when the chief is very community-oriented. Thus, we are arbitrarily saying that the citizens will choose response (1) with probability .50 if the chief is quite military; in other words, 50 percent of the citizens will choose response (1) on the questionnaire. Similarly, the probability of response (5) for the military chief is .03; that is, only 3 percent of the citizens will give response (5) if the chief is militaristic.

For the community-oriented chief, on the other hand, the highest probability—.65—was assigned to the response designating the chief as caring about community needs above military style. That is, we say that 65 percent of the citizens will choose response (5). At the other end, we say that only 1 percent of the citizens ($P = .01$) will designate the community-oriented chief as heavily militaristic by choosing response (1).

Let us illustrate the operation of the three properties of probability that we have indicated earlier. This time we will demonstrate the conditions where we do not have equally likely outcomes. Let's go back to the target-shooting contest. The properties of probability in that case, as in all others, are:

1 The probabilities are all positive numbers (or zero).

2 The probability that either officer A or officer B will win is 1/4 + 1/5. The common denominator that allows these numbers to be added together is 20 (the lowest number that can be divided by both 4 and 5). We therefore have 5/20 + 4/20 = 9/20 as the probability that either officer A or officer B will win the contest. If we wanted to calculate the probability that either officer B or

officer T will win, the relevant numbers would be 1/5 + 1/1000 = 200/1000 + 1/1000 = 201/1000.

3 The probability that the contest will be won by officer A or B or C or D or E or some other officer of those competing is one: that is, *somebody* is going to win in the normal course of events.

Similarly, in the case of the questionnaires administered in the shopping center about the respondents' perceptions of the police chief, we can appreciate that:

1 The probabilities are all positive.

2 The probability of a response among the choices is the sum of the separate probabilities; that is, the probability of choice (4) or (5) is .18 + .65 = .83, in the case of the community-oriented chief.

3 The sum of all probabilities is one; that is, .01 + .02 + .14 + .18 + .65 = 1 or .50 + .25 + .12 + .10 + .03 = 1.

PROBABILITY DISTRIBUTIONS

Numbers are associated with possible outcomes in most research investigations in the field of criminal justice. Even when dealing with a descriptive property such as sex, we most often express results in some form such as the percentage of boys or girls, men or women. When there are two categories of outcome, as we discussed previously, the proportion is a mean when the number 1 is assigned to the category for which the proportion is computed and the number 0 is assigned to the other category.

Binomial Distribution

Consider again the experiment of tossing a coin once. The coin is unbiased, so that the probability of a head is 1/2 and the probability of a tail is 1/2. If we assign the number 1 to heads and the number 0 to tails, we have a state of affairs that can be represented in the following form:

Outcome or a sample point	Number assigned	Probability
H(eads)	1	1/2
T(ails)	0	1/2

The column containing the assigned numbers is a variable in the sense that its particular value depends upon the outcome. In the statistical world, a variable whose value is a number associated with the outcome of an experiment or trial is called a *random variable*. There is a set of probabilities associated with the values of the random variable by virtue of mutual pairing with the outcomes. Thus, in the foregoing example, the probability ½ is associated with the value 1 because 1 is the number assigned to the outcome H, and $P[H] = \frac{1}{2}$. This is quite straightforward; it is also a very important point in the logic of probability.

The set of paired outcomes or points in the sample space and their probabilities define what is called a *probability function*. A probability function differs from a *probability distribution* in that the former associates probabilities with all possible outcomes while the latter associates probabilities with all possible events.

Suppose we now toss a coin twice and assign a number to each outcome in accordance with the number of heads it contains. Thus, for example, the outcome (HH) contains two heads and is assigned the number 2. In tabular form, the situation looks as follows:

Outcome or sample point	Number assigned	Probability
HH	2	1/4
HT	1	1/4
TH	1	1/4
TT	0	1/4

The random variable now is "number of heads in two tosses" and has values of 0, 1, 2. The probability function is the set of pairs from the first and third columns: HH-1/4, HT-1/4, TH-1/4, TT-1/4.

But notice that the values of the random variable impose three events on the sample space. The three events are: the event "two heads," containing the outcome HH; the event "one head," containing the outcomes HT and TH; and the event "zero heads," containing the outcome TT. The pairing of probabilities and these three events, therefore, specifies a probability distribution. That distribution is shown in the following form:

Event: number of heads	Probability
2	1/4
1	1/2
0	1/4

The foregoing representation indicates that in two coin tosses, our chances of getting one head are even (one out of two) and of getting no heads (or all heads) are 1 in 4.

We move next to the experiment of three coin tosses under the same specifications as above. The following illustrates the sample space values of the random variable, and associated probabilities:

Outcome or sample point	Number assigned	Probability
HHH	3	1/8
HHT	2	1/8
HTH	2	1/8
HTT	1	1/8
THH	2	1/8
THT	1	1/8
TTH	1	1/8
TTT	0	1/8

The random variable is "number of heads in three tosses," with values 0, 1, 2, 3. The probability distribution over the events defined by these four values is shown in the following chart. The chart also indicates the outcomes that are included in each event:

Number of heads in three tosses	Event outcomes included	Probability
3	HHH	1/8
2	HHT, HTH, THH	3/8
1	HTT, THT, TTH	3/8
0	TTT	1/8

The probability of the event "two heads" is 3/8; that is, it is likely to occur three times in every eight tosses. Or, to put it another way, there are three outcomes favorable to the event and a total of eight equally likely outcomes. The probability for the event "one head" is arrived at by means of similar kinds of reasoning.

We can now move to the general case where there are n tosses, rather than proceeding in this step-by-step fashion through four tosses, five tosses, six tosses, and so on. It obviously is not feasible to show the sample space, the values of the random variable, and the probabilities. An outcome would be a form (HHTT...H), where the dots represent the variability allowed by the generality of n. The values of the random variable are $0, 1, 2, 3, 4, 5, \ldots (n-1)$, n, indicating every possible integral value btween 0, representing zero heads, and n, representing all, or n, heads.

In the general case of n tosses of an unbiased coin, the probabilities of various events are shown in Table 30.

The final three columns in Table 30 show the actual probabilities for 3, 4, and 5 tosses of the coin. These have been computed from the formulas in the second column. The blank in the table for $(n-1)$ heads in 3 tosses occurs because $(n-1)$ heads in 3 tosses is 2 $(3 - 1)$ heads, which is entered in the row above for the event "2 heads."

TABLE 30

PROBABILITIES OF VARIOUS NUMBERS OF HEADS IN n COIN TOSSES

Event or number of heads	Probability	Illustrative examples of probabilities		
		$n=3$	$n=4$	$n=5$
0	$(1/2)^n$	1/8	1/16	1/32
1	$n(1/2)^n$	3/8	1/4	5/32
2	$\dfrac{n(n-1)}{2}\left(\dfrac{1}{2}\right)^n$	3/8	3/8	5/16
3	$\dfrac{m(n-1)\,(n-2)}{6}\left(\dfrac{1}{2}\right)^n$	•	•	5/16
•	•	•	•	•
•	•	•	•	•
•	•	•	•	•
$n-1$	$n(1/2)^n$	•	1/4	5/32
n	$(1/2)^n$	1/8	1/16	1/32

The distribution shown in Table 30 is called the *binomial distribution*. It can also be expressed in the form of an equation in the following manner:

$$P[r \text{ heads}] = \frac{n!}{r!\,(n-r)!}\left(\frac{1}{2}\right)^n$$

The equation looks quite formidable and forbidding, but the chances are that our reaction to it stems more from lack of familiarity with the meaning of a symbol than from the overwhelming complexity of the formula itself. Let us work toward some clarification. When an exclamation mark follows a number, it specifies a set of products. In particular, the exclamation marks are a shorthand for the following longer sets:

$$2! = 2{\cdot}1 \text{ (that is, 2 times 1)}$$
$$3! = 3{\cdot}2{\cdot}1$$
$$4! = 4{\cdot}3{\cdot}2{\cdot}1$$
$$5! = 5{\cdot}4{\cdot}3{\cdot}2{\cdot}1$$
$$6! = 6{\cdot}5{\cdot}4{\cdot}3{\cdot}2{\cdot}1$$
$$10! = 10{\cdot}9{\cdot}8{\cdot}7{\cdot}6{\cdot}5{\cdot}4{\cdot}3{\cdot}2{\cdot}1$$
$$20! = 20{\cdot}19{\cdot}18{\cdot}17\cdots4{\cdot}3{\cdot}2{\cdot}1$$

Just to take 10! and multiply it out will give us 3,628,800. It can readily be seen that the shorthand 10! expresses a very large number in very simple form. In the general case, where we employ the letter n to designate any number, we have the formula:

$$n! = n(n - 1)(n - 2)(n - 3)\ldots 4\cdot 3\cdot 2\cdot 1$$

Similarly:

$$r! = r(r-1)\ (r-2)\ (r-3)\ldots 4\cdot 3\cdot 2\cdot 1$$

Let us illustrate how we can apply the formula with a simple example. Suppose we toss a coin five times and are interested in the probability that we will get two heads from that number of tosses. In this case, therefore, $n = 5$, $r = 2$, and

$$P[2 \text{ heads}] = \frac{5!}{2!\ (5-2)!} \left(\frac{1}{2}\right)^5 = \frac{5\cdot 4\cdot 3\cdot 2\cdot 1}{(2\cdot 1)\ (3\cdot 2\cdot 1)}\frac{1}{32}$$

$$= \frac{10}{32} = \frac{5}{16}$$

Notice that 5/16 is the value shown in Table 30 as the probability of two heads when $n = 5$.

And for the probability of three heads in four tosses, we then have

$$P[3 \text{ heads}] = \frac{4!}{3!(4-3)!} \left(\frac{1}{2}\right)^4 = \frac{4\cdot 3\cdot 2\cdot 1}{(3\cdot 2\cdot 1)(1)}\frac{1}{16} = \frac{4}{16} = \frac{1}{4}$$

And, again, the entry can be compared with that in Table 30, which shows that for 4 tosses the probability of 3 (or 4 − 1) heads is 1 in 4.

A special case for the binomial distribution occurs when the two possible alternative outcomes do not have the same probabilities of occurrence, as is the case with the toss of an unbiased coin when $P[\text{head}]$ and $P[\text{tail}]$ are equal to ½. Suppose, on the other hand, we are doing some research in regard to the sex distribution of the cadets at a police academy. There has been an affirmative action drive to increase the number of women going into police service, and in this class there are 65 females and 35 males. We want to choose one person randomly from the class roster. If we examine the choice from the perspective of whether we will draw a male or a female, we have a binomial situation much like that for a toss of a coin. Only this time $P[\text{female}] = 65/100$, not ½, and $P[\text{male}] = 35/100$, not ½.

Let's go back to the coin toss, since we have become familiar with some of the probability techniques in regard to it. Suppose that you were a member of the detective bunco squad (a *bunco squad* controls swindling of the public by various kinds of schemes), and during your work you had arrested a professional gambler who made a living by betting with visitors to the city in the local bars. The gambler would at first use an unbiased coin but later would substitute one with extra metal in it. This metal biased the coin, and when you conducted your own trials with it, you discovered that the likelihood of heads was 65 times in a hundred throws. You could represent the probabilities for this biased coin in the following fashion:

$$P[\text{head}] = .65$$

and $$P[\text{tail}] = .35$$

If you toss this coin n times, the probability of r heads is

$$P[r \text{ heads}] = \frac{n!}{r!(n-r)!} (.65)^r (.35)^{(n-r)}$$

The general formula, where p is the probability of one outcome (.65 for heads in the foregoing example) and q is the probability of the other outcome (.35 for tails in the example), is

$$P[r \text{ heads}] = \frac{n!}{r!(n-r)!} p^r q^{(n-r)}$$

where p is the probability of a head. You must understand that the formula applies to any series of trials where there are two outcomes (like heads and tails, or like female and male), where the probability of each outcome remains the same on each outcome, and where the random variable of interest is the number of occurrences. To reflect that generality, the formula may be written as:

$$P[r \text{ of the outcomes whose probability is } p] = \frac{n!}{r!(n-r)!} p^r q^{(n-r)}$$

The binomial distribution is given in tabular form in Table 31. The table sets out the probabilities of various outcomes, $r = 0, 1, 2, 3$, etc., when the binomial trial is repeated n times, $n = 5, 10, 15$, or 20.

To illustrate the manner in which Table 31 may be used, suppose we select 15 individuals ($n = 15$) from a large pool of people, where the probability of a positive attitude toward the police is .70 ($p = .70$), and the probability of a negative attitude toward the police is .30 ($q = .30$). The probabililty that exactly 10 of the 15 people selected will have a positive

TABLE 31
BINOMIAL PROBABILITIES: $\dfrac{n!}{r!(n-r)!}\, p^r q^{(n-r)}$

Values of r	Values of p								
	.1	.2	.3	.4	.5	.6	.7	.8	.9
					$n = 5$				
0	.5905	.3277	.1681	.0778	.0312	.0102	.0024	.0003	.0000
1	.3280	.4096	.3602	.2592	.1562	.0768	.0284	.0064	.0004
2	.0729	.2048	.3087	.3456	.3125	.2304	.1323	.0512	.0081
3	.0081	.0512	.1323	.2304	.3125	.3456	.3087	.2048	.0729
4	.0004	.0064	.0284	.0768	.1562	.2592	.3602	.4096	.3280
5	.0000	.0003	.0024	.0102	.0312	.0778	.1681	.3277	.5905
					$n = 10$				
0	.3487	.1074	.0282	.0060	.0010	.0001	.0000	.0000	.0000
1	.3874	.2684	.1211	.0403	.0098	.0016	.0001	.0000	.0000
2	.1937	.3020	.2335	.1209	.0439	.0106	.0014	.0001	.0000
3	.0574	.2013	.2668	.2150	.1172	.0425	.0090	.0008	.0000
4	.0112	.0881	.2001	.2508	.2051	.1115	.0368	.0055	.0001
5	.0015	.0264	.1029	.2007	.2461	.2007	.1029	.0264	.0015
6	.0001	.0055	.0368	.1115	.2051	.2508	.2001	.0881	.0112
7	.0000	.0008	.0090	.0425	.1172	.2150	.2668	.2013	.0574
8	.0000	.0001	.0014	.0106	.0439	.1209	.2335	.3020	.1937
9	.0000	.0000	.0001	.0016	.0098	.0403	.1211	.2684	.3874
10	.0000	.0000	.0000	.0001	.0010	.0060	.0282	.1074	.3487
					$n = 15$				
0	.2059	.0352	.0047	.0005	.0000	.0000	.0000	.0000	.0000
1	.3432	.1319	.0305	.0047	.0005	.0000	.0000	.0000	.0000
2	.2669	.2309	.0916	.0219	.0032	.0003	.0000	.0000	.0000
3	.1285	.2501	.1700	.0634	.0139	.0016	.0001	.0000	.0000
4	.0428	.1876	.2186	.1268	.0417	.0074	.0006	.0000	.0000
5	.0105	.1032	.2061	.1859	.0916	.0245	.0030	.0001	.0000
6	.0019	.0430	.1472	.2066	.1527	.0612	.0116	.0007	.0000
7	.0003	.0138	.0811	.1711	.1964	.1181	.0348	.0035	.0000
8	.0000	.0035	.0348	.1181	.1964	.1771	.0811	.0138	.0003
9	.0000	.0007	.0116	.0612	.1527	.2066	.1472	.0430	.0019
10	.0000	.0001	.0030	.0245	.0916	.1859	.2061	.1032	.0105
11	.0000	.0000	.0006	.0074	.0417	.1268	.2186	.1876	.0428
12	.0000	.0000	.0001	.0016	.0139	.0634	.1700	.2501	.1285
13	.0000	.0000	.0000	.0003	.0032	.0219	.0916	.2309	.2669
14	.0000	.0000	.0000	.0000	.0005	.0047	.0305	.1319	.3432
15	.0000	.0000	.0000	.0000	.0000	.0005	.0047	.0352	.2059

(Continued)

Source: Adapted from Hoffman, Lawrence D., and Orkin, Michael. 1979. *Mathematics with Applications.* New York: McGraw-Hill. Pp. 410–411. Copyright © 1979 by McGraw-Hill, Inc. Used with the permission of McGraw-Hill Book Company. [From: (1) Chao, L.C. 1974 *Statistics: Methods and Analyses* (2d ed.) New York: McGraw-Hill. (2) National Bureau of Labor Standards. 1950. *Tables of Binomial Distribution,* Applied Mathematics Series, no. 6.]

TABLE 31 (CONTINUED)

Values of r	Values of p								
	.1	.2	.3	.4	.5	.6	.7	.8	.9
					$n = 20$				
0	.1216	.0115	.0008	.0000	.0000	.0000	.0000	.0000	.0000
1	.2702	.0576	.0068	.0005	.0000	.0000	.0000	.0000	.0000
2	.2852	.1369	.0278	.0031	.0002	.0000	.0000	.0000	.0000
3	.1901	.2054	.0716	.0123	.0011	.0000	.0000	.0000	.0000
4	.0898	.2182	.1304	.0350	.0046	.0003	.0000	.0000	.0000
5	.0319	.1746	.1789	.0746	.0148	.0013	.0000	.0000	.0000
6	.0089	.1091	.1916	.1244	.0370	.0049	.0002	.0000	.0000
7	.0020	.0545	.1643	.1659	.0739	.0146	.0010	.0000	.0000
8	.0004	.0222	.1144	.1797	.1201	.0355	.0039	.0001	.0000
9	.0001	.0074	.0654	.1597	.1602	.0710	.0120	.0005	.0000
10	.0000	.0020	.0308	.1171	.1762	.1171	.0308	.0020	.0000
11	.0000	.0005	.0120	.0710	.1602	.1597	.0654	.0074	.0001
12	.0000	.0001	.0039	.0355	.1201	.1797	.1144	.0222	.0004
13	.0000	.0000	.0010	.0146	.0739	.1659	.1643	.0545	.0020
14	.0000	.0000	.0002	.0049	.0370	.1244	.1916	.1091	.0089
15	.0000	.0000	.0000	.0013	.0148	.0746	.1789	.1746	.1319
16	.0000	.0000	.0000	.0003	.0046	.0350	.1304	.2182	.0898
17	.0000	.0000	.0000	.0000	.0011	.0123	.0716	.2054	.1901
18	.0000	.0000	.0000	.0000	.0002	.0031	.0278	.1369	.2852
19	.0000	.0000	.0000	.0000	.0000	.0005	.0068	.0576	.2702
20	.0000	.0000	.0000	.0000	.0000	.0000	.0008	.0115	.1216

attitude toward the police is .2061, while the probability that they will have a negative attitude is .003.

Normal Distribution

It probably is not much of an exaggeration, if any, to state that modern statistics is built upon a foundation that consists of the *normal distribution*. The normal distribution not only is important in its own right but also represents a key element in determining the nature of various other distributions.

The normal distribution, to state the matter simply, is a particular way of assigning probabilities to intervals of numbers. The intervals may be considered events encompassing all numbers within the specified bounds.

The association of intervals and probabilities can best be visualized by referring to what is called the *normal curve*. The equation of this curve is:

$$y = \frac{1}{\sqrt{2\pi}} \, e^{-z^2/2}$$

TABLE 32
X AND Y PAIRS FOR
A NORMAL DISTRIBUTION CURVE

z	y
− 4.00	.0001
− 3.50	.0009
− 3.00	.0044
− 2.50	.0175
− 2.00	.0540
− 1.50	.1295
− 1.00	.2420
− .50	.3521
0	.3989
+ .50	.3521
+ 1.00	.2420
+ 1.50	.1295
+ 2.00	.0540
+ 2.50	.0175
+ 3.00	.0044
+ 3.50	.0009
+ 4.00	.0001

The variable z can take any value from minus infinity (− ∞) to plus infinity (+ ∞). Infinity, for those not familiar with the concept, refers to a limit without bound—that is, an endless process. The concept is extremely difficult to grasp, in part because of our linguistic heritage, which does not confortably embrace ideas such as infinity. (In fact, persons with pragmatic minds often say, "Well, now that we have reached infinity, why can't we add to it and have infinity plus something else?") The effective range for the normal curve, that is, its most usual and useful bounds, is between − 4.00 and + 4.00. The value of π in the formula just above is approximately 3.142; the symbol is the Greek letter *pi*. The value of e is approximately 2.718. To plot the normal curve, you insert a value for z (the abscissa) and then compute a value for y (the ordinate). For example, letting z = + 4.00 and solving for y produces y = .0001.

Other z, y pairs are set out in Table 32.

When the paired z's and y's are plotted on graph paper, the resulting curve takes the form shown in Figure 10.

The value of z (positive or negative) indicates the distance of a point from the center in the right-left direction, and the value of y indicates the height of the curve at that point (which is always positive).

The following special features of the normal distribution curve are important to bear in mind:

1 It is symmetrical about the y axis. This symmetry can be seen by direct

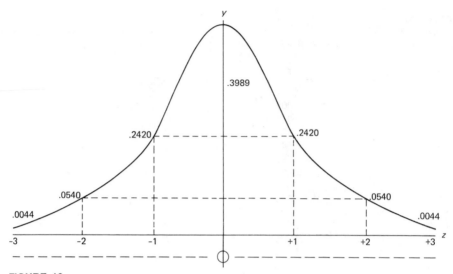

FIGURE 10
Normal distribution curve.

observation of the shape of the curve. It also can be appreciated by the fact that positive and negative values of z have the same ordinate value (or height of curve).

2 The highest point in the curve is at the value $z = 0$, when $y = .3989$.

3 Almost all the area of the curve falls between $- 3.00$ and $+ 3.00$. In fact, it is the case that the entire area under the curve (that is, between $- \infty$ and $+ \infty$) is equal to 1.000. And the area between -3.00 and $+3.00$ is .9974.

4 The curve approaches the z axis asymptotically. This means that it moves closer and closer to the axis as it moves out to the left and right but never reaches the axis.

The probability assigned to a given interval on the z axis is the area under the curve between the limits of the interval. For example, the area in the interval between $z = 0$ and $z = 1.50$ is equal to .4332. The probability of obtaining a z between 0 and 1.50, therefore, is .4332. This area is shown by shading in Figure 11.

The areas under the normal curve between $z = 0$ end various interval end points are shown in Table 33.

Table 33 indicates that the probability of a z between $z = 0$ and $z = .25$ is .0987; the probability of a z between 0 and .50 is .1915, and the probability of a z between 0 and .75 is .2734, and so on. Since the curve is symmetrical, all the preceding probabilities apply in the negative direction as well, so that, for example, the probability of a z between $z = - .25$ and $z = 0$ is .0987.

It has been demonstrated over the years through the collection of empirical data that many human characteristics follow the pattern of a

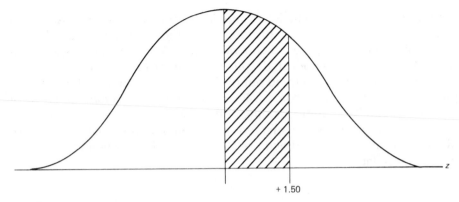

FIGURE 11
Normal curve with shading to indicate the interval between $z = 0$ and $z = 1.50$.

normal distribution. Height, weight, intelligence, reaction time to emergencies, jumping ability, skill at various sports, arm strength, and a host of other matters are normally distributed. Because intelligence as measured by the usual kinds of tests is normally distributed, we can readily determine the probability that a randomly selected person will have an IQ on the Stanford-Binet test that lies somewhere between 116 and 124 (remember, this means that an outcome—the person's IQ—will be in the event 116–124).

The concept of probability pervades research and judgments throughout the criminal justice system. Virtually every action that a detective takes is based upon an estimate of probabilities. One of the major reasons why experienced persons often perform their jobs better (assuming they have

TABLE 33
NORMAL CURVE AREAS FOR
VARIOUS INTERVAL END POINTS

Interval z = 0 to z =	Area under curve
.25	.0987
.50	.1915
.75	.2734
1.00	.3413
1.25	.3944
1.50	.4332
1.75	.4599
2.00	.4772
2.25	.4878
2.50	.4938

not burned out or lost initiative or intelligence) is that their exposure to a variety of circumstances has afforded them the opportunity to calculate probabilities more accurately than a newcomer. When a male suspect who is drunk reaches into a pocket, despite instructions to keep his hands up, is it likely that he is going to try to put his hands on a weapon and shoot? The probability of such an outcome will dictate the corresponding behavior of the officer. Similarly, understanding of the characteristics of a normal curve allows much more sophisticated judgments about distributions of phenomena and their standing in relationship to similar phenomena in the general population.

CHAPTER 11

STATISTICAL INFERENCE

CHAPTER OUTLINE

SAMPLING
   Simple Random Sampling
   Stratified Sampling
   Cluster Sampling
STATISTICAL INFERENCE
   The Logic of Statistical Inference
   Estimation
   Testing Statistical Hypotheses

SAMPLING

A *population* consists of the entire set of people or objects or numbers in which we are interested at a particular time. A *sample* is some subset of that population. One of the functions of statistics is to make decisions about a population on the basis of a sample. This is done when it proves impossible or inconvenient, and perhaps much too expensive, to obtain the entire population. Only in the rarest of cases can we make statements about a population with complete certainty when less than the entire population is available. Suppose, for instance, we want to get a range of data regarding embezzlers who are imprisoned in the federal penitentiaries for that offense. We discover that there are 276 such persons. We would be foolhardy if we interviewed only 26 of them and suggested without qualification that what they tell us represents totally accurately what we would have learned had we also interviewed the other 250.

Therefore, because of this, it is highly desirable to have some notion of sampling variability—that is, the variations in a characteristic of successive samples—in order to state the probable accuracy of our results or, in other words, the amount of confidence we have in them as accurate portrayals of the total population. It is possible to make statements about sampling variability only when the sampling has been performed according to the rules of probability.

Let us consider an example. Suppose we wished to estimate the mean IQ of all inmates of the jails and prisons in the state of Nebraska. Our population, then, consists of the IQs of all such inmates. It might be possible to administer the intelligence test to all inmates, but that might not be practical in terms of the time constraints that we are operating under, with an early due date for our report set by our superiors. Therefore, we select a small number of inmates, determine their IQs, and then use the mean of the sample to estimate the population mean.

If the selection of a sample has been accomplished in an entirely haphazard manner, we will not be able to make any confident statements regarding the estimate. By haphazard selection we mean selection where the probabilities that the various numbers in the population will appear in the sample are unknown. There have been horrendous examples of research done haphazardly in which the samples in no manner can be said to reflect the population. Suppose, for example, that we had gone into the jail at Grand Island and done our IQ testing on those inmates found in the library, because they were the most accessible. Obviously, it is not unlikely that inmates in the library will tend to have higher IQs than the general inmate population. And it may have been that the persons in the Grand Island jail at the time were notably different—suppose there had been a flurry of arrests for civil protest marches in that city—than the inmates in the remainder of the state's penal institutions. Therefore, if we obtain a sample mean by a haphazard process, we cannot specify its probable accuracy, or the amount of confidence we have in the estimate.

If we had, on the other hand, selected in such a way that each inmate had an equal probability of being drawn, we would have been able to make important qualifying statements about our estimate based on a sample.

An example of a qualifying statement indicating confidence is: The chances are 95 in 100 that the interval from $\bar{x} - 4$ to $\bar{x} + 4$ will include the population mean. Another example might be: The chances are 95 in 100 that the interval $\bar{x} - 8$ to $\bar{x} + 8$ will include the population mean. Notice that this is equivalent to saying that the second case involves a less accurate estimate than the first case. If the sample that we are employing has a mean equal to 111, for purposes of illustration, then in the first case our 95 in 100 interval is

107 (that is, 111 − 4) to 115 (111 + 4), while for the second it is 103 (111 − 8) to 119 (111 + 8).

To sample in accord with known probabilities, certain standard selection procedures are adopted. Of these, the most important for our purposes is random sampling. Sampling is said to be random when each unit or associated number has an equal opportunity of being included in the set of selected numbers or units. In everyday language "random" refers usually to selection without aim or purpose, but in statistics it has a much more precise definition; for aimless choice, we have earlier used the term *haphazard*. Haphazard selection is rarely random, since there is usually some bias at work, even though it may not be obvious to the casual observer. Bias, of course, implies that some units are more likely to be chosen than others.

It should be emphasized that "random" refers to a sampling process and not to any particular sample. When the expression *random sample* is employed, it means that the sample was selected by a random process, and it carries no implications for the characteristics of the particular sample. A sample is random if it was selected by means of a random sampling process, no matter how unrepresentative it may prove to be of its own population.

Take, for example, a study that sought to measure the number of persons driving on an interstate highway who do not possess valid driving licenses. We know that about 2000 cars traverse the highway each day, and we decide to stop 50 cars on a specified day. We do so by flagging down every fortieth car that goes by, starting at a random early point. We find that 30 of the 50 drivers have invalid licenses or no license at all. That result seems unusually high to us, so we increase the sample to 200 by stopping every tenth car. This time we discover that only 10 of 50 drivers do not possess proper licenses. Since in both cases we sampled in such a manner that each of the approximately 2000 cars to traverse the highway on the day of the sampling had an equal probability of being drawn, our sample in both instances would be considered random, no matter how disparate the results that we obtained. The most likely explanation for the different outcomes, of course, is that in the first instance the luck of the draw biased the result, just as sometimes when we throw a coin up 10 times we get 8 heads and 2 tails, rather than 5 heads and 5 tails. Obviously, the greater the number of tosses, the more likely we are to approach the 50–50 head-tail result.

A special case of random sampling occurs when every unit has an equal probability of occurrence in the selected group and, in addition, every possible combination of n units has an equal likelihood of occurring as a given sample of size n. This is called *simple random sampling*. We are assured of simple random sampling if the probability of each unit is equal on each draw.

Not all random sampling falls into the category of simple random sampling. Suppose, for instance, we are interested in determining the running abilities of members of a recruit class at the police academy for a large urban state. Affirmative action to equalize the sex distribution of officers has led to a class which is made up of 500 women and 500 men. But we know on the basis of a variety of experimental work that the men as a group are likely to be better runners, though there may be a not insignificant number of the women who perform better than some of the men. But we would prefer to be certain that we have an equal number of men and women in the sample, without allowing that outcome to be dictated by the probabilities of random sampling. What we do is merely to select our sample in equal amounts from the two groups, say 50 men and 50 women. Then we can generalize our results back to the female and male populations much more adequately. Instead of saying that the average recruit runs the mile in 5 minutes and 47 seconds, we can differentiate the performance of the women as a group and the men as a group. In this sense, we have taken steps to eliminate the possibility of a poor or unrepresentative sample, such as the highly unlikely but nonetheless possible outcome that would have, say, 80 males and 20 females in the sample. The sampling will remain random if we select our 50 males and 50 females in such a way that evey experimental person has an equal probability of choice. But we no longer have simple random selection, since the probability of getting certain combinations in our selected group is zero; that is, we cannot get a selection of size 100 consisting of 75 males and 25 females or even one of 51 males and 49 females.

Sampling procedures are further classified in terms of whether or not each selected experimental unit is made available for further selection after the appropriate measurement is made upon it. We say that we are sampling *with replacement* when the selection of a given experimental unit has no effect on the probability of its being selected again. The unit is, in this sense, returned to the complete set from which we are doing our selecting.

Consider the process of selecting the persons from the roster of the police academy for our investigation of running speed and endurance. If we draw the names randomly from a file of registration cards in the superintendent's office, we might, say, in one of our first few choices select the name of John Doe. If we sample with replacement, we return Doe's card to the file after each selection in order to make the card available for further random choice. Doe, in this manner, can be chosen two, three, or even more times, and the measurement we are interested in would enter the sample a corresponding two, three, or more times. Sampling *without replacement,* on the other hand, is accomplished simply by not returning the selected card to the files and thereby making it ineligible for further selection. The results for each individual, under these circumstances, could occur in the sample no more than one time. Throwing a coin or a die repeatedly is equivalent to sampling *with replacement,* since the occurrence of a given outcome has no effect on the probability of its occurring again.

Our discussions of statistical inference in this chapter will be based upon simple random sampling from infinitely large populations or from finite populations with replacement. Two other forms of random sampling (cluster sampling and stratified sampling) will also be discussed briefly, but a detailed exposition is beyond the scope of this treatment. Indeed, there are entire volumes devoted to the various kinds of random sampling methods and their variations (see, for example, Cochran, 1963, and Kish, 1965).

It should be noted that as a result of sampling without replacement from a finite or delimited population, the probabilities associated with the selection of the various experimental units change with each draw. Suppose, as an example, our population for study consists of 10 police officers and we use random sampling without replacement. The probability of getting any particular officer into our sample on the first draw is 1/10. The probability of getting any 1 of the 9 remaining officers on the next draw is 1/9, the next probability is 1/8, and so on. It can be convenient to assume that we are sampling with replacement for calculating associated probabilities if the population is finite but extremely large. If there are, say, 639,836 law enforcement officers in our population, and our sample size is but four, the actual probabilities of

$$\frac{1}{639,836} \qquad \frac{1}{639,835} \qquad \frac{1}{639,834} \qquad \frac{1}{639,833}$$

differ so slightly that the assumption of equivalence is supportable.

Simple Random Sampling

What methods are necessary to assure that simple random sampling is achieved? It was stressed earlier that haphazard selection cannot be expected to be equivalent to random sampling no matter how unbiased the individual carrying out the aimless selection is. Even in so simple a task as listing digits aimlessly, we have discovered that people prefer certain digits to others, and therefore these have a higher probability of occurrence. At a task such as choosing children haphazardly in a large play area, a given selector may show a slight, but important, preference for tall children or short children or dark-skinned children or intelligent-appearing children. To the extent that such a bias is allowed to operate, the haphazard sample will not be random and it certainly will not be simple random.

To minimize the play of judgments (and the accompanying biases involved in such judgments) as much as possible, mechanical sampling processes are generally used. Perhaps the most obvious approach is to number all the experimental units of interest, write these numbers on slips of paper, and then withdraw *n* of these slips from a thoroughly mixed hopper. If the hopper is again mixed thoroughly after each and every draw, this procedure will provide simple random sampling. The method is satisfactory in principle, but unfortunately, it suffers from a number of difficulties when translated into actual practice. Aside from the laboriousness involved in its execution, it is very difficult to achieve a thorough enough mixing to assure random selection on each draw. It is altogether too easy for two or more slips of paper to remain in an obscure corner of the hopper, despite the vigor of the mixing process.

Similar procedures, such as assigning numbers to the experimental units and listing them on balls or beads or cards, with subsequent mixing, shaking, or shuffling, suffer from the same sort of difficulties. Empirical evidence indicates that it is impossible to mix balls or beads or to shuffle cards adequately between each draw to obtain uniform probabilities.

Fortunately, for those desiring a simple random sample, a number of research workers have devised optimum techniques for getting such samples and have established these techniques in such a manner that their samples may be used by other investigators. This has been accomplished by sampling from the set of digits from 0 to 9 with replacement and listing the selected units in tables. These tables usually are called *tables of random numbers*. The first table of random numbers was devised by Tippett in 1927. Tippett's table was formed by selecting 40,000 digits at random from census reports and then combining them by 4s to give 10,000 four-digit numbers. The early random sampling experiments were used to check the predictions of theoretical probability laws by comparison between observed and mathematically predicted frequencies.

In a number of subsequent sampling investigations, Tippett's table, when used in the regular way, was found unsuitable for the rigorous demands of random sampling. Kendall and Smith (1939), accordingly, published a number table derived from use of a machine in which a circular disc contained the digits 0 to 9 on 10 equal partitions. The disc rotated at a very high speed, and at haphazard intervals a light flashed for a short enough period to make the rotating disc seem to stand still. When the light flashed, an observer would read the digit in the partition which was aligned with a fixed pointer. This procedure was repeated over and over again until Kendall and Smith had 100,000 random digits. These were grouped in 100 separate thousands and listed in subgroupings of two and four on each page. The following represents a section from Kendall and Smith's table of random numbers:

10	04	00	95	85	04	32	80	19	01
23	94	97	28	60	43	42	25	26	48
35	63	42	90	90	74	33	17	58	77
42	86	03	36	45	33	60	77	72	92
47	26	92	87	09	96	85	37	82	61

In the introduction to the book by Kendall and Smith (1939), Kendall discussed the methods used to test the randomness of their set of numbers. One such test consisted of selecting a block of numbers and comparing the digits (0 to 9) and the pairs of digits in that block with the numbers of digits and pairs of digits expected on the basis of a random process. In the case of the single digits, for example, this means that each digit would occur one-tenth the number of digits in the block.

The testing satisfied Kendall that the numbers in the table did represent simple random samples. The authors did, however, locate sporadic patches which were unsuitable for drawing samples when such patches—or parts of the table—were used alone. Footnotes were placed on the appropriate pages of the table of random numbers to warn the table user against employing only these patches. It should be pointed out that any very large table of random numbers may be expected to have parts which are unsuitable for many sampling purposes, usually sampling purposes in which small n's are involved.

The Rand Corporation (1955) has developed and published a very large table of random numbers. These random digits were produced by a machine which was essentially a 32-place electronic roulette wheel which made about 3000 revolutions per trial and produced one number each second. A converter was employed which handled only 20 of the 32 numbers and ignored the rest. It retained only the final digit of the two-digit numbers that were produced. Slight biases were found in the set of numbers produced by this method, and they were subjected to rerandomization by arithmetic transformation. The numbers which made up the final table were given tests like those used by Kendall and Smith and satisfied rigorous criteria of randomness. The following is a section from the Rand Corporation table:

65027	61184	04285	01392	17974	15077
38807	36961	31649	42096	63281	02023
65122	59659	86283	68258	69577	13798
35583	16563	79246	86686	76463	34222
07500	37992	45134	26529	26760	83637

To use a table of random numbers for selecting from a set of experimental units, a criminal justice researcher should proceed in the following manner:

First: Assign numbers to the entire set of experimental units, using the numbering system employed by the table of random numbers that will be examined to draw the sample. Kendall and Smith have divided their digits into 100 groups of 1000 each and then numbered the rows from 1 to 25 and the columns from 1 to 40 within each group. The lines of the Rand table are numbered from 00000 to 19999 and arranged, for each line, in 10 columns of 5 digits each.

You can choose a starting point with the Rand table, for example, by allowing the book to fall open and selecting a five-digit number grouping haphazardly. If the first digit of this grouping is even, call it zero; if it is odd, call it one. The five digits then give you the starting line. Consider the columns within the line number, 0, 1, 2, 3, . . . , 9, and the second digit in the grouping gives you the starting column within the chosen line.

Second: Ordinarily, the table is read from the starting point as you would read a book, but it can be read vertically or backwards. The reading is in terms of groups of size equal to the number of digits assigned to each experimental unit. Suppose there are *r* digits in each of the assigned numbers. The first set of *r* digits read from the table designates the first unit selected, the second *r* digits the second unit, and so forth until the entire selected group is obtained. If certain *r* digits from the table have not been assigned to any unit, they are ignored and you proceed to the next *r* digits.

For many research problems, the randomization achieved by a table of random numbers may be approximated by a less cumbersome method. The class of approximations is widely referred to as *systematic sampling*. One approach to systematic sampling was illustrated in the example above of estimating the number of persons driving without valid driving licenses. Every fortieth or every tenth car on the highway was selected, with the first car randomly chosen from among the first 40 cars in the first case and the first 10 cars in the second case. The method provides an approximation to simple random sampling because it seems reasonable to assume that licensed and nonlicensed drivers enter the highway randomly and drive with random speeds, so that their probabilities of reaching the checkpoint remain constant after each observation (like tossing a coin repeatedly).

This method, in more general terms, consists of choosing every *k*th unit (frequently from a listing) after randomly selecting the starting unit. Clearly this method does not provide a good approximation to simple random sampling when there are inherent biases in the array of possible choices— as when a listing from which choices are to be made shows periodicity, in that units with similar characteristics occur at regular intervals. For example, a selection of rooms ending in 1 (101, 201, 301, 401, etc.) at a certain hotel may produce only corner suites, and a selection of every twenty-fifth officer in a police department may produce only lieutenants because of an ordering by squads and ranks.

Another approach to systematic sampling, and one that will counteract some periodicity effects, is to use different selection intervals at different parts of the selection roster.

Stratified Sampling

In the case of stratified sampling, the representation of the population in the form of a listing is divided into two or more strata. The grouping of units into strata is based on some relevant criterion or criteria, such as sex, age, socioeconomic status, annual income, party affiliation, or type of school attended. When the stratification is achieved, a simple random sample (or its approximation) is taken from each stratum.

Suppose, for example, we wished to assess by telephone interview the attitudes of the citizens in a certain city toward the "deadly force" policy of the city's police department. Before starting the sampling process, we know that the affluent and the poor tend to have different attitudes toward the police and that similar differences are found between age, ethnic, and racial groups. Consequently, it would seem desirable to have a balance over these groups in our sample; otherwise, the sampling results may not be representative of the population (consisting of all citizens of the city). To illustrate, a simple random sample may produce predominately upper- and middle-class people or younger people or whites.

Stratification in this case would consist of drawing up strata containing citizens of certain types in each stratum, and then selecting citizens from each stratum by simple random sampling. Since the drawing up of strata with so many relevant criteria in a large city would be a formidable task, approximation methods are widely used.

A most simple case of stratified sampling was the example discussed earlier in this chapter: 50 males and 50 females were selected from a recruit class of 500 males and 500 females. The population was stratified into "male" and "female," and then a simple random sample of 50 was taken from each stratum.

Clearly, stratified sampling raises the efficiency of the process by eliminating unrepresentative samples, but the method does require different types of statistical calculations from those discussed in this book. (Cochran, 1963, or Kish, 1965, may be consulted for details.)

Cluster Sampling

Simple random and stratified sampling can be enormously expensive in certain types of research—as, for example, in house-to-house interviewing in a large city or in administering tests to officers in a very large number of metropolitan police departments. Cluster sampling may be a practical alternative.

In cluster sampling, one starts with larger groupings (clusters) of units—like all the households in a certain block or all the officers in a certain grouping—and then samples clusters (rather than units) by simple random or stratified methods.

Suppose that we are interested in the attitudes of police officers in California toward decisions of superior and appellate courts. The method chosen for establishing attitudes is the interview. It is clear that simple random sampling over all police officers in the state is not possible and stratified sampling is not much more feasible. But we can regard police departments as clusters and then sample from a listing of departments in the state. Stratification of clusters can be achieved by grouping departments into some such strata as: departments in cities with more than 250,000 residents, departments in cities with 100,000 to 250,000 residents, departments in cities with 25,000 to 100,000 residents, and departments in cities with fewer than 25,000 residents. Then, to raise the probability of representativeness, we select clusters (departments) from each of these strata. We then have in the sample very large departments, large departments, medium-size departments, and small departments (or approximately so, since there is some difference in officer-to-citizen ratios over departments).

Once a cluster is selected, we sample units from the cluster (or use all units in the cluster). Thus, we may have selected the following clusters in the preceding example (where the clusters were police departments): Oakland Police Department, Fremont Police Department, Anaheim Police Department, Covina Police Department, Laguna Beach Police Department, and Carmel Police Department. We would then direct our interviews only at randomly selected officers from these departments.

Statistical handling of the data from cluster sampling is even more complicated than that of data from stratified sampling.

STATISTICAL INFERENCE

The Logic of Statistical Inference

The methods of statistical inference are employed to help the criminal justice investigator generalize from data that are obtained. The particular form that the generalization takes depends on the interests and goals of the investigator.

An investigator, for example, might be interested in the average number of minutes per day that adults in Chicago spend in efforts to avoid being victims of crime. This could be measured by calculating indirect routes that they follow in going from one place to another in order to avoid areas they consider unsafe, and by similar kinds of measures. Clearly, it will be impossible to get such information from all the residents in the city of Chicago; but it is easy enough to take a sample of such persons. Then, depending on how the sample was drawn, methods of statistical inference to estimate the mean for all Chicago adults can be used. Not surprisingly, this aspect of statistical inference is called *estimation*.

Take another example—those coin tosses that we discussed in some detail in Chapter 10. Suppose you assume that a coin randomly chosen from your pocket is unbiased, that is that $P[H] = P[T] = \frac{1}{2}$. A simple experiment would consist of tossing the coin 50 times and noting the numbers of heads and tails that come up. Suppose that such an experiment is carried out and the result proves to be 30 heads and 20 tails. Should such an outcome lead the investigator to doubt the accuracy of the original idea that the coin is unbiased? The aspect of statistical inference that assists the investigator in arriving at this type of decision is called *hypothesis testing*.

There are other kinds of statistical inference, such as Bayesian inference, a method based on the conception that increasing information alters the subjective probabilities regarding alternative possible "causes" of events. But estimation and hypothesis testing are the two kinds of inference most widely used.

As a basis for discussion of statistical inference, it is essential to provide a logical framework. The logical framework offers a method of thinking about the concepts underlying specific procedures of such inference.

The inferential process starts with a population, such as that of the Chicago adults in the example used earlier, where it is not possible or not feasible to measure or evaluate every one of its members. The population may be thought of in terms of the numbers procured by the measurement or the evaluation process rather than in terms of the actual people (or objects) upon whom (or upon which) the measurements are made. The set of measurements of the population may be distributed as shown in the histogram in Figure 12.

Let us look at the histogram for a moment to derive some information based upon its shape. Assume that the mean of the population it represents is 75.6 and that its standard deviation is 13.5.

The measurements of the population are grouped to facilitate presentation in the histogram. Thus, there is a group that contains all measurements in the interval 50–54, another for the interval 55–59, and so on over the entire range of the measurements, with the highest falling in the interval 100–104.

FIGURE 12
Histogram representation of population measurement.

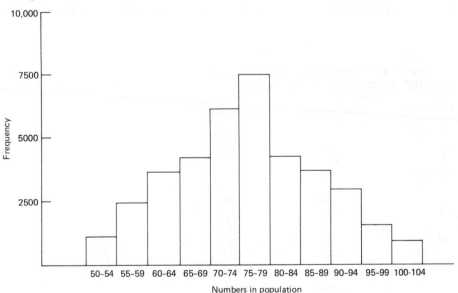

Numbers in population

The ordinate of the histogram shows the frequency with which the measurements in each of the interval groupings occur. Since the bases of all the histogram rectangles are the same length, it can be assumed that the area of the rectangle above each interval represents the frequency of the interval. The same information can be shown in the form of a table (Table 34).

A column has been added to Table 34 to show each frequency as a proportion of the total number of numbers. It can be seen, thus, that .0297 of the measurements fall in the interval 50–54, .0656 fall in the interval 55–59, and .0973 in 60–64, and so on.

The grouping into the intervals 50–54, 55–59, and so forth, is, of course, arbitrary. The groups were set up in order to make it relatively easy to communicate the broad distributive features of measurements in the population. It would have been perfectly possible to use other choices of groupings, and they would work just as well: for example, intervals such as 50–52, 53–55, 56–58, and so on in this manner. But some kind of grouping clearly is essential, since there are 37,831 measurements and that is altogether too large an array to communicate and to absorb individually.

Discussion of the population measurements in this way provides a mechanism for conceptualizing population sets when the actual numbers are not available. Thus, if the population of numbers is specified as the set of weights of all adults in the United States, it is possible to imagine a histogram or a table such as Table 34. The intervals could well be of the order of 50–59 pounds, 60–69 pounds, 70–79 pounds, and so on.

Suppose we want to estimate the mean of the population set shown in Table 34 from a sample size of 50. We are going to sample by a process that gives each individual in the population an equal likelihood of occurring on

TABLE 34
DISTRIBUTION OF POPULATION MEASUREMENT
BY INTERVAL, FREQUENCY, AND PROPORTION

Interval	Frequency	Proportion
50–54	1124	.0297
55–59	2480	.0656
60–64	3682	.0973
65–69	4003	.1058
70–74	6124	.1619
75–79	7489	.1980
80–84	4204	.1111
85–89	3702	.0979
90–94	2641	.0698
95–99	1487	.0393
100–104	895	.0236
	37,831	1.0000

each draw, that is, by simple random sampling. On the first draw, therefore, the probability of a number from the interval 50–54 is 1124/37831, which equals .0297. The probability of a number from the interval 55–59 is 2480/37831 = .0656. The proportion column, in short, shows the probabilities associated with each interval when equal-likelihood sampling is used. The sampling is done with replacement to maintain those probabilities on each draw.

The column of proportions in Table 34 presents probabilities under these sampling conditions. Certain consequences become readily deducible from examining the column. First, you are much more likely in the sample to get values from the center of the distribution (that is, from 65–69, 70–74, 75–79, 80–84, 85–89) than from the ends (that is, 50–54, 55–59, 95–99, 100–104). Put another way, you are more likely to get values near the mean, which is equal to 75.6, than further out. Second, since the distribution is roughly symmetrical, you are about equally likely to get a value above or below the mean on a given draw. Thus, you would expect the high values to balance the low values over the draws.

These consequences lead to an expectation that the mean computed from the sample of 50 will be not far from the population mean of 75.6. Is it possible, however, to come up with a sample mean very far from 75.6, say 53.4 or 101.9? It is indeed possible—but the probability is so low that it might take trillions of samples of size 50 before you could expect so extreme a mean. Of course, the sample means we have noted, such as 101.9, are very extreme; the likelihoods of various possible values for the mean go up sharply as you move closer to 75.6 from 53.4 at one end and 101.9 at the other end. In fact, Figure 13 shows approximately the probabilities of possible sample mean values over the range 50 to 104.

FIGURE 13
Probabilities of possible sample means values over the range 50–104.

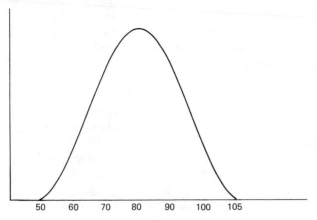

When you examine Figure 13, think of the probabilities associated with any interval as the area under the curve that covers that interval in the manner discussed in Chapter 10 for the normal distribution. Thinking in that fashion is like imagining a histogram embedded under the curve, where the curve smooths the squared tops of the histogram.

As fate would have it, the distribution shown if Figure 13 *is* normal. A statistical theorem, in fact, states that the sampling distribution of means is approximately normal if the sample size is large enough, regardless of the population distribution. If the sample size is small, the sampling distribution of means still is approximately normal if the population of numbers is approximately normal. Also, the mean of the sampling distribution is equal to the mean of the original distribution. For purposes of reasonable approximation, a small sample is usually regarded as one less than 30, while a large sample is considered one of 30 or larger.

The sampling distribution is the heart of statistical inference. All decisions in estimation as well as in hypothesis testing are based on a sampling distribution as a referent.

Estimation

Let us assume that a city's newspapers have been running large feature stories about what they regard as the high injury rate associated with automobiles within city boundaries. The chief of the police department is aware of the literature on automobile accidents and in answer to a request for information from members of the city council, states: "I think the injury rate might well go down greatly if we could get people to use their seat belts. Perhaps we can pass an ordinance requiring the use of seat belts. They have laws like that in Canada and Australia."

Before any action such as this is taken, however, the council members decide that it would be wise to determine the proportion of drivers and riders within the city who use seat belts. You will remember that we discussed a procedure for making such a determination in an earlier chapter. Direct determination is a most difficult task—perhaps an impossible one. Therefore, it becomes necessary to employ a process of estimation, such as the one whereby observers at randomly selected locations in the city note the number of people in cars and the number who use seat belts.

The reports of all observers indicate that the proportion of car occupants who fasten their seat belts is .16. This is, of course, a sampling proportion, not the proportion derived from scrutiny of all cars and all occupants during a specified period in the city.

How reasonable is it to employ the .16 as an estimate of the proportion for all cars? If the observation process has been random, it intuitively seems quite reasonable to generalize to the city at large. The generalization might be questioned if the observation had been based only on large cars, or small cars, or older drivers, or younger drivers, or drivers in residential areas, or drivers in shopping areas, or similar kinds of selective groups. The reason such results with such samples would appear questionable is the known or potential relationship between the factors and the use of seat belts. Older drivers, for example, are known to be more likely than younger drivers to fasten their seat belts. The greater the number of older than younger drivers in the observed sample in terms of their proportion in the population of interest, the more you are likely to be overestimating the finding of central interest.

Let's take another example. Suppose it is proposed in a session of the state legislature in Salem, Oregon, that police officers should be required, before being hired, to have a high level of sophistication in the social and behavioral sciences, such as sociology and psychology. The argument is made that their primary role is interpersonal intervention; they must deal with family disputes and neighborhood complaints and question a variety of persons of quite different backgrounds. Yet, it is maintained, the average police officer in the state does not know as much about social or behavioral science as the average freshman in college.

The aides of a legislator interested in this measure are asked to seek some firmer information in support of (or in opposition to) the proposed measure. They locate a standard test measuring social science information that has been used widely to test first-year college students. They administer this test to a random sample of law enforcement officers throughout the state. The test has been standardized so that the average for college freshmen is a score of 400.

After administering and scoring the tests, the legislator's aides discover that the mean score for the officers is 435. Since the 435 was not the result of testing every police officer in the state of Oregon, it is at best only an estimate of the average score for all officers. Is it a reasonable estimate? As before, it would appear reasonable if the sampling was random. We would not want too many bright officers in the sample, or dull officers or well-educated officers or poorly educated officers—or any similar kinds of biasing items.

Note—most important—that the word *reasonable* has been used prominently in describing the possible utility of the estimation process. Our task now becomes that of providing formal underpinning to the intuition that lies behind use of the concept of "reasonableness."

Let us look at another example in order to pin down the numerical and inferential logic of the relationship between samples and the population they are expected to represent. Suppose we have taken a random sample of 20 from a large population of private enforcement officers who are assigned the duty of patroling a marina which docks a large number of boats. The question of interest concerns the swimming ability of the officers, since we are interested in determining whether the force is of adequate quality to guard against water emergencies that may arise in connection with boating activities. If we have enough competent swimmers, we will be able to make guarding assignments so that at least several harbor officers will be able to assist in rescue operations if needed.

We find that 4 of the sample of 20 officers are not competent swimmers. Again, the sample value, the 4/20 or .20, seems a reasonable estimate of the proportion of the population which is not competent in swimming.

As the first step toward justification for our intuition of what is reasonable, we turn to Table 31 (Chapter 10) and look within the box headed $n = 20$, in the row where $r = 4$. The first value in that row is .0898, which is in the column labeled .1. This means that if the proportion of noncompetent swimmers in the population is .1, then the probability of getting 4 noncompetent swimmers in a sample of 20 is .0898. The next value to the right is .2182, which is the probability of getting 4 noncompetent swimmers in the sample of 20 if the proportion of noncompetent swimmers in the population is .20. The remainder of the entries in that row are similarly interpretable.

Now note that the highest of these entries is .2182, under the column headed .20. That specifies that of all the possible population proportions specified in the table, the one that provides the highest probability, or maximum likelihood, for the obtained result is .20. Indeed, even if there were many more possible population proportions given in the table (e.g., .18, .19, .21, .22) the proportion giving the maximum for the obtained result would still be .20.

Consequently, the estimate of 4/20 = .20 for the population proportion is called a *maximum-likelihood estimate*. That is, the population proportion of .20 (over all possible population proportions) produces the highest probability for the obtained result (4 in 20 nonswimmers).

As another example, suppose that our sample is 15 and that 6 in the sample show themselves not to be competent swimmers. What is the maximum-likelihood estimate for the population proportion given the obtained proportion of 6/15 = .40? We turn again to Table 31 and look at the row where $r = 6$ within the box headed by $n = 15$. The first entry in the row is .0019, meaning that the probability of obtaining 6 swimmers who are not competent in a simple random sample size of 15 is .0019 if the actual proportion of noncompetent swimmers in the population is .1. As we move along the row, we find that the maximum value is .2066. For the entries in the table, then, the highest probability, or maximum likelihood, for the particular sampling results occurs when the proportion of swimmers who are not competent in the population is .40. And that would be the case even if the table contained proportions of .37, .38, .39, .41, .42, .43, etc.

The maximum-likelihood estimate of the population proportion, therefore, is .40, which corresponds to one's intuition of a reasonable estimate.

In point estimation, such as that illustrated thus far, there is no way to assign a probability value to the accuracy of the estimate. One can be sure only that the estimation process produced a reasonable result—the maximum-likelihood estimate.

Probability statements come with *interval* estimates. An interval estimate with associated probability takes this form: the probability is 95 in 100 (.95) that the interval 435 − 6.1 to 435 + 6.1 encompasses the population mean.

The probability is based on the sampling distribution. Let us illustrate the approach by using the population summarized in Table 34. A sample of 50 is taken by simple random sampling—the sampling distribution is shown in Figure 13. The mean of the sampling distribution, like the mean of the population, is equal to 75.6. Using that mean and the standard deviation of the sampling distribution (which is equal to the standard deviation of the population divided by $\sqrt{n}$), we can establish the probabilities associated with getting sample means of varying degrees of difference from the population mean. Thus, as one example, the probability of getting a sample mean larger than 79.3 or smaller than 71.9 is less than .05. The interval is 71.9 to 79.3, that is, 7.4 in total length.

But in an actual estimation problem, we do not know the value of the population mean—we are trying to estimate it. We can, however, use the sampling results to produce the interval length (or approximately so). We can then use the interval obtained from our sample to set bounds about our sample mean and have the probability of .95 (1 − .05) that the bounds encompass the population mean.

Let us illustrate the process for the example where we were interested in the knowledge of the social sciences by officers in Oregon. The sample mean obtained with a sample of size 50 was 435. Suppose the sample standard deviation was 22. That gives a standard deviation for the sampling distribution of 3.1 ($22/\sqrt{50}$).

An interval with a .95 confidence of covering the population mean becomes (435 − 6.1) to (435 + 6.1), or 428.9 to 441.1. We could, similarly, move to a .99 confidence interval, which would be 427.0 to 443.0. Notice that the interval increases in length as we move to a position of greater confidence that the population mean lies in the interval.

It should be noted, in concluding, that one uses $\sqrt{n-1}$ rather than $\sqrt{n}$ (that is, $\sqrt{49}$ rather than $\sqrt{50}$ in the preceding example) when one uses the sample standard deviation in place of the population standard deviation, but the difference is too small to be of much significance for present purposes.

Testing Statistical Hypotheses

Suppose you reach into your pocket, remove a coin, and conjecture that the coin is unbiased, in the sense that tossing it will be as likely to produce a head as a tail. The conjecture that a coin is as likely to show a head as a tail is often referred to as an *empirical hypothesis*. From a broader perspective, an empirical hypothesis in a conjectural statement about the condition of some aspect of the world.

The conjecture about the coin, of course, may or may not be true. That uncertainty may well lead to a decision to test the empirical hypothesis by a simple experiment. The experiment consists of tossing the coin 10 times and observing the numbers of heads and tails that appear in the 10 tosses. The possible outcomes for the experiment are: 10 heads, 0 tails; 9 heads, 1 tail; 8 heads, 2 tails; and so on to 1 head, 9 tails; 0 heads, 10 tails. But we must decide now which of these outcomes could lead us to believe that the original conjecture or empirical hypothesis can be believed and which results will lead us to doubt the conjecture. When members of a class in criminal justice research were asked about the basis for such a decision, widespread agreement was achieved that outcomes 5, 5; 6, 4; and 7, 3 (regardless of which of the figures were heads and which tails) would lead to belief in the conjecture while outcomes 8, 2; 9, 1; and 10, 0 (again, regardless of the direction) would lead to doubt.

Dividing the outcomes into two sets in this fashion—with one set leading to belief in the conjecture and the other to doubt—is referred to as establishing a *decision rule*. The decision rule in this instance is: (1) Outcome 5, 5; 6, 4; or 7, 3 = believe conjecture. (2) Outcome 8, 2; 9, 1; or 10, 0 = doubt conjecture. This appears quite reasonable, but is it?

When members of the class were asked why they had established the cutoff between 7, 3 and 8, 2 rather than between, say, 8, 2 and 9, 1, they could provide no justification.

It is at this point that the theory of testing statistical hypotheses profitably enters the picture, because it provides a consistent and rational method for setting up decision rules. In addition, it establishes a probability for making a wrong decision.

Step 1 in statistical hypothesis testing is to convert the empirical hypothesis to a statistical hypothesis. A statistical hypothesis is a formal statement about a population characteristic or about several such character-istics; these characteristics, in statistical form, are called *parameters*. The empirical hypothesis that a head is as likely as a tail becomes the statistical hypothesis:

$$P[H] \;=\; P[T] \;=\; \frac{1}{2}$$

Step 2 is to pretend that the statistical hypothesis is true and to refer to the sampling distribution that results from use of the parameter or parameters. In our particular case, the sampling distribution that results from the pretense that $P[H] = P[T] = 1/2$ is the binomial with $p = q = \frac{1}{2}$. Since $n = 10$, the sampling distribution is:

$$\frac{10!}{r!\,(10-r!)} \left(\frac{1}{2}\right)^{10}$$

Or, equivalently, the sampling distribution is set out in Table 31 (Chapter 10) for $n = 10$, under the column headed .50. Using this table with $p = 1/2$, the probability of 10 heads, 0 tails is .0010; the probability of 9 heads, 1 tail is .0098; the probability of 8 heads, 2 tails is .0439; and so on. Similarly, the probability of 10 tails, 0 heads is .0010; the probability of 9 tails, 1 head is .0098; the probability of 8 tails, 2 heads is .0439; and so on.

To illustrate the advance that we have made, by the use of step 1 and step 2, beyond the intuitive guess of the members of the criminal justice research class about the decision rule, we can compute the probabilities of two classes of outcome—under the condition that the statistical hypothesis that $p = 1/2$ is true. The probability of each possible outcome is shown in Table 35.

Since the outcomes are mutually exclusive, the probability of either event (5, 5; 6, 4; 7, 3) or, equivalently, of event (8, 2; 9, 1; 10, 1) can be computed by adding the probabilities of the outcomes within each event. If the statistical hypothesis is true, the probability of an outcome leading to belief in the hypothesis is .891 and the probability of an outcome leading to doubt of the hypothesis is .109. (We have dropped the last digit of each probability figure owing to the slight discrepancy that comes about from rounding).

TABLE 35
PROBABILITIES OF OUTCOMES IN REGARD TO
STATISTICAL HYPOTHESIS THAT $p = 1/2$

**Outcomes leading to
belief in hypothesis**

Heads	Tails	Probability
5	5	.2461
6	4	.2051
4	6	.2051
7	3	.1172
3	7	.1172
		.8907

**Outcomes leading to
doubt of hypothesis**

Heads	Tails	Probability
8	2	.0439
2	8	.0439
9	1	.0098
1	9	.0098
10	0	.0010
0	10	.0010
		.1094

We can state, therefore, that if we follow the decision rule advocated by the class members, we will be wrong with a probability of .109 when the coin really is unbiased. That is, if the coin is unbiased so that $p = q = 1/2$, there is a probability of .109 that one of the following outcomes will occur: 8 heads, 2 tails; 8 tails, 2 heads; 9 heads, 1 tail; 9 tails, 1 head; 10 heads, 0 tails; 10 tails, 0 heads. That would seem to put us a bit further along than we were when the intuitive-decision rule was propounded.

Let us return to the steps necessary for testing a statistical hypothesis. We formulated a statistical hypothesis (step 1); then we referred to a sampling distribution resulting from the pretense that the statistical hypothesis was true (step 2). Step 3 involves choosing a decision rule on the basis of some arbitrarily selected, low probability of an erroneous decision when the statistical hypothesis really is true.

As before, the decision rule assigns all possible outcomes to two categories. The language of the resulting decision, however, differs somewhat from that used in the informal manner above. The outcomes that fall into the category that is unlikely if the statistical hypothesis is true—(the 8, 2; 9, 1; 10, 0 above)—lead to the expression *rejection of the statistical hypothesis.* If the statistical hypothesis really is true, then an outcome in that category is an unlikely eventuality.

It can be noted, in this context, that a good deal of nonsense has been written to the effect that a research worker may reject a statistical hypothesis but may never accept it. This argument would have it that the protocol of research requires us to say that rather than accepting the hypothesis, what we have done is failed to reject it. This argument strikes us as quite odd, as if its advocates were fearful of being less than absolute purists, so that they end up in very awkward verbal postures. There is nothing at all wrong with stating that one "accepts the hypothesis" when an appropriate outcome occurs. Accepting the hypothesis means nothing more than that the obtained data provide no basis for doubting the truth of the statistical hypothesis. For further discussion of this point see Binder (1963).

Using the foregoing language, the category of outcomes leading to acceptance of the statistical hypothesis is called the *acceptance category* or, because reference often is made to points under a curve, the *acceptance region.* Similarly, the category of events leading to rejection is called the *rejection category* or *rejection region.*

Typically, the low probability chosen for selecting the rejection region is either .05 or .01. Assume for the moment that our criterion is .05. The rejection category will then include the most extreme of the possible outcomes such that their accumulated probabilities of occurrence are .05. In the instance of the example regarding the testing of the hypothesis that the coin is unbiased, or that $p = q = 1/2$, we initially placed in the rejection category the outcomes 10 heads, 0 tails and 10 tails, 0 heads. The probability of either of these outcomes is .002, or 2 times in 100. Since this is short of the goal of .05, we enlarge the category to include 9 heads, 1 tail and 9 tails, 1 head. The accumulated probability now is .022. This remains short of .05, but if we include 8 heads, 2 tails and 8 tails, 2 heads in our rejection category, the accumulated probability becomes .109. This is considerably above .05. With discrete data of this sort, it ordinarily is not possible to achieve a rejection probability of exactly .05 (or .01), so that the research worker has to be satisfied with an approximation.

In this particular case, therefore, we place 9, 1 combinations and 10, 0 combinations in our rejection category and we state that the probability of rejecting the statistical hypothesis when it is true is .022. A result that falls into the rejection category is commonly said to be *statistically significant*.

A final word is in order about the relationship between the process of statistical inference and the basic theme of this book: systematic decision making. Clearly, estimation by the methods discussed earlier in this chapter provides a systematic approach to that mode of inference. Rather than haphazard guessing of the value of a population variable, we have systematic methods that maximize the probability of a correct estimate and minimize the probability of being wrong.

The procedure for testing a statistical hypothesis is in actuality a method for guarding against a pervasive alternative plausible hypothesis. That alternative plausible hypothesis is that a given event has occurred as a result of chance rather than on the basis of the central hypothesis.

REFERENCES

Binder, A. 1963. Further Considerations on Testing the Null Hypothesis and the Strategy and Tactics of Investigating Theoretical Models. *Psychological Review,* **66**:553–559.

Cochran, W. G. 1963. *Sampling Techniques* (2d ed.). New York: Wiley.

Kendall, M. G., and Smith, B. B. 1939. *Tracts for Computers. No. XXIV. Tables of Random Sampling Numbers.* London: Cambridge University Press.

Kish, L. 1965. *Survey Sampling.* New York: Wiley.

Rand Corporation. 1955. *A Million Random Digits with 100,000 Normal Deviates.* Glencoe, Ill.: Free Press.

Tippett, L. H. C. 1927. *Tracts for Computers. No XV. Random Sampling Numbers.* London: Cambridge University Press.

INDEX

Abortion issue, 23
Abstractions, higher- and lower-level, 17–18
Abstracts on Criminology and Penology
     (publication), 57
Academy of Criminal Justice Sciences, 28
Acceptance category (region), 258
Accidental death in Hanawalt study, 101, 102
Accretion measures, 93, 95–98
AD (mean absolute deviation from the median),
     179, 180, 182–183
Addiction:
   advocacy by evaluator on policy toward,
        157–158
   causes of, 50
   and halfway house for paroled addicts, 104,
        105, 163
   heroin, 11, 12
   literature on narcotics, 56
   urinalysis as accretion measure in
        determining, 96–97
   (*See also* Marijuana)
Adjusted behavior of boys, 98
Administration of Criminal Justice (Tompkins),
     56
Advertising, placebo effect of, 108
Aggravated assaults:
   Uniform Crime Reports and, 84–86
   in victimization surveys, 111

Agriculture, literature on, 56
Airplane hijackings, 80
Albert (child) as subject of experiment, 24–25
Alcohol, Tobacco and Firearms, Bureau of, 5, 6
Alcohol use, 58, 77, 107–108
Alexander the Great, 49
Allbrecht, G. L., 15, 16
Alt, F. B., 147, 148
Alternative explanations for phenomena, 5
Alternative plausible hypotheses, 60–89
   control groups eliminating, 104
   experimenters as sources of error in, 83–84
   internal and external validity in, 62–63
   pitfalls in measurement methods in,
        76–82
   placebo control groups and, 109
   and problems in crime statistics, 84–88
   quasi experiments and, 146
   in research methodology, 15–17
   situational factors as sources of error in,
        82–83
   and subjects as sources of error, 63–76
   true experiments and, 140
American Psychological Association (APA),
     28–29
American Society of Criminology, 28
Anderson, C. L., 49
Anecdotal evidence, 7–8, 154–156

Anonymity:
  and APA principles, 29
  as right in research, 27–28
APA (American Psychological Association),
    28–29
Applied research, defined, 17–19
Applied science, literature on, 56
Arapesh (tribal group), 122
Archival records, use of, 93, 100–102
  in systematic observation, 138
Arrests:
  sexual distribution of, in U.S., 64
  vice, 129
  of youths as percent of population, 153
Arson, 14
  as research issue, 48–50
  Uniform Crime Reports and, 86
Arts, literature on the, 56
Aschaffenburg, G., 49
Assaults:
  aggravated: *Uniform Crime Reports* and,
    84–86
  in victimization surveys, 111
  with gun before and after Massachusetts gun
    control law, 147
  in victimization survey, 112, 113
Attention, center of (see "Center of attention"
    effects)
Authority:
  defiance of police, 131, 132
  research methodology and dependence on,
    6–7
*Author's Guide to Journals in Law, Criminal
    Justice, and Criminology* (Mersky, Berring,
    and McCue), 58
Automobile accidents, 252–253
  prevention program, 167–169
Automobile thefts:
  Uniform Crime Reports and, 86
  in victimization surveys, 111–112

Banks, W. C., 31, 33
Bard, M., 54
Bedford, S., 41
Belsey, A., 158
Berliner, L. S., 162
Berring, R. C., 58
Beveridge, H. I. B., 5
Biases:
  and errors of interpretation, 5
  experimenter bias effect, 83–84
  influencing behavior, 65
  in probability, 219
  in unstructured observation, 127–128
Biasing of programs, 161
Bibliography of Crime and Criminal Justice
    (Culver), 56
Bickman, L., 134
Biderman, A. D., 111, 115

Bier, V. M., 162
Bimodal set, 178
Binder, A., 82, 92, 108, 258
Binomial distribution, 234–238
Biological equipment, as source of error, 64, 66
Biological and psychological alterations
    distorting studies, 70–73
Biology, literature on, 56
Birkett, W. N., 40
Black children, murder of (Atlanta; 1980 and
    1981), 45
Blacks, 15–17
  Tuskogee study on, 24
Blalock, H. M., Jr., 213
Blixen, K., 122
Bohnstedt, M., 167
Bok, S., 109
Borden, L., 47
Botein, B., 40
Bowker, A. E., 40
Brainwashing to recruit prostitutes, 50
Braithwaite, J., 200
Bridgman, P., 123–124
Brown, C. E., 146, 163
Brown, E., 167, 169
Browne, T., 6
Buddha, 49
Burglary:
  study involving victims of, 68–69
  and *Uniform Crime Reports*, 86
  in victimization surveys, 111–113

Cadwallader, M. L., 14
Caesar, Julius, 49
Campbell, D. T., 62, 76, 98, 103, 138, 145, 214
Candid Camera (television program), 102
Capital punishment:
  abandonment of, 23
  knowledge of date of, 41
Care and skill in experiments, Nuremberg Code
    and, 25
Case studies, use of, 47
Causation:
  correlation and, 214–215
  crime, as research issue, 46–50
Census, U.S. Bureau of the, 114
"Center of attention" effects:
  control groups and, 104
  distorting studies, 67–70
  placebo control groups and, 109
  and questionnaires and interviews, 134
  reactive effect of measurement as, 76–77
  situations producing, 91
  victimization and, 114
Center for Studies in Criminology and Criminal
    Law, 56
Central tendency:
  indicators of, 172
  measures of, 173–178

Central tendency, measures of (Cont.):
  mean, 172–175
  median, 176–178
  mode, 178
  proportion, 175–176
Change(s):
  crime statistics and population, 86
  defined in concept of outcome, 166
  in measuring instruments, 80–81
Chappell, D., 86
Cheap guns (Saturday night specials), 5–6
Chein, I., 157
Chemical sciences, literature on, 56
Children:
  murder of black (Atlanta; 1980 and 1981), 45
  raising IQ in, with glutamic acid, 74
  as subjects of experiments, 24–25
Classification of research, 119–121
Clinical practice, literature on, 56
Cloward, R. A., 18, 19
Cluster sampling, 247–248
Cochran, W. G., 243, 247
Cohen, A. K., 18
Comparison in research methodology, defined, 14–15
Complete observer, 125, 126, 144–145
Complete participant, observer as, 125–127
Computation of the mean, 174
Concepts, quantification of, 10
Consent, free (voluntary), 21–22, 25, 26
  in APA principles, 28
  of federal prisoners, 21–22
  in simulated prison experiment, 34
  surrogate informed, 30–31
Consistency, ideal of, 41
Constructs, as sources of error, 65
Control:
  and advancement of knowledge, 121–124
  of guns, Massachusetts study and, 147–148
  in true experiment, 140–143
  over variables, classification by, 121
Control groups for avoiding errors, 104–110
  equating treatment and control groups, 105–108
  ethical considerations, 105
  placebos as controls, 108–110
Controlled variables, 140–143
Cook, S. W., 138
Cook, T. D., 145, 214
Corporations, interviewing executives of, on criminal laws bearing on business, 133
Correlation, 188–215
  causation and, 214–215
  meaning of, 196–202
  other measures of, 202–213
  product-moment correlation coefficient, 190–196
Correlation ratio, 203–204
  number of sets as basis for, 204

Correlational analysis, defined, 120
Cost-benefit analysis, 167–169
Counseling:
  for juvenile delinquents, 161
  resistance to, 62–63
Courtrooms (see Trials)
Cressey, D. R., 85
Crime statistics (see Statistics)
Criminal insanity, literature on, 56
Criminal Justice Abstracts (formerly Crime and Delinquency Abstracts; publication), 57
Criminal Justice Newsletter (publication), 57
Criminological Foundation (Netherlands), 57
Criminology (journal), 54
Criminology—A Bibliography: Research and Theory in the United States (Center for Studies in Criminology and Criminal Law), 56
Criminology and the Administration of Criminal Justice: A Bibliography (Radzinowicz and Hood), 56
Cronbach, L. J., 79
Cross-sectional studies, 120, 121
Culver, D. C., 56
Current Contents (publication), 56
Curvilinear relationships, defined, 202–204

Darwin, C., 17
Debriefing:
  after experiments, 27–28, 30–31
  in simulated prison experiment, 33
Deception:
  in APA principles, 28
  arguments for and against, 29–30
  freedom from, as right in research, 27–28
  in simulated prison study, 32
  and surrogate informed consent, 30–31
Decision rule, 256
Decker, D. L., 116
Defiance of police authority, 131, 132
Demand characteristics of experimental situation, 69–70
De Mause, L., 23
Dependent variables (outcomes):
  defined, 140–143
  (See also specific studies)
Descriptive research, 119–120
Descriptive statistics, 171–215
  correlations (see Correlation)
  indicators of variability in (see Indicators, of variability)
  measures of central tendency as (see Central tendency, measures of)
  standard scores as, 183–187
Design(s):
  interrupted time-series, 145–147
  Solomon four-group, 142–143
  of study or experiment or investigation, 16–17

Destouches, L. F., 8
Deutsch, S. J., 147, 148
Deviation from the mean, 174–175
Dichotomous data, 205–209
Dickson, W. J., 68
Dieckman, D., 146, 163
Difference in concept of outcome, defined, 166
Dillinger, J., 47
Divorces and import of apples into Great
    Britain, 215
Dostoyevski, F., 49
Double-blind experiments, 110
    example of, 144–145
Driving behavior:
    marijuana and, 66–67, 69
    and seat belts, 144–145
    (See also Automobile accidents)
Drug addiction (see Addiction; Marijuana)
Due process for youths, 23
Duplication in research methodology, 12–13
Durrell, L., 17
Dying declaration, 42

Earth sciences, literature on, 56
Eckels, T. J., 162
Economic indices, poverty, crime and, 200,
    201
Economics, issue of, in program evaluation,
    167–169
Education:
    matching in terms of achievement in, 106,
        107
    performance and, of police officers, 209,
        210, 212, 213
Eisworth, R. S., 126, 144–145
Empirical hypothesis, 255–256
Engineering, literature on, 56
Ennis, P., 111, 112
Environmental sciences, literature on, 56
Epilepsy, arson and, 48–49
Equal likelihood in probability, 218–223
Equating treatment and control groups,
    105–108
Erikson, M. L., 137
Erosion measures, 93–95
Errors, avoiding (see Control groups for
    avoiding errors; Nonreactive measures for
    avoiding errors)
Estimation, 252–255
Eta coefficient, 203–204
    number of sets as basis for, 204
Ethical relativism, 23–25
Ethics, 21–36
    anonymity, deception and, 27–28
        (See also Deception)
    APA standards on, 28–31
    consent and (see Consent, free)
    control groups and, 105
    issues of, 31–35

Ethics (Cont.):
    Nuremberg Code and, 25–27
    placebos and, 109
    and shoplifting study, 102
    and study on honesty, 94
    and survey of youths, 137
Ethnocentrism, 84
Etiology of crime as research issue, 46–50
Evaluation research, 18
    (See also Program evaluation)
Evans, F. J., 69
Events:
    and conditions, effect of array of immediate,
        preceding behavior, 65–66
    mutually exclusive, in probability, 223–224
    in probability, 220–221
Evidence:
    exclusionary rule of, 23
    judge warning on improper, 42–43
    research methodology and inappropriate use
        of, 7–8
Excerpta Crimologica (publication), 57
Exclusionary rule, 23
Execution (see Capital punishment)
Experimentation as approach to research,
    140–148
    approaches having less control compared
        with, 123
    design in, 16–17
    ethics of (see Ethics)
    nonlaboratory experiment, 143–148
    true experiment, 140–143
    (See also specific experiments)
Experimenter bias effect, 83–84
Experimenters as sources of error, 83–84
Explanatory research, 119–120, 124
External validity:
    defined, 62–63
    of naturalistic observation, 126

Face validity, 154
Fahey, R. P., 15, 16
Faison, A., 15
Falk, P., 154
Favorable outcomes, probability of, 222
FBI (Federal Bureau of Investigation), 84–86
Fear(s):
    of crime: erosion measures to determine,
        94–95
        by sex, 205–207
    and errors of interpretation, 5
Federal Bureau of Investigation (FBI), 84–86
Ferracuti, F., 18–19, 54
Ferrero, W., 9
Field comments, 126–127
Field experiments, 143–144
Fienberg, S. E., 114
Finckenauer, J. O., 155–157, 166
Finckenauer reports, 155–157

Fingerprints, 95–96
Fode, K. L., 83
Force:
    police use of deadly, 138, 247
    police use of excessive, 129–132
Fowles, J., 123
Frank, B., 42
Frank, J., 42
Frankfurter, F., 6–7
Free (voluntary) consent (see Consent, free)
Fruchter, B., 204
Fyfe, J. J., 15, 16

Galliher, J. F., 30
Galvin, R. T., 134
Gang activities, participating in, for research,
    28
Gang behavior, 18–19
Garofalo, J., 112
Geis, G., 86, 105, 163
General case, probabilities in the, 225–227
Generalizability, program evaluation and issues
    of, 159–160
Generalization, research methodology and
    incorrect, 5–6
Gerard, D. L., 157
Giordano, P. C., 202
Glueck, E., 120
Glueck, S., 120
Gold, M., 125, 137
Gordon, W., 47
Gorer, G., 44
Government, federal, sources of information on
    publications of, 57
Grant, J. D., 134
Gross, H., 3
Group(s):
    approval of peer, female delinquency and,
        202
    nonequivalent group designs, 145, 146
    reference, support for juvenile delinquents
        in, and self-reported involvement,
        202
    sociometry and, 138–139
    (See also Control groups for avoiding errors)
Group therapy for juvenile delinquents,
    151–152
Grove, J. B., 62, 98, 103, 138
Grunbaum, A., 108
Guide to Material on Crime and Criminals, A
    (Kuhlman), 56
Guide to U.S. Government Publications
    (publication), 57
Guilford, J. P., 204
Guns:
    law on, in Massachusetts study, 147–148
    use of cheap, 5–6
    (See also Police officers, weapons and)
Guttmacher, M., 17

Haddon, W., Jr., 126, 144–145
Hale, M., 13
Halleck, J. W., 15, 16
Hanawalt, B., 100–102
Haney, C., 31, 33, 34
Haphazard selection, 240, 241, 243
Harding, R. W., 15, 16
Hartshone, C., 51
Hartshorne, H., 24, 94
Hathaway, S., 120
Hawthorne effect, 67–68
Hay, R. A., Jr., 147, 148
Hearsay evidence, admissibility of, in court, 42
Heisenberg, W., 76
Heisenberg principle, 76
Henchy, T., 134
Hepburn, J. R., 54
Himelson, A. N., 105, 163
Hindelang, M. J., 112
Hines, T. C., 58
Hirschi, T., 4
Hispanics, 15–17
Holmes, O. W., 51
Homicide:
    of black children (Atlanta; 1980 and 1981),
        45
    classic study of, 54
    finding common ingredient in, 47
    gun control and, 147–148
    Hanawalt study on, 101, 102
    literature on, 54, 55
    Uniform Crime Reports and, 85, 86
Homosexual episodes, experiment involving,
    34–35, 126, 127
Honesty, studying degree of, among students,
    94
Hood, R., 56
Hoover, J. E., 96
Human beings as subjects of research (see
    Ethics)
Human rights, changes in attitudes toward,
    23–27
Humanities, literature on, 56
Hume, D., 214
Humphreys, L., 34–35, 126, 127
Hypothesis:
    statistical testing of, 248, 255–259
    term, defined, 3
    (See also Alternative plausible hypotheses;
        Experimentation as approach to
        research)

Impact assessment, 160, 165–167
Independent variables (treatments),
    140–143
    (See also specific studies)
Indeterminacy, principle of, 76
Index to Legal Periodicals (publication), 56–57
Index Medicus (publication), 56

Index to U.S. Government Periodicals
(publication), 57
Indicators:
of central tendency, 172
mean, 172–175, 192
median, 176–178
mode, 178
proportion, 175–176
of variability (dispersion; spread), 173,
179–183
mean absolute deviation from the median,
179, 180, 182–183
range, 179, 183
standard deviation, 179–182
variance, 179–181
Individuals:
changes in attitude toward rights of, 23–27
factors influencing behavior of, 64–65
(*See also* Biases; Ethics)
Infanticide, 23
Institute for Scientific Information, 56
Intelligence quotient (*see* IQ)
Internal validity of study, defined, 62–63
*International Guide to Periodicals in Criminal
Justice* (McDowell, Russell, and Hines), 58
Interpretation:
research methodology and errors of, 5, 14
(*See also* Program evaluation)
Interrogations, 79–80
Interrupted time-series designs, 145–147
Interval estimates, 255
Interviewer effects, 81–82, 91
Interviews:
National Crime Survey and, 114–116
survey, 134–138
compared with questionnaires, 136
Investigational mortality as problem in
selection of subjects, 74–76
IQ (intelligence quotient):
of criminals and police, 173
of inmates, 240–241
in matching, 106–107
standard deviation for, 181
Irresistible impulse, doctrine of, 66
Irvine, W., 17

Jenkins, B., 15
Jennings, H., 139
Johnson, L. A., 111
Jones, J. H., 24
*Journal of Criminal Law, Criminology, and
Police Science* (publication), 54
Journal of Marriage and the Family
(publication), 54
Joyce, J., 96
Juries:
last address to, 40–41
as research issue, 39–40
Jury trials (*see* Trials)
Justice, U.S. Department of, 119

Justice Assistance News (publication), 119
Justice Statistics, Bureau of, 85
Juvenile Awareness Project Help ("Scared
Straight" program), 153–159, 165–166
Juvenile delinquents, 14–15, 62, 63
classic studies on, 120–121
counseling services for, 161
dispersion of inner-city, to suburbs,
159–160
diversion program and, 167
gang behavior of, 18–19
group therapy for, 151–152
literature on, 57
reference group support for, and self-reported
involvement, 202
Juvenile Justice Digest (publication), 57
Juvenile offenders (*see* Juvenile delinquents)
Juveniles (*see* Juvenile delinquents; Youths)

Kaplan, E. H., 162
Kelley, A. B., 126, 144–145
Kelling, G. L., 146, 163
Kelven, H., Jr., 40
Kendall, M. G., 212, 244–245
Kendall's tau, 211–213
Keve, P. W., 43
Keynes, G., 6
Kinsey, A., 79
Kirk, R. E., 141
Kish, L., 243, 247
Klein, M. W., 18
Knowledge:
example of damage to, from human error,
9–10
and purpose of theory, 4
Kuhlman, A. F., 56

Larceny:
Uniform Crime Reports and, 86
victimization surveys and, 112, 113
Lardner, J., 15, 16
Larson, R. C., 162
Law Enforcement Assistance Administration
(LEAA), 114
"Learning to learn" phenomenon, 78–79
Lee, R. S., 157
Legal aspects of criminal justice, literature on,
57
Leopold, N., 22, 47
Lewis, N. D. C., 48, 49
Lewis, R., 167
Library of Congress catalog, 56
Lie detectors, 99–100
Life history, as source of error, 64
Life sciences, literature on, 56
Lindesmith, A. R., 50
Literature, review of, as preparation for
research, 53–58
Loeb, R., 47

Lombrosian "stigmata," 9
Lombroso, C., 9, 10, 49
Longitudinal studies, 120–121, 124
Luke, Saint, 49

McCabe, S., 39
McCall, G. J., 134
McCleary, R., 147, 148
McConnell, D., 82
McCue, J. K., 58
McDowell, C. P., 58
McIntyre, J., 111
"Mad bomber" (incident), 65
Madden, E., 10
Maltz, M. D., 46
Manslaughter in Hanawalt study, 101, 102
Marchi, S. A., 167, 169
Marijuana:
    driving behavior and, 66–67, 69
    experiments using, 22–23
    (See also Addiction)
Martienssen, A., 44
Martin, C. E., 79
Matching of experimental and control groups,
        105–107
Mattingly, C., 162
Maximum-likelihood estimate, 254
Maxwell, G., 215
May, M. A., 24, 94
Maze problem, effect of rat, on student
        experimenters, 83–84
Mead, M., 122
Mean(s):
    measure of central tendency, 172–175
    regression toward the, 73–74
    for sets of numbers, 192
    statistical distribution of, 252
Mean absolute deviation from the median (AD),
        179, 180, 182–183
Measuring instruments, changes in, 80–81
Median:
    mean absolute deviation from the, 179, 180,
        182–183
    measure of central tendency, 176–178
Medical experiments, 24
Medicine, literature on, 56
Mersky, R. M., 58
Merton, R. K., 47
Milgram, S., 33
Mill, J. S., 214
Miller, D. E., 105, 163
Miller, W. B., 18
Millett, K., 50, 51
Milner, C., 50, 51
Milner, R., 50, 51
Milton, C. H., 15, 16
Miranda warning, 23, 32
Mock juries for research, 39, 40
Mode, measure of central tendency, 178
Mohammed, 49

Monachesi, E. D., 120
Moneymaker, J., 27
Monitoring delivery of services in process
        assessment, 160–163
Monthly Catalog of United States Government
        Publications (publication), 57
Moreno, J., 138, 139
Mortality, investigational, as problem in
        selection of subjects, 74–76
Motor vehicles (see Automobile accidents;
        Automobile thefts)
Motor Vehicles, Department of (California),
        167, 168
Murder (see Homicide)
Mutually exclusive events in probability,
        223–224
Myers, J. L., 141

Napoleon I, 49
Narcotics:
    literature on, 56
    (See also Addiction; Marijuana)
National Council on Crime and Delinquency,
        57
National Crime Survey (NCS), 114–116
National Criminal Justice Reference Service
        (NCJRS), 53
National Highway Traffic Safety
        Administration, 169
National Research Council, 114
National Rifle Association, 147
National Safety Council, 169
Natural sciences, literature on, 55
Naturalistic observation, 121–123, 125–134
    true experiment compared with, 140
Nazi atrocities, 23–24
NCJRS (National Criminal Justice Reference
        Service), 53
NCS (National Crime Survey), 114–116
Negative relationship, 195
"Negligent Operators" (Neg-Ops; program),
        167–169
New York Times, The (newspaper), 49
Newman, J. H., 92
Nonequivalent group designs, 145, 146
Nonlaboratory experiment, 143–148
Nonreactive measures for avoiding errors,
        91–104
    accretion measures, 93, 95–98
    archival data, 93, 100–102, 138
    erosion measures, 93–95
    general forms of, 102–104
    physical evidence, 93, 98–100
Nonreactive Measures in the Social Sciences
        (Webb), 92, 93, 103
Normal curve, 234–237
Normal distribution, 234–238, 252
Nuisance events in studies, 66, 67
Numerical value of correlation coefficient, 195
Nuremberg Code, experiments and, 25–27

O'Brien, R. M., 116
Observer(s) and observation(s):
  complete, 125, 126, 144–145
  complete participant, 125–127
  as form of nonreactive measure, 102–103
  participant, 125, 126, 128–134, 163–165
  research methodology and errors of, 4–5
  role of, in naturalistic observation, 125–126
  uncontrolled observations, 121–122
  (See also Naturalistic observation; Systematic
    observation as approach to research)
O'Donnell, J., 97
Offender: A Bibliography, The (Tompkins), 56
Ohlin, L. E., 18, 19
O'Neal, P., 120
O'Neill, B., 126, 144–145
Opiates:
  transforming casual user into addict, 50
  (See also Addiction)
Orne, M. T., 69
Owens, M. E. B., III, 114

PAIS (Public Affairs Information Service;
    publication), 57
Palmer, T., 167
Parameters in statistical hypothesis testing, 256
Parisi, N., 58
Parole, 73–74
Participant, observer as, 125, 126, 128–134,
    163–165
Participation:
  literature on victim, in homicide, 54
  of target populations in process assessment,
    160–161
Pascal, B., 8
Pate, T., 146, 163
Patterns in Criminal Homicide (Wolfgang),
    54
"Patterns in Criminal Homicide in Chicago"
    (Voss), 54
Pearson, K., 193, 210
Peer group approval, female delinquency and,
    202
Penick, B. K. E., 114
Personal biases (see Biases)
Peter the Great, 49
Phi coefficients, 207–209, 211
Phillips, H. B., 7
Physical evidence, 93, 98–100
Physical sciences, literature on, 56
Physical traces in systematic observation, 138
Physical traits of criminals, 9–10
Pierce, B., 51
Pilot research, 119–120, 124
Placebo control approach, 109
Placebo control groups, 109
Placebo effect, 108–110
Point-biserial correlation coefficient, 205–207,
    211

Police officers:
  behavior of, studies, 45–46, 61, 77, 78,
    126–138, 146, 163–167
  literature on training of, 53
  performance and education of, 209, 210,
    212, 213
  salaries of, 177
  use of excessive force by, 129–132
  weapons and, 44–45
    shooting blacks and hispanics, 15–17
    target shooting, 71–74
    in use of deadly force, 138, 247
  weights of, in two cities, 173
Policy debate, involvement in, 157–159
Polsky, H., 98–99
Pomeroy, C. W., 79
Popper, K. B., 48, 214
Population:
  crime statistics and changes in, 86
  defined, 63, 239
  distribution and measurement of, by interval,
    frequency, and proportion, 250
  (See also Sampling; Statistical inference)
Positive relationship, 195
Poverty, crime and, 200, 201
President's Commission on Law Enforcement
    and Administration of Justice, 78
Pretesting effect, 78–79
Prison(s):
  behavior in simulated, 31–34
  guards of, 160–161, 189
  literature on, 57
  prisoners in: behavior of, 67
    free consent for research, 21–22
    parole of, 73–74
Probability(ies), 216–227
  equal likelihood in, 218–223
  formal definition of, 220
  in the general case, 225–227
  mutually exclusive events in, 223–224
  properties of, 224
  sample space in, 217–218
  sampling in accord with known, 240–241
  (See also Statistical inference)
Probability distribution, 227–238
  binomial, 227–234
  normal, 234–238
Probability function, 228
Probation officers, 43–44
Process assessment in program evaluation,
    160–165
Product-moment correlation coefficient,
    190–196
Productivity study, 67–68
Program evaluation, 150–170
  assessing impact in, 160, 165–167
  assessing process in, 160–165
  conclusions on, 169–170
  defined, 151–152
  and evaluator as advocate, 157–159

Program evaluation *(Cont.):*
  issues of economics in, 167—169
  and issues of generalizability, 159—160
  of "Scared Straight," 153—159
Project Identification (Bureau of Alcohol,
    Tobacco and Firearms report), 5
Property offenders, 14—15
Proportion, measure of central tendency,
    175—176
Prosser, W., 92
Prostitutes, motives of customers of, 50—51
Protection of humans in experiments,
    Nuremberg Code and, 25—27
Psychological Abstracts (publication), 57
Psychological and biological alterations
    distorting studies, 70—73
Psychological characteristics of criminals,
    9—10
Psychotherapy:
  group, for juvenile delinquents, 151—152
  placebo effect of, 108
  (*See also* Counseling)
Public Affairs Information Service (PAIS;
    publication), 57
Punishment:
  capital: abandonment of, 23
    knowledge of date of, 41
  dying declaration and fear of, 42
  theory of, 3—4
Purpose, classification of research by,
    119—120
Purves, R., 39
Pyromania (*see* Arson)

Quasi experiment, 141, 143—146
  to evaluate "Scared Straight," 156
Questionnaires, 116
  survey, 134—138
    compared with interviews, 136
Quine, W. V., 214

Radzinowicz, L., 56
Rahway State Prison, program at, 153—159,
    165—166
Rand Corporation, 245
Rand Corporation table, 245
Random numbers, tables of, 244, 245
Random sampling, 241—247
  cluster, 247
  simple, 241, 243—247
  stratified, 246
Random variable, defined, 227
Randomization:
  in field experiment, 145
  in matching, 106—107
  quasi experiments and, 144, 146
  in true experiment, 140—143
Range as indicator of variability, 179, 183

Ranked data, 209—213
Rape, 64
  forcible, *Uniform Crime Reports* and, 85, 86
  statistics and, 87—88
  in victimization surveys, 112, 113
Rayner, R., 24—25
Reactive effect (reactivity) of measurement,
    76—77
  placebo control groups and, 109
  situations producing, 91
Reader's Guide to Periodical Literature
    (publication), 57
Reading to gain ideas for research, 39
Reality, variations in perception of, 65
Reasonableness in estimation process, 253
Recidivism, program seeking to deal with,
    153—159, 165—166
Regression toward the mean, 73—74
Reichman, N., 162
Reiner, R., 77
Reiss, A. J., Jr., 111, 126, 128—133, 137
Rejection category (region), 258, 259
Rejection of the statistical hypothesis, 258
Relation (relationship):
  defined, 189
  (*See also* Correlation)
Reliability of observations, 128
Replacement, sampling with, 242—243
Research:
  classification of, 119—121
  impetus to, 38—39
  systematic observation as approach to,
    124—139
Research issues, 39—51
  causes of crime as, 46—50
  police behavior as, 45—46
  probation work as, 43—44
  trials as, 39—43
  weapons in police work as, 44—45
Research methodology, 1—20
  and basic and applied research, 17—19
  defined, 4
  essential features of, 13—17
  failings guarded against by, 4—9
  as a process, 11—13
Research preparation:
  review of literature as, 53—58
  site exploration and related details as, 51—53
Response set, 79—80
Reynolds, P. D., 30
Rice, R., 47
Risk in experiments:
  and APA principles, 29
  Nuremberg Code and, 25
Robbery(ies):
  gun control and armed, 147
  Uniform Crime Reports and, 85, 86
  victimization surveys and, 111—113
Robertson, L. S., 126, 144—145
Robin Hood, 47

Robins, L. N., 120
Roebuck, J. B., 14
Roethlisberger, F. J., 68
Rosenfeld, E., 157
Rosenthal, R., 83, 84
Rosenthal effect, 83–84
Rossi, P., 160
Rubin, S., 17
Rubin, Z., 30
Rubinstein, J., 45, 46, 126, 128–129, 131
Russell, B., 214
Russell, G. L., 58

Sackett, G. P., 134
Sagarin, E., 27
Saint Luke, 49
Sample, defined, 239
Sample space in probability, 217–218
Sampling, 239–248
    in accord with known probabilities,
        240–241
    cluster, 247–248
    random, 241–247
    simple random, 241, 243–247
    stratified, 246–248
Sampling variability, 240
Scared Straight! (film), 154, 155
"Scared Straight" (Juvenile Awareness Project
    Help; program), 153–159, 165–166
Scatter diagrams, 196–200
Schafer, S., 86
Scheibe, K. E., 69
Schwartz, R. D., 62, 98, 138
Science Citation Index (publication), 55
Seat belts, study involving use of, 144–145
Sechrest, L., 62, 98, 103, 138
"Seerbohm report," 170
Selection distorting studies, 73–76
Selective observation, research methodology
    and, 5
Self-reports, 7, 137
Selltiz, C., 138
Semmelweis, P.-I., 8
Sex, matching in terms of, 105–106
Sexual behavior:
    homosexual, 34–35, 126, 127
    hypotheses on criminalized, 50
    interviews to study, 79
    literature on sex offenders, 56
    (See also Rape)
Shadow jury, 39–40
Shapiro, A. K., 108
Shichor, D., 116
Shoplifting, 14, 94, 102
Shumway, F., 155
Siegel, L., 86
Signal Companies, 155
Simmons, J. L., 134
Simple random sampling, 241, 243–247

Site exploration as preparation for research,
    51–53
Situational factors as sources of error, 82–83
Sjoholm, N., 82
Skill and care in experiments, Nuremberg Code
    and, 25
Smith, B. B., 244, 245
Smith, H. W., 138
Smudging as accretion measure, 96
Social Science Citation Index (SSCI), 53–54
Social Science and Humanities Index
    (publication; formerly, *International
    Index*), 57
Social structure of institution for youth, 98–99
Social value of research, Nuremberg Code and,
    25
Sociograms, 138
Sociological Abstracts (publication), 57
Sociometry in systematic observation,
    138–139
Socrates, 49
Solomon four-group design, 142–143
Sourcebook in Criminal Justice Statistics
    (publication), 58
*Sources for the Study of the Administration of
    Criminal Justice* (Tompkins), 56
*Sources of National Criminal Justice Statistics:
    An Annotated Bibliography* (Parisi), 58
Spearman's rank-order correlation coefficient,
    209–211
Spergel, I., 18
Squire, L., 167
SSCI (*Social Science Citation Index*), 53–54
Standard deviation:
    as indicator of variability, 179–182
    for sets of numbers, 192, 193
Standard scores, 183–187
Stanley, J. C., 62, 76
Statistical classification, 120
Statistical hypothesis testing, 248, 255–259
Statistical inference, 239–259
    estimation in, 248, 252–255
    logic of, 248–252
    sampling in (see Sampling)
    testing statistical hypotheses, 248, 255–259
Statistically significant result, 259
Statistics:
    alternative plausible hypothesis and
        problems in crime, 84–88
    (See also Alternative plausible hypotheses)
    dealing with flaws in crime, 110–111
    descriptive, 171–215
    inferential, 239–259
    literature on information based on, 58
    National Crime Survey, 114–116
    problems in crime, 84–88
    Uniform Crime Reports, 64, 84–87, 111,
        115, 116, 137, 201
Stori, J. R., 155–157
Stratified sampling, 246–248

Street behavior of police, questionnaire on, 134–137
Structured observation in naturalistic observation, 126–134
Subculture of violence, 18–19, 54
"Subcultures, Violence, and the Subculture of Violence: An Old Rut or a New Road?" (Hepburn), 54
Subjects:
  investigational mortality as problem in selection of, 74–76
  as sources of error, 63–76
  using, as their own controls, 107
  (See also Individuals; specific studies)
Suchman, E. A., 165
Sum of the deviations from the mean, 175
Sums of products for sets of numbers, 193
Surrogate informed consent, 30–31
Survey(s):
  to evaluate preventive patrol program, 163–165
  as systematic observation, 134–138
  telephone techniques for, 115–116
  (See also Victimization surveys)
Sutherland, E. H., 47
Symbolic set of instructions, 174
Systematic observation as approach to research, 124–139
  naturalistic observation, 125–134
  physical traces and archival records, 138
  questionnaires and interviews, 134–138
    compared, 136
  sociometry, 138–139
Systematic sampling, 246

Tarde, G., 10
Tearoom Trade (Humphreys), 34
Technology, literature on, 56
Telephone survey techniques, 115–116
Telescoping in surveys, 114
Temporal classification of research, 120–121
Termination of experiments:
  in APA principles, 29
  as right of human subject, 25–27
Thaw, H. K., 47
Theory, research and, 3–9
Time, elapsed, as research difficulty, 70–71
Time samples for observational studies, 133
Time-series designs, interrupted, 145–147
Tippett, L. H. C., 244
Tippett's table, 244
Toch, H., 134, 137
Tompkins, D. C., 56
Topinard, P., 10
Traffic citations issued during 10-day period, 178
Trials:
  media reporting on criminal, 6–7
  research issues in, 39–43

Trials (Cont.):
  sentences of judges in simulated, 197
Tribal beliefs, 121–122
Trimodal set, 178
True experiments, 140–143
Tuskegee study on blacks, 24

UCR (see Uniform Crime Reports)
Ulysses (Joyce), 96
Uncontrolled observations, 121–122
Uniform Crime Reports (UCR), 64, 84–87, 111, 115, 116, 137, 201
Unimodal set, 178
Unionization, police attitudes toward, 77
Units of assignment, 140
Unreported crime, 87–88
Unstructured observation in naturalistic observation, 126–134
Used-car dealers, crimes of, 93
Uses of Criminological Literature (Wright), 58

Van der Tak, H. G., 167
Van Hoffman, N., 35
Variability, indicators of (see Indicators, of variability)
Variables:
  classification by control over, 121
  dependent and independent, 140–143
    (See also specific studies)
  random, 227
Variance as indicator of variability, 179–181
Victim participation in homicide, literature on, 54
Victimization surveys, 111–116, 137
  National Crime Survey and, 114–116
  proportion of known victims in police files and, 113
Victims (see specific types of crime)
Violence:
  crimes of, heat and, 189
  death in fourteenth- and early fifteenth-century England, 100–102
  subculture of, 18–19, 54
  (See also Homicide)
Vitamin E, anecdotal evidence on, 7–8
Voluntary (free) consent in experiments (see Consent, free)
Voss, H., 54
Vulgar Errors (Browne), 6

Warwick, D. P., 29–30, 34, 35
Washington Crime News Services, 57
Watson, J. B., 24–25
Weapons (see Guns)
Webb, E. J., 62, 92, 98, 103, 138
Weihofen, H., 17
Weir, A., 111

Weiss, P., 51
Whitney, R., 47
Wife-beating as crime, 112
Wilson, C. W., 126
Winer, B., 142
Winick, C., 65
Witches, 13
Witnesses:
confrontation between, in Italian criminal
trials, 41
evidence and right to cross-examine, 42
Wixon, C. W., 144–145
Wolfe, J. L., 6
Wolfgang, M. E., 18–19, 54, 86
Wright, M., 58
Wrightsman, L. S., 138

Yablonsky, L., 18
Young, W., 41
Youths:
due process for, 23
exploratory research of offenders among,
119
program to reduce incidence of crime
among, 153–159, 165–166
social structure of institution for, 98–99
surveys of, reporting on violations of law,
137
(*See also* Juvenile delinquents)

Zeisel, H., 40
Zimbardo, P. G., 31, 33